JOURNAL FOR THE STUDY OF THE PSEUDEPIGRAPHA
SUPPLEMENT SERIES

7

Editor
James H. Charlesworth

Associate Editors
Philip R. Davies
James R. Mueller
James C. VanderKam

JSOT Press
Sheffield

TEMPLE SCROLL STUDIES

Papers presented at the
International Symposium on the Temple Scroll

Manchester, December 1987

Edited by
George J. Brooke

Journal for the Study of the Pseudepigrapha
Supplement Series 7

Published by JSOT Press
JSOT Press is an imprint of
Sheffield Academic Press Ltd
The University of Sheffield
343 Fulwood Road
Sheffield S10 3BP
England

Typeset by Sheffield Academic Press
and
printed in Great Britain
by Billing & Sons Ltd
Worcester

British Library Cataloguing in Publication Data

Temple scroll studies.
    1. Dead Sea scrolls. Temple scroll
    I. Brooke, George J.   II. Series
    221.4'4

ISBN 1-85075-200-1

To the memory of

Professor Yigael Yadin

Our teacher in all things to do with
the Temple Scroll

CONTENTS

ACKNOWLEDGMENTS

The International Symposium on the Temple Scroll (Manchester, 14-17 December, 1987) was made possible through a grant from the University of Manchester's Joint Committee on University Development. To this was added a grant from the University's Department of Biblical Criticism and Exegesis. To my colleagues in the University, especially Professor Barnabas Lindars, S.S.F., I am grateful for support and encouragement since the inception of the idea of holding the Symposium. All the participants in the Symposium appreciated the hospitality of Hulme Hall in Manchester.

I am also very grateful to Professor James H. Charlesworth, the editor of the *Journal for the Study of the Pseudepigrapha and Related Literature*, for welcoming the Symposium's papers enthusiastically into the Supplement series of the journal. Thanks are also due to Dr James R. Mueller, associate editor of *JSP*, and especially to Dr David E. Orton of Sheffield Academic Press for editorial advice. I am grateful too to Professor John Strugnell for giving Professor Lawrence H. Schiffman permission to include in his paper many details of the as yet unpublished 4QMMT. Thanks are also due to the Israel Exploration Society for permission to reproduce an illustration from *Qadmoniot*, Vol. V, Nos. 19-20; to M. Ben-Dov for permission to reproduce an illustration from his *In the Shadow of the Temple*; and to Dr John Wilkinson for permission to reproduce illustrations from his *Jerusalem as Jesus Knew It* (Thames & Hudson, 2nd edn, 1982).

The publication of technical books of this sort with complex charts and diagrams, and involving several different languages, is an expensive business. It is, therefore, with very deep appreciation that I thank the Manfred and Anne Lehmann Foundation of New York for the very generous financial support which it has given to enable the speedy and successful publication of this volume.

George J. Brooke

ABBREVIATIONS

Abbreviations in this volume follow the standard format of the *Journal for the Study of the Pseudepigrapha and Related Literature*; in nearly all cases these are the same as those used in the *Journal of Biblical Literature*.

For the Temple Scroll itself the abbreviation 11QT refers to the principal copy of the text, probably to be labelled 11Q19 by the Royal Dutch Academy of Sciences; 11QT^b refers to the second, but probably earlier, copy of the text (Dutch Academy No. 11Q20; PAM Nos. 43.975-78).

In the first note to several of the papers there is full reference to Yadin's *editio princeps* of the scroll, *Megillat ham-Miqdaš* (3 Vols.; Jerusalem: The Israel Exploration Society and the Shrine of the Book, 1977); English translation with some additions and corrections, *The Temple Scroll* (3 Vols.; Jerusalem: The Israel Exploration Society and the Shrine of the Book, 1983). In some cases scholars refer particularly to either the Hebrew or the English version of Yadin's work; in all other cases references are given to both versions, the English first, then the Hebrew in brackets, with the volume number in large Roman numerals, followed by the page numbers, in a form such as: *The Temple Scroll*, II, pp. 300-301 (Heb.: II, pp. 211-12).

References to the works of Josephus are self-explanatory: *Ag.Ap.* = *Against Apion*, *Ant.* = *Jewish Antiquities*, *War* = *The Jewish War*.

LIST OF CONTRIBUTORS

George J. Brooke is Lecturer in Intertestamental Literature at the University of Manchester, Manchester, UK.

Johann Maier is Professor for Judaic Studies, Martin-Buber-Institut für Judaistik der Universität zu Köln, West Germany.

Margaret Barker teaches mathematics in Borrowash, Derbyshire, UK.

Mathias Delcor is Professor at the Ecole Pratique des Hautes Etudes, Sorbonne, Paris, France.

E.-M. Laperrousaz is Professor at the Ecole Pratique des Hautes Etudes, Sorbonne, and the Université de Paris-Sud, Orsay, France.

Barbara Thiering lectures in the School of Divinity, University of Sydney, New South Wales, Australia.

Hartmut Stegemann is Professor at the University of Göttingen, Göttingen, West Germany.

Phillip R. Callaway is German Instructor, Clayton State College, Morrow, Georgia, USA.

Jacob Milgrom is Professor in the Department of Near Eastern Languages, University of California at Berkeley, California, USA.

Philip R. Davies is Senior Lecturer in Biblical Studies, University of Sheffield, Sheffield, UK.

James C. VanderKam is Professor of Religion, North Carolina State University, Raleigh, North Carolina, USA.

Lawrence H. Schiffman is Professor of Hebrew and Judaic Studies, New York University, New York, USA.

Hans Burgmann is a freelance writer and Judaist living in Offenburg, West Germany.

Manfred R. Lehmann is a businessman, scholar and bibliophile based in New York, USA.

Zdzisław J. Kapera is Librarian at the Institute of Oriental Philology, Jagiellonian University, 31-120 Kraków, Poland.

INTRODUCTION

George Brooke

University of Manchester

This volume contains the papers that were presented to the International Symposium on the Temple Scroll which was held at Hulme Hall in Manchester, 14th-17th December, 1987. The purpose of the Symposium was to celebrate the tenth anniversary of the publication of Professor Yigael Yadin's *editio princeps* of the Temple Scroll by bringing together scholars from around the world who have spent much of their research time in the last ten years studying the scroll. Although many articles have been written on particular aspects of the Temple Scroll, so far only one complete monograph (by Ben Zion Wacholder) has been devoted to it. This volume also serves, therefore, as a compendium of ideas about the scroll, ideas which will variously set the tone of the debate about the Scroll for the next decade.

The symposium could not attempt to cover all aspects of the scholarly debate about the Scroll, but four areas of research were addressed by four principal speakers: Professors Maier, Milgrom, Schiffman and Stegemann. Their papers stand at the head of each section of this book; for convenience's sake the other papers submitted to the symposium have been grouped with one or other of these principal papers and are printed in each section in the alphabetical order of their authors. In addition Dr Z. Kapera presented a short review of research on the Temple Scroll in Eastern Europe which complements in particular the bibliographical work of F. García Martínez (*RevQ* 12 [1985-87], pp. 425-40).

To some extent the division of the papers of the symposium into these four main sections is somewhat arbitrary because, while addressing their own particular topics, many speakers found themselves talking about the compositional nature of the work, its purpose, its possible historical setting and date. As with the study of many pieces of ancient literature, the questions asked by scholars all interrelate until certain matters become more or less established through a consensus of scholarly opinion. However, something of the general trend of the symposium was presented in a final seminar in which the four principal speakers addressed various questions of date, setting, redaction, genre, and purpose.

It was agreed that we have two manuscript copies of the Temple Scroll, both from Cave 11. The principal exemplar is that which is commonly labelled 11QT, whose palaeographical date is probably within a generation of the turn of the era. That is the scroll that forms the basis of Yadin's exemplary work. The second exemplar, labelled 11QT^b, was the editorial responsibility of J.P.M. van der Ploeg and was published by him and by Yadin almost simultaneously; some further small fragments of this second scroll have yet to be published (see Professor Stegemann's paper in the present volume, esp. n. 8). This second text is to be dated approximately half a century earlier than 11QT, though all palaeographic datings are highly relative, as more than one contributor to the symposium pointed out. There was general acknowledgment that the three fragments numbered Rockefeller 43.366 are not a second century BCE copy of the scroll but some other composition.

Although there was thus some general agreement about the dates of the actual manuscripts of the text, there was little firm agreement about the date of its literary composition. Of the principal speakers Professor Stegemann was concerned to date the text to the early post-exilic period and proposed, as he has done in other papers, that 11QT is a sixth book of the Torah which contains traditions that have parallels in the contemporary or slightly later books of Chronicles. Professor Maier, while sympathetic to Professor Stegemann's view, envisioned a time at the end of the Persian period when the restoration of the monarchy in Judah might have been possible; perhaps the Statutes of the King in 11QT 56-59 were drawn up in anticipation of such an eventuality. Professors Milgrom and Schiffman, however, preferred to associate the Statutes of the King with the reality of the rulership of the Hasmoneans. Professor Milgrom suggested that much of the scroll could have been composed in the late third century BCE under the stimulus of the reforms in Judah and Jerusalem during the time of Antiochus III; this would account for the absence of reference in rabbinic literature to the strict rules of purity for Jerusalem proposed in the scroll. For Professor Milgrom the scroll was then redacted in the second century BCE—which explains its concern with some matters that are often particularly associated with Hasmonean rulers. But while Professor Schiffman was sympathetic to understanding the Statutes of the King against a Hasmonean background, he argued that the lack of reference to the strict purity proposals in later rabbinic allusions to the Hasmonean period could not be taken as decisive for suggesting that major parts of the scroll were composed at an earlier time. All four speakers agreed that some help for solving the date of the composition of the scroll as a whole or in its parts would be discovered from further detailed work on the relation of the Temple Scroll to the books of Chronicles. None of the principal speakers dated the composition of the scroll to the same time as the palaeographic dating of the actual manuscripts themselves, though Dr Thiering had proposed this in her paper.

From their differing perspectives all four major speakers pointed to the differences between the Temple Scroll and the writings that could be clearly assigned to the group that lived and worked at Qumran in the first centuries BCE and CE. The priestly character of the scroll could not be denied, but the identification of its priestly authors was as yet difficult to establish. Professor Milgrom came the closest to arguing that although there were differences between 11QT and other Qumran literature, these were not of such an order that they would force the conclusion that 11QT was produced by a group other than that which later lived at Qumran. Professor Schiffman pointed out how the differences reflected differing theologies of law amongst priestly groups in the late Second Temple period; as yet the precise setting of these various theologies was hard to ascertain, though it might be that there was some interaction between those at Qumran and the Sadducees in some form and that this interaction might account for the presence of 11QT in Cave 11. Professor Maier opened the issue wider still by reflecting upon how 11QT might be the text which forces us all to reconsider the nature of the make-up of the Qumran community by seeing that too rigid or narrow a definition of that priestly group would lead to the pre-judging of a whole range of questions which only the complete publication of all the Qumran texts might help us to clarify.

When considering the genre of the Temple Scroll, Professor
Schiffman took up the terminology of Ben Zion Wacholder's
monograph and proposed that 11QT is re-redacted *Torah*; it is not a
replacement for the *Torah* but a codification modelled on the *Torah*
itself designed to show the *Torah*'s true meaning by supplementing it,
especially through its adaptation of the pentateuchal traditions
concerning the tent of meeting. As such 11QT suggested that the
Law of the Pentateuch was not exhaustive and its own claim that its
cultic regulations had divine authorship was intended to give it
authority. Once again Professor Maier both sought to reserve
judgment whilst asking larger questions than whether or not 11QT
was *torah*. He suggested that for the moment it was best to consider
the text as *sui generis*, though scholars should pay attention to its
obvious systematization of earlier materials. In particular, too, there
was an interesting agreement that the term *halakhah* was not
altogether appropriate for describing the Temple Scroll.

The association of 11QT with *torah* led to certain typical proposals
for the text's setting in life. Professor Stegemann proposed that
11QT represented the priestly giving of *torah*; priestly decisions,
perhaps originally given orally, had been collected together and
combined into a literary form with particular attention to the
significance of the Sinai pericope; all had been done with an explicit
concern for Jerusalem. Professor Milgrom acknowledged that the
whole was written under the perspective of the re-entry into the
promised land after the exile. Professors Maier and Schiffman,
however, argued caution, since a possible reading of the text might
lead one to the conclusion that, in some matters at least, ideals rather
than actualities were the controlling factors motivating the authors
and editors. As such no narrow description of the text's setting would
be possible. For Professor Maier 11QT was primarily retrospective,
offering the picture of what the ideal past should have been; for
Professor Schiffman 11QT was more forward-looking, depicting an
ideal society in which there would be no divine condemnation.

In this shift towards considering the text's purpose, Professor
Milgrom took up and developed Professor Schiffman's views
concerning the prospective nature of 11QT. For Professor Milgrom
11QT was almost prophetic, written to offer hope, in a way similar to
how some scholars have viewed the *Mishnah*. The clue for this could
be seen in 11QT's attention to Deuteronomy which may have been

written with a similar purpose. As such 11QT was a kind of blueprint for the near future, perhaps a blueprint for a future akin to that for which the later members of the Qumran community hoped. Professor Schiffman was more inclined to notice that 11QT's attention to the text of the *Torah* meant that it had an overall exegetical purpose; although the various sections of the scroll may have had an independent origin, they had been skilfully combined so that there was virtually no internal contradiction in the final form of the text. Professor Stegemann reverted to his understanding of the text's setting and argued that because it was not possible to imagine one author being responsible for the whole text, so it was not really possible to describe the text as having a single overall purpose. 11QT contained a collection of the results of many priestly debates, debates which had been going on for at least as long as there had been a temple building; its early post-exilic setting showed how one group intended to offer a sixth book of the Law in order to safeguard Jerusalem, but 11QT contains many other matters as well.

When asked to characterize their impressions of the Temple Scroll the four major speakers offered once more a diverse set of opinions, but a diversity couched in questioning terms rather than dogmatic statements. For Professor Milgrom the rules on the place for the latrine posed precisely the question concerning whether 11QT reflected actual practice or offered an ideal theoretical construct. The rules for sabbath abstinence seemed to offer an unacceptable ideal that might turn the 'sabbath of exaltation' into the 'sabbath of constipation'! And yet the material in Josephus on the actual practice of Essenes echoed some of the concerns of 11QT. For Professor Maier the text's composition seemed to characterize its puzzling nature. It was clearly remarkably, almost artificially consistent; it was also wide-ranging. Study of its composition would clarify how its contents were to be understood and used for our better comprehension of the realities of the Second Temple period. For Professor Stegemann, the Temple Scroll pointed to the need for scholars to reevaluate the writing and passing on of *torah* in the post-exilic period. In the light of the Temple Scroll, the Samaritan Pentateuch, the Septuagint, and the books of Chronicles (together with the [as yet unpublished] 'Rewritten' texts of the Pentateuch from Qumran), would have to be taken into account in a fresh way; they should no longer be consigned to the edges of scholarly interest, but taken in their own right as pieces in a jigsaw more varied and exciting than previously imagined. For Professor Schiffman the importance of the Temple Scroll lay in the way that it challenged existing assumptions about Judaism in the Second Temple period, especially the supposed consensus in Qumran studies; the hallmark of investigation into the Temple Scroll was a diversity that showed that the scholarly understanding of the Qumran library was in need of a return to the drawing board.

All the papers in this volume are offered as an instalment in this process of scholarly revision. It is impossible to say that there were any firm interpretative conclusions to which all the participants in the symposium agreed. Yet there were tendencies. For the Temple Scroll itself there was a general sense that it could not be associated straightforwardly with the Qumran community. For many this was quite simply because it completely or largely predated that community, possibly by centuries; for some the lack of quotation of 11QT in the other Qumran texts was best explained by dissociating it from the Qumran community. Although they could not agree on its detailed interpretation, several participants pointed to how their understanding of the Statutes of the King gave them a basis for describing the nature and purpose of the scroll as a whole. Many thought that the Temple Scroll offers a glimpse into Second Temple period affairs which no other text from Qumran so far published has been able to offer.

More broadly, it was acknowledged that the Temple Scroll can represent how Qumran studies need to be adjusted onto a wider basis. Similarities with a work like *Jubilees* meant that the Qumran scrolls could no longer be put into a neat compartment, and considered by themselves as an entity largely uninfluenced by the general climate of the time. Furthermore it was noted that the priestly exegetical activity attested in 11QT offers many clues into the diversity of the religious understandings of the time. Some at the symposium also had their opinions (and even their way of speaking) about law, and the *Torah* in particular, adjusted or completely altered by the discussion of 11QT. Still further it was admitted that the Temple Scroll characterizes how the assumptions of biblical scholars may be challenged afresh from Qumran. It was observed that if the Temple Scroll had been the first text from Qumran to be published forty years ago, how very different our understanding would have been; and yet, if the Temple Scroll had been published first of all the scrolls, the real challenge it offers to our picture of Second Temple period Judaism might well have gone unnoticed. The papers in this volume represent the variety of the challenge of the Temple Scroll; any scholarly consensus about it will be at least another ten years in the making. The general purpose of the symposium was to celebrate the tenth anniversary of the publication of Professor Yadin's *editio princeps* of the Temple Scroll. Without all his careful editorial work the progress in scholarship represented by the papers here would not have been possible; his influence is detectable on nearly every page. It is to Professor Yigael Yadin's memory that this book is respectfully and most gratefully dedicated.

PART I

ARCHITECTURE, ARCHAEOLOGY AND DATE

THE ARCHITECTURAL HISTORY
OF THE TEMPLE IN JERUSALEM
IN THE LIGHT OF THE TEMPLE SCROLL*

Johann Maier

University of Cologne

1. *The Date of the Scroll and its Contents*

Yigael Yadin, to whom we owe the impressive edition of the Temple Scroll together with a comprehensive commentary, favoured a rather late date for the whole composition. Yet, when the assumption that the scroll had a single author is doubted, mainly because of the differing contents of the individual parts of the scroll, then the scroll can be considered as a well-planned composition rather than as a work written by one author.[1] In relation to the sections concerning the sanctuary (11QT 3-13, 30-45), the professionalism of their architectural contents provokes the impression that they constitute an entity in themselves of older origin, to be dated in the early Hellenistic or even in the Persian period. An examination of their architectural character and terminology confirms this literary impression.[2] The Temple Scroll represents in this respect a source between the design of Ezek. 40-48 and the first great architectonic transformation of the sanctuary in the Hellenistic style under Antiochus III, namely that by the High Priest Simon (about 200 BCE).

This design as a whole and in its details is not to be evaluated as a mere product of phantasy, for it reflects realistic concepts, traditions and experiences as well as the dreams and expectations of the Jerusalem school of architecture. This school developed plans for an ideal sanctuary, whether eschatological or heavenly, and for a City of the sanctuary.[3] Or, as in the case of the Temple Scroll, a plan was developed of an ideal sanctuary for the twelve tribes as it should have been built as the first temple.

2. Basic Architectonic Information from the Temple Scroll

a. From the cultic point of view, it was the task of an architect to find appropriate architectural solutions for the various cultic areas in their graded holiness in order to preserve their ritual purity in accordance with the ritual functions of the sanctuary. Certain points, however, seem to have been subject to differences of opinion.

In consequence, the demarcation of cultic areas varied from time to time or from design to design. The architects had to consider several spheres of holiness or ritual purity and to provide for their demarcation by appropriate architectonic means:

1. The Temple house (with its inner division);
2. the area of the sacrificial cult for priests in service;
3. a court of priests;
4. a court of men;
5. an area for all Israelites in a state of ritual purity (and off limits to gentiles);
6. eventual outer precincts with certain ritual restrictions with appropriate transition zones between sanctuary and 'city of the sanctuary'.

b. The design in the Temple Scroll (Fig. 1) consistently applies the square shape to cultic areas as well as describing architectonic enclosing structures for their demarcation according to their functions and according to the distribution of their components to the twelve tribes of Israel with special shares for the tribe of Levi (its priestly clan, and the levitical clans). Three areas are demarcated by the massive enclosing structures in the form of concentric square porticoes:

I. The court of priests, with four gates; 280×280 cubits inside, 300×300 outside. Functionally corresponding to Ezekiel's inner court which, however, has no gate at the west.

II. The court for men, with twelve gates; 480×480 cubits inside, 500×500 outside, 100 cubits in width.

III. The court of Israel, with twelve gates; 1600×1600 inside, 1700×1700 outside, 600 cubits in width.

The real extent of these measurements depends upon the cubit applied (see the following table). Only the court of Israel deviates from the traditional and topographically suitable extent of the sanctuary in Jerusalem (Fig. 2). The middle and inner courts were obviously designed according to the existing cultic areas, but their real extent (depending upon the length of the cubit to be applied) and the function of these areas were matters of dispute.

Temple Scroll Design in Figures

cubits		meters (:7)				
		0.42	0.4375	0.4666	0.525	0.56
I.	1700 (outside)	714 (102)	743.75 (106.25)	793.33	892.5 (127.5)	952 (136)
	1600 (inside)	672 (96)	700 (100)	746.66	840 (120)	896 (128)
II.	500 (outside)	210 (30)	218.75 (31.25)	233.33	262.5 (37.5)	280 (40)
	480 (inside)	201.6	210 (30)	224 (32)	252 (36)	268.8
III.	300 (outside)	126 (18)	131.25 (18.75)	140 (20)	157.5 (22.5)	168 (24)
	280 (inside)	117.6	122.5 (17.5)	130.66	147 (21)	156.8
Width of court: II : 100		42 (6)	43.75 (6.25)	46.666	52.5 (7.5)	56 (8)
×6 = III : 600		252 (36)	262.5 (37.5)	280 (40)	315 (45)	336 (48)

3. *Enclosing Structures in the History of the Sanctuary of Jerusalem*

a. In the Bible almost nothing is said about the necessary structures for service and administration of such important institutions as the temple and palace. It is obvious that in the course of centuries, with increasing tasks and developing institutions, the demand for such structures grew in proportion to new requirements; this was one of the most important motivations for enlarging the areas and for re-shaping the architectonic ensemble. From the beginnings under Solomon royal and cultic administration were largely identical. But biblical texts hint at an increasing tendency to separate the cultic from the royal realm, an issue subject to disputes and political controversies.[4] It is significant that the *terminus technicus* for such service or administration units was the same one in both realms, namely the royal and the cultic: לשכה (niche, store, chamber, cell, department, office, lodging). The meaning and importance of such units are well attested by Ezek. 40–48 and by the Temple Scroll, yet the sources differ in the technique of construction. In Ezek. 40–48 these units form a series of cells on an apparently elevated level, as a whole called רצפה. This רצפה-technique was not suited for constructing more than one storey or floor. The only way to accomplish that is described in the design of Ezekiel in connection with two buildings south and north of the temple house. The aim was achieved by forming steplike recessing storeys with an open terrace for access before the לשכות. The Temple Scroll, however, employed a new technique, namely designing storeys of equal dimensions and putting a gallery-like construction in front of it. The *terminus technicus* for this structure is פרור/פרבר, a Persian loanword. It appears already in 2 Kgs 23.11: King Josiah removed the horses and chariots of the sun-god from the place between the entrance to the 'House of the Lord' and a certain לשכה in the פרורים. The LXX translator did not understand this term and transliterated it φαρουρειμ, in the other two instances (1 Chron. 26.18) paraphrasing the text. In fact he could have used περίστυλον or στοά because technically there is no difference between the פרבר/פרור and a building with a stoa in front of it except the difference of style.[5] The term פרור/פרבר was a riddle for lexicographers before the publication of the Temple Scroll. The non-technical use of this word suggested only a synonym for חצר in its sense of 'suburb', 'hamlet' (in relation to a city). But in 1 Chron. 26.18, in the list of the doorkeepers, the term appears in a technical sense: doorkeepers were appointed for the פרבר in the west, four for the מסלה, two for the פרבר itself, here obviously part of an enclosing structure at the western side of the outer court of the sanctuary.

b. A לשכה for cultic purposes is already mentioned in the narrative of the anointing of Saul (1 Sam. 9.22), but as part of a במה-sanctuary.

The fact that a sacrificial meal should have taken place at a sanctuary of that type embarrassed the LXX translator who in consequence chose the rather rare and profane term κατάλυμα. The Chronicler reports (2 Chron. 31.11-12; without parallel in 2 Kgs 18) that king Hezekiah ordered לשכות for tithes and cultic taxes to be established in the sanctuary, appointing levitical officials in charge of them. The passage resembles 1 Chron. 9.26 where, in an evidently post-exilic list, levitical functionaries are in charge of the לשכות and the אוצרות (the chambers and stores) of the House of God. In any case the close relationship between לשכות and cultic administration is evident and of course this had consequences for the architectonic development of the sanctuary, as attested by 2 Kgs 23.11. The Chronicler, however, eliminated this information perhaps on purpose, not least because of the fact that cultic and royal לשכות appeared too close together within the sanctuary. Further evidence for the same period is provided in Jer. 35-36 where the term is used several times in connection with conflicts between the prophet and royal authorities: in most instances for rooms in the palace area, but Jer. 35.2-4 locates the לשכה of Hanan ben Yigdaliah within the 'House of the Lord' near a לשכת השרים above that of Maaseyah ben Shallum, the keeper of the threshold. Jeremiah had to invite the Rechabites into a לשכה in this environment and to offer them wine. The mixture of royal and cultic purposes was well felt by the LXX translator. For the first instance of לשכה (v. 2) he used the more general word αὐλή (court), (without concrete location), the room of Hanan ben Igdaliah (in v. 4) the cultic term παστοφόριον, but in the two last instances he preferred οἶκος (house) as in all instances of a לשכה within the palace area. The postexilic uneasiness about the intermingling of cultic and laical לשכות is also reflected in the conflicts between Nehemiah and the priest Eliashib. Nehemiah regarded it as illegitimate that Tobiah got a לשכה within the temple area and stopped this practice by force after his failure to carry into effect a first command (Neh. 13).

c. In the historical development before the exile and in the postexilic discussions as reflected in the works of the Deuteronomist and the Chronicler, the Levites played a considerable part.[6] They served in both realms, the cultic and the royal, and this obviously from the beginning, firstly as the yahwistic nucleus behind Davidic political and religious endeavours and, subsequently, in the organizing and executive staff of Solomon's emerging cultic and royal administration. Their allegiance to the Davidic dynasty had several consequences. They became the protagonists of the yahwistic (and Davidic) claim to the whole of Israel. After the division of the Davidic-Solomonic empire they found themselves in a difficult position within the northern kingdom of Israel. In Jerusalem/Judah they played a major political role between the two emerging focuses of political and religious life, the royal one and the priestly one, the latter represented by the leading priestly family and their head, the forerunner of postexilic High-priesthood. Their advantage was their mediating function, not only between cultic and royal realms but also between both of them and the public. Levites seem to have been the most influential opinion makers in pre- and post-exilic Judaism, at the same time of course also pursuing their own group interests. This does not necessarily imply a continuous monolithic group nor uniform group interests, for the diversity in functions certainly resulted in differing aims and needs within the group as a whole.

4. *Sanctuary and Palace*

a. The developing uneasiness concerning cultic and royal institutions had its roots in the Solomonic concept of a Palace sanctuary. With its increasing functions as a central sanctuary of the kingdom of Judah and its claimed function as a sanctuary for all Israel, in addition to the increasing weight of the priestly institutions and the development of their concepts of holiness and ritual purity, by the end of the period the Solomonic concept almost became topsy-turvy. And indeed, it was the sanctuary which survived, at least as a holy area, both destruction and exile. An extreme view from the cultic perspective against the proximity of palace and sanctuary is expressed by Ezekiel in his polemics (43.7-9), which denounce the palace as a source of defilement:

> And he said unto me: 'Son of man, this place of my throne, and this place of the soles of my feet, where I will dwell in the midst of the children of Israel for ever, and my holy name (too), shall the house of Israel no more defile, neither they, nor their kings, by their whoredom, nor by the corpses of their kings when they die; (8) by placing their threshold next to my threshold, and their doorpost to my doorpost, and (with only) a wall between me and them'...

The Deuteronomistic redaction and the Chronicler in its footsteps eliminated from the extant sources almost everything which contradicted the new norms concerning the holiness and ritual purity of the sanctuary, norms which had been developed during a continuous struggle with the ups and downs of political life in Judah and Jerusalem. The Deuteronomist as well as the Chronicler conceived every political change as a kind of cultic reform pro or contra their own tendency and shaped their sources according to it. But such events had also a concrete significance in connection with the architectonic changes carried out by the kings concerned. And there was a practical aspect which even the Deuteronomist and the Chronicler could not ignore.

The northern side of the city of Jerusalem was throughout its history the weakest strategic point of defence. The temple hill was the decisive stronghold of the city and in this respect the cultic and secular architectural considerations met again even after the destruction of the first sanctuary and the palace. The architects had throughout all the centuries to combine solutions for both cultic and strategic purposes, and the priests had to come to terms with this concept which found its most impressive realization under King Herod. But a military function with all its implications concerning the ritual purity and the sanctity of the holy place could not be regarded as adequate for the cultic norms. The Deuteronomist was more easily ready for compromise as he was stressing the political position and role of the chief priest. The Chronicler, however, followed more or less the line of Ezekiel, which was stated even more strictly in the Temple Scroll; the Chronicler stressed the political significance of the Davidic king, notwithstanding his tendency to exclude any cultic-priestly function for the king.

b. *Building Activities in the Santuary during the Period of the first Temple*

(1) The first reform with architectonic implications relevant to our point of view is attributed to King Jehoshaphat, but only by the Chronicler. The king convoked an assembly in 'the House of the Lord' before the 'new court'. Does the expression 'new court' imply an expansion of the court areas between Solomon and Jehoshaphat?
(2) King Jotham built (according to 2 Kgs 15.35) the שער בית יהוה העליון, the upper gate of the house of the Lord (mentioned already with

2 Chron. 23.20). The Chronicler (2 Chron. 27.3) has the same wording but adds additional information about Jehoshaphat's building activities on the Ophel and in Judaean cities. The expression שער עליון reminds one of Jer. 36.10, where חצר עליון seems to be identical with חצר פנימית. The erection of this upper gate probably marks a change in the demarcation between the inner and the outer court, symptomatic of an increasing priestly self-consciousness. According to Jeremiah 36 Baruch reads a scroll with Jeremiah's words to the people approximately from the position in the 'new gate', between inner and outer court. Josephus (in *Ant.* 9.237) used a source which knew more about Jotham's building activities. It mentioned the erection of στοαί and προπύλαια for the sanctuary, of embankments or walls and towers, in addition to cultic and strategic structures. The Chronicler stressed (2 Chron. 27.2) the correct conduct of this king who followed the example of his father Uzziah except that he did not try to enter the temple and to act as a priest like Uzziah according to 2 Chronicles 26, with the consequence that God punished him with leprosy. This story, with no parallel in 2 Kings, indicates a change in the relationship between king and priesthood during the eighth century.

(3) Jotham's successor Ahaz appears (2 Kgs 16) again as a king with priestly aspirations but in the sense of a counter-reform. He initiated grave changes in sacrificial practice and even in the architectonic structure. The Chronicler (2 Chron. 24) replaced this by the remark that this king shut the doors of the temple and erected various altars in and outside Jerusalem.

(4) Of special importance is King Hezekiah, at least in the eyes of the Chronicler who dedicated to this king a long report in 2 Chron. 29–31 without parallel in 2 Kings. Hezekiah opened the doors of the temple and re-established its cult after a ritual purification. In ch. 31 he is credited with far-reaching reforms and reorganizations. In this context, connected with regulations for the cultic-ritual taxes, the installation of לשכות is mentioned.

(5) The last king according to this model (or rather its prototype) was Josiah, the prominent reformer. Like King Joash he ordered the collection of money for the repair of the temple, organizing a staff of experts and hiring labourers on a great scale (2 Kgs 23.4-14; 2 Chron. 34.8-18; Josephus, *Ant.* 10.48-59). Scholars of the Old Testament were always divided about the evaluation of the Chronicler's

Sondergut and certainly the schematic description of the reforms is obvious.[7] But the archaeological evidence confirms at least the fact that some of these kings indeed carried out architectonic changes in the city and, therefore, we may assume that the temple was involved, for cultic or for strategic reasons or for both of them.

c. The connection between royal and cultic purposes found its architectural expression in the application of identical techniques in both spheres as is attested by 1 Kgs 6.36: 'And he—Solomon—built the "inner court" with three rows of hewed stones and a row of cedar beams'. According to 1 Kgs 7.12, the same mural technique was applied in the palace area for the 'great court', which is not the 'outer court' of the sanctuary but probably an area comprising palace and sanctuary. It is significant that the Chronicler omitted the passage about the palace, but formulated in 2 Chron. 4.9 a similar statement restricted solely to the sanctuary: 'Furthermore he made the court of the priests (חצר הכהנים) and the great court (העזרה הגדולה) and doors for the court (עזרה) and overlaid the doors of them with brass'. The LXX translated both חצר and עזרה with αὐλή as in 2 Chron. 6.13. The term עזרה, which in Ezek. 43.14, 17, 20 and 45.19 is applied to certain extensions of the altar structure, appears here for the first time applied to a cultic area, perhaps a reaction to 'wrong' demarcations between royal and cultic spheres, as for instance in 1 Kgs 8.22: 'And Solomon stood before the altar of the Lord in the presence of all the congregation of Israel and spread forth his hands toward heaven'. The Chronicler did not eliminate this passage but he corrected the impression that Solomon's position was in fact near the altar. He added 2 Chron. 6.13: 'For Solomon had made a brass scaffold and had set it in the midst of the עזרה', which according to 2 Chron. 4.9 must be understood as the great עזרה outside the priest's court, at the border between the two areas in front of the altar. Ezek. 46.1-2 forbids the ruler to enter the inner court area, allowing his approach through the eastern gatehouse as far as the inner threshold. The king's position in the sanctuary and later on his podium at the border of the court of priests was a point of controversy which gained new actuality when after the exile the possibility of a Davidic restoration or at least of a monarchical reign emerged. The issue received a special colour as soon as the High Priests acted also as political representatives, and, of course, such old controversies could be used again when High Priests acted at the same time as kings.

For the period of the First Temple, we have some texts which reflect this controversy as seen through the eyes of the Deuteronomist and Chronicler. The first concerns the revolt of the priest Jehoiada against the queen Athaliah (2 Kgs 11 and 2 Chron. 23). In 2 Kgs 11.14 the king's position during the enthronement and covenantal ceremony is described as כמשפט, 'according to the regulation'. The Chronicler (2 Chron. 23.13) added in accordance with his correction in 2 Chron. 6.13 that this position was in the entrance. Moreover, Chronicles's Jehoiada warns explicitly that nobody but priests and Levites should be entitled to enter the holy area and even the king's guards are in this case Levites (2 Chron. 23.6-7).

A similar correction occurs in 2 Chron. 23.20 where שער הרצים, a gate (according to 2 Kgs 11.19 connected with the palace), is replaced by שער העליון, which seems to be the eastern gate, which king Jotham had built (2 Kgs 15.35 and 2 Chron. 27.3). The Chronicler's correction corresponds to Ezekiel's regulation in 46.1-8, where the king is told to use exactly this gate at the eastern demarcation between the court of priests and the outer court. Significant too is the episode of the collecting of money for the repair of the Temple in 2 Kings 12 compared with 2 Chronicles 23. In 2 Kgs 12.9-12 it was the priest Jehoiada who installed the chest for the money near the altar and gave the orders to the doorkeepers and the king's scribe. According to 2 Chron. 23.8, it was the king who ordered a chest to be placed outside the gate of the House of the Lord. This is typical of the Chronicler's tendency to stress the political role of the king, removing him at the same time from the holy area proper. It is interesting that Josephus, a priest and politician, in *Ant.* 9.161-62 (combining both sources) shared in this respect the view of the Deuteronomist.

d. From a comparison of Ezekiel, the Deuteronomist and the Chronicler emerges the impression that the relationship between king and sanctuary was one of the major themes of dispute during the exilic and Persian period.[8] This fact is significant in face of the common assumption that discussions about this subject presuppose an existing royal regime, an argument often used also for the date regarding the king's law in the Temple Scroll,[9] explaining it as a reaction to Hasmonean rule. This point should perhaps be reconsidered in the light of the discussions in the exilic-postexilic literature.[10] The

Temple Scroll law for the king fits well into the frame of such discussions, containing however some new topics and representing a more developed phase of the discussion. But there is no single hint of the central problem of Hasmonean kingship—the combination of both the priestly and the royal functions. The pre-exilic claims of kings to perform priestly rites were already a settled issue at the end of the first commonwealth. The question of a priest performing the function of a king had never occurred before the Hasmoneans, notwithstanding the fact that already in the Persian period the High Priest[11] represented the temple state of Judah. The difference was that between political representation and direct exercise of power and military functions. From a strictly ritualistic point of view the latter was scarcely tolerable for a Priest. The historical problem of the Maccabean claim to power was the combination of political rule with the High priesthood, beginning with Jonathan and culminating in the later Hasmonean combination of High priesthood and kingship. Exactly this point is recorded in Josephus[12] and in rabbinical sources[13] as a matter of serious dispute. If the law for the king in the Temple Scroll was provoked by Hasmonean rule, it should have included something about this matter of dispute. In this respect a Herodian date would be more plausible for the Temple Scroll than a Hasmonean one, but the issue itself had its roots in the history of the first commonwealth and was subject to differences of opinion already present in Persian times.[14]

5. *Temple Scroll Design and Ezekiel 40–48* (Fig. 3a-b)

a. Despite the similarity in their square shape and the identical measurement of 500 × 500 cubits, the two designs differ in a significant manner.

1.   Ezekiel's figure of 500 × 500 refers to his outer court, the whole area of the sanctuary. In the Temple Scroll it is the area of the middle court, the court of men. Unless Ezekiel's sanctuary was planned as off limits to women, there is a shift of function from the centre outwards in accordance with the remarkable expansion of the whole area of the sanctuary in the Temple Scroll.

2.   The Temple Scroll divides the enclosing structures symmetrically (according to its device of describing a sanctuary for

the twelve tribes of Israel) by twelve gate buildings, three at each side. Ezekiel's design has three gate buildings symmetrically distributed on the N-S and E-W axis leaving the western enclosure without a gate, the same scheme applying to the inner court.

3. The Temple Scroll's inner court (= the court of priests as in Ezekiel) has four gate buildings in symmetrical axial positions like Ezekiel, but: Ezekiel's court has no gate at the western side; his court differs in size and shape, being a rectangle of 200 cubits in N-S extension and of 350 cubits from the western wall towards the east. The Temple Scroll retains the scheme of concentric squares, its inner court with 300 × 300 cubits enclosing Ezekiel's court in a distance of 50 cubits except in the west where it borders the western side of the Temple house.

4. In the Temple Scroll an inner square of 200 × 200 covers the sacrificial area with the Temple house, the area for priests in service. In Ezek. 40–48 the rectangle of 200 × 350 with enclosing structures 50 cubits deep leaves for the same functional area a rectangle of 100 × 200, divided into two squares, the eastern forming the court of the altar, the western including the Temple house.

5. Consequently, the positions of the altar and the Temple house differ in the two designs by 50 cubits.

	0.42	0.525	0.56 m
50 cubits	21	26.25	28 m

This remarkable difference, a shifting of the cultic focus, means that in the Temple Scroll the centre of the whole scheme is in the entrance to the Temple house (the *ulam*) while in Ezekiel's design it coincides with the altar.

The shifting of the centre is of course a consequence of differing demarcations of the holy areas. The Temple Scroll and Ezek. 40–48 represent two contradicting traditions within the Jerusalem school of temple architecture. Only a partial harmonization is possible, either by shifting the cultic focus within the given area to its geometrical centre (Fig. 3a) or by shifting the whole area, the cultic focus being a fixed geographical point (Fig. 3b). In any case it is quite clear that the question of shape and extent had its bearing upon fundamental cultic matters and vice versa.

It is striking to see that the architectural problem in this context is not the distance between Temple house and western wall as in most modern reconstructions but the disposition of the area at the eastern side. The altar as centre seems from this point of view to be the preferable variant. The author of the Temple Scroll design, however, was not concerned about topographical circumstances outside the sanctuary of 500 × 500 cubits. For the ideal design of the First Temple (as it should have been built) the expanded areas beyond the 500 × 500 square were of rather theoretical significance. Within the 500 × 500 square the author's outlook was different because of the traditional and topographically fixed sites of altar and temple house, already subject to cosmological and religious symbolism. As a result of such presuppositions, he was probably ready to shift the whole (anyway expanded) area to the west, but scarcely to do the same with the altar and the temple house. Otherwise a difference of opinion with far-reaching consequences also for Herod's reconstruction of the Temple would have to be considered.

b. Ezekiel's design reflects the ideal two-court sanctuary according to a cultic scheme at the end of the First Temple period. Additional courts which may have been constructed during the period of the Judaean kings had no place in this design. In postexilic times this restrictive plan had to be changed and finally the descriptions of the late Second Temple period preferred to speak of at least three precincts, regarding an exterior enclosing area with an outermost wall more and more as part of the sanctuary. The traditional holy square area remained nonetheless the true sanctuary. This centrifugal shift was done for obvious practical reasons, one in the interest of the sanctuary to provide the necessary space for the increasing visiting masses, the other was the old one, namely the requirements of defence at the city's weak northern side and/or the endeavour of the political power to secure control over and in the whole area.

6. *Evidence for a Square of 210 × 210 m*

a. Ezekiel (42.15; 45.2), the Temple Scroll (implicit in col. 38) and the *Mishnah* (*Mid.* 2.1) are witnesses to the concept of a square sanctuary of 500 × 500 cubits. In the Temple Scroll, however, this concerns the middle court. Some scholars have seen in this figure nothing more than a conventional motif derived from Ezekiel.

Others, and especially authors of the nineteenth century, applied the square shape in their reconstructions of Jerusalem's sanctuary. But it seemed impossible to give a more accurate measurement for this traditional square, the less so since differing cubits obviously were in use.

b. The square shape was also a conventional device for Josephus as a matter of course. Unfortunately, the figures given in his writings seem contradictory.

(1) In *Ant*. 8.95-98 Josephus relates the great works which Solomon had to perform to provide the necessary space for the sanctuary at the top of the hill to the north of the city. In §97 Josephus gives a strange figure apparently referring to the height of the circumvallation as of 400 cubits, topographically an evident nonsense.[15] But the figure in question makes good sense if it does not refer to the direct height but to an area extending 400 cubits, accomplished by building enclosing walls and filling up the space with them, arriving finally at the level of the top of the hill.

(2) In *Ant*. 15.400 the circumference of the holy area is said to have been four stades, one stade on each side. Presupposing the Roman stade (of about 185 m) this figure does not match the 400 cubits of *Ant*. 8.97 or the 500 traditional cubits.

(3) *Ant*. 20.221 (cf. 15.401-402; *War* 5.185) mentions 400 cubits for the length of a so-called Stoa of Solomon at the east side of the *hieron*, probably a pre-Herodian structure of the same length as the square *hieron*.[16]

(4) Finally in *Ant*. 15.415 the length of the Herodian Royal stoa at the south of the court of gentiles is one stade.

c. Josephus used sources from different times and of different origin and consequently, differing cubits and stades have to be taken into account. For the passages in question a striking correlation between the old Judaean cubit and the Hellenistic foot and stadion resolves the contradictions in the given measurements:

$$210 \text{ m} = 600 \text{ feet of } 0.35 \text{ m} = 1 \text{ stadion}$$
$$= 400 \text{ cubits of } 0.525 \text{ m}$$
$$= 500 \text{ cubits of } 0.42 \text{ m}^{[17]}$$

During the last centuries of the Temple its holy square *temenos* was 210 m in length. At its east side stood a portico of pre-Herodian (allegedly Solomonic) origin of the same length, and Herod built his new 'Royal stoa' on the southern side of the 'court of the gentiles' to the same extent, probably aligned to the holy square. Considering these figures and circumstances it seems plausible that Herod based his building activities for the sanctuary on a plan in accordance with the traditional square. In fact it would have been almost impossible not to consider the traditional shape and position of this holy site.

7. *Herodian Plans for the Surface Areas of the Sanctuary*

a. *Evidence for a Plan Underlying Herod's Constructions*
Hints at a plan of this kind are perceptible in the appearance of the Haram esh-sharif (Fig. 4). An architectonic fact of fundamental significance is the south-west corner of the Haram as a right angle. Considering its position in relation to the city it may be regarded as a starting point for planning and building alike. And it suggests itself that this right angle was aligned to the corresponding angle of the holy square.

The southern wall, now largely excavated by Israeli archaeologists,[18] is in its 280 m length divided by the Hulda gates. From them tunnels led beneath the Royal stoa into the area of the 'court of the gentiles' to stairs which came to light in front of the Royal stoa. At least here a symmetrical plan is reasonable, but on the outside a symmetrical division of the wall is lacking at first sight, the extreme eastern part being too short.

At the west and at the east of the Royal stoa stood corner buildings connected with outside staircases, the western one now definitively established by the Israeli excavations (Fig. 5) with its remains still visible as 'Robinson's arch'. The eastern wall is not of one cast and is essentially a pre-Herodian wall. Herod used it and thus here at the south east angle the rectangle scheme had to be relinquished. Only the last part at the southern end of the wall is evidently a Herodian construction in connection with the expansion of the area towards the south and the substructures for the monumental buildings above the southern wall.[19]

The course of the eastern part of the wall at the north side is still uncertain; it borders on a ravine which was filled up some time later. The western part was connected with the porticoes and stairs which linked the sanctuary with the fortress Antonia. From here the western wall, probably entirely constructed by Herod for strategic

reasons, bordered the Tyropoeon valley. Since nothing from the
north-western parts remains (i.e., can be excavated), a reconstruction
of the Herodian building plan has to rely on the findings at the
southern part of the western wall and at the southern wall. Herod
began his work with the Antonia and the north-western angle, the
weak point of defence, continued with the southern wall at a right
angle to the former and joined it at the eastern end to the old wall.
From an architectural point of view, already this rough sketch of the
situation gives rise to the assumption of an uncompleted undertaking,
the eastern and north-eastern parts having been left as a temporary
solution, only more or less fitting the scheme as a whole. The reason
is obvious as a new wall at the east and the inclusion of the ravine at
the north implied enormous expenditure. Considering the tendency
towards symmetry and regularity in Hellenistic large-scale architecture, it should be possible to reconstruct the Herodian plan
underlying his uncompleted work.

An incomplete realization of an underlying plan presupposes,
nevertheless, certain reasons as far as given dimensions are concerned.
It seems that the structure of the southern wall and of the buildings
above it contains the clue to the problem if seen in its relation to the
traditional square with its metrological implications.

Of special significance is the shape of the surrounding area of the
Haram esh-sharif. The fortress Antonia was probably part of the area
which Herod included in his surface plan for the sanctuary. At the
northern border of this area, a symmetrical plan corresponding to the
division of the southern wall by the Hulda entrances is indicated by
the existing north-south streets, probably more or less in line with
streets of Herod's times (Fig. 6). The division of the western wall by
its ancient gates presupposes a symmetrical plan too; its verification
will be possible as soon as Israel's archaeologists who excavated the
western wall (up to about 450 m from the southern corner) publish
the exact measurements.

b. *The Architectonic Structure of the Southern Enclosure and the
Western Wall*
(1) *The Real Length (280 m) of the Southern Wall.* The usual starting
point for an architectural analysis of Herod's buildings at the
southern enclosure is of course the actual length of the enclosing
wall. The measurement given in the descriptions range, however,
from 277 m to about 283 m, the most probable and recently affirmed

figure being 280,[20] also preferable from a metrological point of view, resulting in 500 long cubits of 0.56 m. The length of Herod's realized wall was, therefore, not only due to topographical conditions such as the existence of an older wall at the east, but also to numerological symbolism, or/and to the fact that in pre-Herodian times, according to certain traditions, the cultic area had been calculated as a square of 500 × 500 cubits, of this same length (280 m).[21]

The striking figure, 280 m = 500 cubits, provides, however, no clue to the architectonic structure of the southern wall in its division by the Hulda entrances. A symmetrical plan requires a symmetrical division of the dimension 280 m by the Hulda entrances and a corresponding symmetrical proportion between this whole structure and the Royal stoa of 210 m length in its central position above it, so that the Hulda gates would also divide the Royal stoa in a symmetrical manner. But the north-south axis of a 280 m long construction, 140 m from the south western corner to the east, does not coincide with half the distance between the Hulda entrances.

(2) *The Length according to Plan: 294 m.* (a) The bipartition of the distance between the Hulda tunnels results in a north-south axis at 147 m from the south-western corner to the east, indicating a planned length of 294 m, 14 m more than the actual length of the wall (25 cubits of 0.56 m). Before any further step of analysis, the divisibility of the dimensions 210 m (Royal stoa), 280 m (actual length of the wall) and 294 m (planned wall length) has to be taken into account.

:	210	280	294
2	105	140	147
3	70	93.333	98
4	52.5	70	73.5
5	42	56	58.8
6	35	46.666	49
7	30	40	42
8	26.25	35	36.75
9	23.333	31.111	32.666
10	21	28	29.4
14	15	20	21
21	10	13.333	14

Already this simple table contains figures which indicate metrological units (feet and cubits) of 0.35; 0.42; 0.4666; 0.525; 0.56 m.

For comparison, here are some archaeologically attested dimensions: the diameter of a Herodian column, the inner width of Barclay's gate, the distance of Robinson's arch from the south west corner, and the length of Robinson's arch at the western wall, in metres and in feet/cubits:

	0.35	0.42	0.4375	0.4666	0.525	0.56
1.4 m	4	3.333	3.2	3	2.666	2.5
5.6 m	16	13.333	12.8	12	10.666	10
11.9 m	34	28.333	27.2	25.5	22.666	21.25
15.75 m	45	37.5	36	33.75	30	28.125

(b) For a preliminary orientation here are two tables for the same dimensions in metres with their equivalents in feet and cubits, in units of 3 cubits and in perches of 6 and 7 cubits:

A.		0.35 (foot)	0.42	0.4375	0.4666	0.525	0.56
210 m		600	500	480	450	400	375
280 m		800	666.66	640	600	533.33	500
294 m		840	700	672	630	560	525
B. Perches							
(a) of 3		1.05	1.26	1.3125	1.4	1.575	1.68
(b) of 6		2.1	2.52	2.625	2.8	3.15	3.36
(c) of 7		2.45	2.94	3.06285	3.2666	3.675	3.92
210 m	(a)	200		160	150		125
	(b)	100		80	75		62.5
	(c)						
280 m	(a)			200			
	(b)			100			
	(c)						
294 m	(a)	280		224	210		175
	(b)	140		112	105		87.5
	(c)	120	100	96	90	80	75

(c) The planned length of 294 m is divisible into seven parts of 42 m or into six parts of 49 m, basic units also for the division of the whole surface of the planned area. The next table illustrates the relationship between these basic divisions (a-b) and the measurement of the components of the construction (c-h). From the table it is evident that the two old cubits, 0.42 m and 0.525 m, were of restricted significance, resulting in round numbers only for the figures 42, 210 and 294. The traditional long cubit of 0.56 m, however, fits in all instances, as does each of the other cubits (0.4375 and 0.4666).

	West		Centre (The Royal stoa (1 stade))			East	
A.	metres						
a	49	49	49	49	49	49	
b	42	42	42	42	42	42	42
c	42	56	14 · 35	35 · 14	56	42	
d	42	70	70	70	42		
e	42		210		42		
f	42		210		28	14	
g			280			14	
h			294				
B.	cubits 0.42 (cf. 0.525: 80, 400, 560)				reed: 2.94 (3.675)		
a							
b	100	100	100	100	100	100	100
c	100						100
d	100						100
e	100		500				100
f	100		500				
g							
h			700				
C.	cubits 0.4375				reed: 3.0625		
a	112	112	112	112	112	112	
b	96	96	96	96	96	96	96
c	96	128	32 · 80	80 · 32	128	96	
d	96	160	160	160	96		
e	96		480		96		
f	96		480		64	32	
g			640			32	
h			672				
D.	cubits 0.4666				reed: 3.2666		
a	105	105	105	105	105	105	
b	90	90	90	90	90	90	90
c	90	120	30 · 75	75 · 30	120	90	
d	90	150	150	150	90		
e	90		450		90		
f	90		450		60	30	
g			600			30	
h			630				

Temple Scroll Studies

	West	Centre					East	
		The Royal stoa (1 stade)						
E.	cubits 0.56						reed: 3.92	
a	87.5	87.5	87.5	87.5	87.5	87.5		
b	75	75	75	75	75	75	75	
c	75	100	25	62.5	62.5	25	100	75
d	75	125		125			125	75
e	75			375				75
f	75			375				50	25
g				500					25
h				525					

(d) The actual division of the southern wall by the Hulda gates and of the facade of the Royal stoa by the Hulda entrances within the court in front of it depended of course on the dimension of the original architectonic appearance of the entrances. The actual distance between the Hulda tunnels of about 63 m and the width of the tunnels (differing measurements of between 11.90 and 12.50, and 12.74 and 14.59 respectively) are not decisive figures for the original dimensions of the entrances in their architectonic structure. It is not impossible that both Hulda gates were of the same width in their outside architectonic appearance, notwithstanding their differing division into a double and a triple gate. In this case a width of 14 m each would fit well:

m	105	14	56	14	105 (91)
feet/					
cubits					
0.35	300	40	160	40	300 (260)
0.4375	240	32	128	32	240 (208)
0.4666	225	30	120	30	225 (195)
0.56	187.5	25	100	25	187.5 (162.5)

But this ideal scheme fails because of the distance between the western wall and the western Hulda tunnel, evidence for the plausible assumption that both gates were not of equal width, the double gate being smaller. Except for this detail, the division of the plan length of 294 m seems to be symmetrical, based on the tripartition into three lengths of 98 m:

98	14		63		21		98
The gates:	0.70	5.6	0.70	5.6	0.70		
	1.05	5.6	1.05	5.6	1.05	5.6	1.05
	or similar						

This small deviation from the symmetrical plan probably did not occur at the entrances within the court and thus, they divided the facade of the Royal stoa symmetrically, producing from an architectural point of view an important effect.

(3) *The Western Wall.* (a) As reliable information and measurements will be attainable only in the near future, the following remarks should be regarded as preliminary. The archaeological evidence so far published and the general character of the wall in its function within the whole architectonic ensemble of the Herodian sanctuary, including the fortress Antonia, allow, however, some observations. There obviously exists a more or less accurate relation between some of the gates of the Haram and the ancient gates of the Herodian enclosure, indicating the architectonic division of the wall as a whole. A table with ideal divisions (see below) of a maximal length of 490 m (see (2) above) confirms this impression at first sight. At least three gates, 'Robinson's arch', 'Barclay's gate' and 'Wilson's arch', are now archaeologically established as two or three of the four western gates mentioned by Josephus. The northern gates should be located in proportions symmetrical to the southern gates and to the possible variants in the plan for the surface inside the enclosure (see c. below).

The reappearance of figures found in the ideal divisions of the southern wall is additional evidence for a symmetrical scheme. This presupposes a similar situation at the eastern wall, but in a restricted sense since this wall is of pre-Herodian origin. Lines drawn from the western gates and intersecting in the geometrical centre of the planned area or of the 'holy square' cut the eastern wall at interesting points. The relationship between western and eastern gates requires further investigation, for it is possible that the Herodian symmetrical scheme had at least some pre-Herodian antecedents.

(b) Western wall and 'holy square':

490 m length = 280 (500 cubits of 0.56m)
+ 210 (500 cubits of 0.42m)

98				294				98	
105				280				105	
140				210				140	
				98					
84	56	56		49	49		56	56	84
84	56	40.25	15.75	49	49	15.75	40.25	56	84
84	56	42	42	42		42	42	56	84
84	56	49	7	49	49	7	49	56	84
84	56	42	14	49	49	14	49	56	84

(c) Division by 98:

98		98		98		98		98	
49	49	49	49	49	49	49	49	49	49
15.75	82.25	82.25	15.75	49	49	15.75	82.25	82.25	15.75

(d) The breadth of Robinson's arch:

m	cubits					
	0.35	0.42	0.4375	0.4666	0.525	0.56
15.75	45	37.5	36	33.75	30	28.125
×2 = 31.5	90	75	72	67.5	60	56.25
×4 = 63	180	150	144	135	120	112.5
×8 = 1.'6	360	300	288	270	240	225
×12 = 189	540	450	432	405	360	337.5
×14 = 220.5	630	525	504	472	420	393.75
×16 = 252	720	600	576	540	480	450
×20 = 315	900	750	720	675	600	562.5
×24 = 378	1080	900	864	810	720	675
×28 = 441	1260	1050	1008	945	840	787.5
×32 = 504	1440	1200	1152	1080	960	900

The resulting figures (in metres and cubits/feet) clearly indicate the significance of the actual extent of this small component in its relation to the construction as a whole.

(e) Division of the southern half on the basis of real dimensions (presupposed length 490m ÷2 = 245):

11.9m	SW corner → Robinson's arch
15.75	Robinson's arch, Wilson's arch
82.25	SW corner → Barclay's gate
5.60	Barclay's gate (inner width)

			A	B	C	D	E	F	G
I.		(a)	82.25			5.60	92.40	15.75	49
		(b)	11.90	15.75	54.60	5.60	92.40	15.75	49
	0.35	(a)	235			16	264	45	140
		(b)	34	45	156				
	0.525	(a)	156.66667			10.66	176	30	93.333
		(b)	22.666	30	104				
	0.56	(a)	146.875			10	165	28.125	87.5
		(b)	21.25	28.125	97.5				
II.			11.90	15.75	53.9	7	91.7	15.75	49
	0.35		34	45	154	20	262	45	140
	0.56		21.25	28.25	96.25	12.5	163.75	28.125	87.5

A = distance SW corner → Robinson's arch
B = Robinson's arch
C = distance Robinson's arch → Barclay's gate
D = I D: inner width of Barclay's gate
II D: architectural frame included
E = distance Barclay's gate → Wilson's arch
F = Wilson's arch
G = distance Wilson's arch → axis

(f) Alternative division on the basis of table (d) (see above) and a length for the western wall of 441m (axis: 220.5m):

I. Total:

	441	
220.5		220.5
73.5	294	73.5
80.5	280	80.5
115.5	210	115.5

II. Southern half:

115.5					105		
82.25			5.6	27.65	56		49
27.65		54.6	5.6	27.65	40.25	15.75	49
11.9	15.75	54.6	5.6	67.9		15.75	49

c. Herodian Surface Plan
(1) General Remarks

The symmetry of the planned length of the southern wall is the best starting point for the reconstruction of Herod's plans for the whole area. When the lengths of the parts of the wall (see preceding section 7.b) are used as the measurements of the sides of squares, a number of larger rectangles of reasonable proportions can be made up out of these squares. The possible number of rectangles is, however, restricted by the fact that a square of 210 × 210 m, aligned with the royal stoa at the south, has to be placed in a convincing position with regard to its east-west axis, its north-south axis being fixed anyway in line with the axis of the southern construction (see Figs. 7 and 8). Automatically a second large square appears, with sides 294 m long, in which the 210 × 210 m square is inscribed. Any reconstructions are therefore limited by the number of possible positions for these two concentric squares within the whole area at our disposal. Unfortunately, this area is not restricted to that of the present Haram; the fortress Antonia in the north west corner has in the end to be included within any comprehensive surface plan. On that basis the maximum extent to the north can be demarcated by a line which runs from Stephen's Gate (on the east) to form a right angle with the extended line of the western wall. This line is 11 × 49 m from the southern wall and the rectangle of the whole area thus delineated has its east–west axis at 269.5 m from the southern wall. Taking into account the extent of the Antonia fortress, this axis appears rather problematic for any symmetrical division of the area of the sanctuary. The north–south distances which must be carefully considered are thus 490 m, 441 m, 420 m and 392 m, with their east–west axis at 245 m (= the axis of the Dome of the Rock), 220.5 m (without apparent topographical significance), 210 m, and 196 m (at the northern side of Wilson's arch).

(2) *Surface Area 294 × 490 m* (proportion 3:5; see Figs. 7 and 8)
(a) Axes. The east–west axis 245 m from the southern wall coincides with the axis of the Dome of the Rock and most notably its length of 294 m corresponds exactly with the actual distance between the western wall and the existing eastern wall of the Haram. The north–south axis intersects the east–west axis in the Dome of the Chain.
(b) Divisibility. The area of 294 × 490 m can be divided into squares as follows:

2940 (42 × 70) squares of 7 × 7 m or
60 (6 × 10) squares of 49 × 49 m or
15 (3 × 5) squares of 98 × 98 m.

(c) Concentric scheme

A. The central square of 294 × 294 m is divisible into
1764 (42 × 42) squares of 7 × 7 m or
49 (7 × 7) squares of 42 × 42 m or
36 (6 × 6) squares of 49 × 49 m or
9 (3 × 3) squares of 98 × 98 m.
B. The inscribed circle of the large square A (294 × 294 m) is the circumscribing circle for the 'holy square' of 210 x 210 m; inside square A the 'holy square' is framed by 24 squares of 42 × 42 m. The 'holy square' consists of
900 (30 × 30) squares of 7 × 7 m or
25 (5 × 5) squares of 42 × 42 m or
16 (4 × 4) squares of 52.5 × 52.5 m or
9 (3 × 3) squares of 70 × 70 m or 4 (2 × 2) squares of 105 × 105 m.
C-D. The southern and northern parts, 294 × 98 m each, consist of
588 (42 × 14) squares of 7 × 7 m or
12 (6 × 2) squares of 49 × 49 m or
3 squares of 98 × 98 m.

The area as a whole is not divisible into 42 × 42 m squares; only the large central square (294 × 294 m) and the 'holy square' (210 × 210 m) are so divisible. The 'holy square', however, is not divisible into squares of 49 × 49 m.

(d) Northern and southern parts. The southern construction with the royal stoa is functionally a public rather than a cultic area. A similar plan appears for the northern part, the Antonia with its connecting structures covering the western part of the area in the north, at least in its northern half. Stairs led from the Antonia into the court of the gentiles, reminding one of the Hulda entrances in the south which come to the surface in a corresponding area. Thus both the rectangular strips of 98 × 294 m in the north and the south functioned as transition zones and as strategic areas, connected not only by the court of the gentiles but also by the enclosing porticoes on the west and on the east (their roofs being accessible from the Antonia).

(3) *Variations with shorter north-south distances, but with the east-west axis at 245 m north of the southern wall (as (2) above)*
(a) 441 × 294 m (see Fig. 8). This surface area leaves a strip of 49 m breadth to the north of the 294 × 294 m square. This would contain porticoes and stairs between the sanctuary and the Antonia and would correspond with the 49 m broad strip between the 294 × 294 m square and the royal stoa in the south; the Hulda entrances would then correspond functionally with the stairs of the Antonia. The circumference inside the porticoes is about 1260 m = 6 stades of 210 m (cf. Josephus, *War* 5.192).
(b) 420 × 294 m (see Fig. 8). This leaves a strip 28 m broad to the north of the 294 × 294 m square, just sufficient for enclosing the porticoes and stairs. Notable in this variation is that 420 m is twice the length of the side of the 'holy square' (210 m).
(c) 392 × 294 m (see Fig. 8). This results in the northern enclosing porticoes and the Antonia stairs coming within the 294 × 294 m square. All three of these variations, and especially the first two, are worth further consideration, the southern extent of the Antonia being the decisive factor in each case.

(4) *Variations with shorter north-south distances and with the east-west axis shifting to the south*
(a) 441 × 297 m. In this variation the east-west axis falls 220.5 m

from the southern wall. South of the 294 × 294 m square there is a strip 73.5 m wide, a measurement exactly one quarter of the length of the southern wall, and so the strip consists of four squares of 73.5 × 73.5 m.

(b) 420 × 294 m. In this variation the east–west axis is 210 m north of the southern wall; there is a strip 63 m broad south of the 294 × 294 m square.

(c) 392 × 294 m. In this variation the east–west axis falls 196 m north of the southern wall, a point which corresponds with the northern side of Wilson's arch. To the south of the 294 × 294 m square there are only 49 m so the Hulda entrances come within that square.

In none of these three cases is there visible any satisfactory relation to the gates of the western wall.

(d) 378 × 294 m. In this variation the east–west axis is 189 m north of the southern wall. To the south of the 294 × 294 m square there is only a strip 42 m wide so that the royal stoa practically borders the square. The east–west axis in this variant seems to coincide with the line from Wilson's arch to the street to the royal palace on the western hill. This then provides a good architectural argument for supporters of a southern position for the Temple,[22] but this is rather problematic from a religious point of view.

d. *The Square of 280 × 280 m*

(1) As already mentioned (7.b) the actual dimension of the southern wall (280 m) is by no means incidental; it corresponds to 500 cubits of 0.56 m. Probably in pre-Herodian times there existed a square cultic area with sides of this length, which came to be regarded as הר הבית. The possibility that Herod's architects chose the 294 × 294 m square not only because of its metrological implications but also with regard to an existing 280 × 280 m square is an intriguing one, and that not only theoretically: with an identical centre and with axes in line Herod's new enclosing wall remained outside the old *temenos* (see Fig. 8).

(2) It may at first sight appear more reasonable to assume that the Herodian surface plan was worked out on the basis of 280 m, the actual length of the southern wall, rather than on the basis of 294 m. But, as already stated (7.b), the obvious symmetrical plan of the construction work in the southern wall and the evident advantages of the variations obtainable with the 294 m plan exclude a Herodian plan

based on 280 m. First of all it would result in the shifting of both axes, the north-south one 7 m to the west, and the east-west one towards the south depending on whatever measurement was given for the northern extent of the platform. Furthermore, the largest circle that can be inscribed within the 280 x 280 m square is not large enough to circumscribe the 210 × 210 m square as is the case in the Herodian 294 m plan. As a result the 280 × 280 m square is to be regarded as a pre-Herodian reality, ingeniously integrated by Herod's architects into their plans which were based on a proposed length for the southern wall of 294 m.

e. *Herodian Plans and the Temple Scroll (Fig. 2)*
(1) Measurements and functions of the square areas:

	Temple Scroll (11QT)		Herodian Plan 294 × 490 (420)
I.	Outer court	I.	Ideal square
	= court of Israel		490 × 490 m
	1700 × 1700 cubits		(420 × 420)
II.	Middle court	II.	Within the Haram
	= court of men		(a) 294 × 294
	500 × 500 cubits		(b) 280 × 280
			(c) 210 × 210 = court of Israel
		III.	Court of men
III.	Inner court	IV.	Court of priests
	= court of priests		
	300 × 300 cubits		

In two instances there are striking correspondences in the proportions between the cultic areas. Firstly, in 11QT the inner length of a side of the middle court is 480 cubits; the inner length of a side of the outer court is 1600 cubits, giving a proportion of three to ten (0.3) (1600 × 0.3 = 480). For the Herodian plan the length of the side of the court of men would be 126 m (3 × 42 m; 3 × 100 cubits of 0.42 m); the length of a side of the ideal square is 420 m, also giving a proportion of three to ten (0.3) (420 × 0.3 = 126). Secondly, in 11QT the length of a side of the inner court is 300 cubits, that of the middle court is 500 cubits, a ratio of 3 to 5 (0.6). In the Herodian plan this proportion occurs twice: in the first place the ratio of 294 m, the length of a side of the court of Israel, to 490 m, the length of the side of the ideal square, is 3 to 5 (0.6) (490 × 0.6 = 294); in the second place the ratio of the side of the court of men, 126 m, to the length of a side of the court of Israel of 210 m is also 3 to 5 (210 × 0.6 = 126).

The differences in function of the courts involved are remarkable. As the court of Israel the outer court of the Temple Scroll corresponds with the Herodian square of 210 × 210 m. The middle court of the Temple Scroll corresponds with the Herodian court of men. The inner court of the Temple Scroll corresponds with the Herodian court of the priests. These correspondences indicate two entirely opposite tendencies: that underlying the Temple Scroll is an exclusive one, expanding the area that is off-limits to certain groups (lay Israelites, women, gentiles); the Herodian tendency on the contrary restricts the cultic areas to a smaller area and expands the areas that have non-cultic purposes.

In the Temple Scroll the three architectural enclosures strictly demarcate areas of different functions. In Herod's sanctuary there are also three areas demarcated by massive architecture: (1) the inner court as (a) a court of priests including (b) a small part as a court of men; (2) the same entity enlarged by the court of women at the eastern side only; and (3) the outer enclosure. Perhaps the square of 500 × 500 cubits, the 'Mountain of the House (of the Lord)', הר הבית, had an enclosing wall with gates more or less as it is described in *m. Middot*,[23] but apparently not of such impressive dimensions that Josephus, for example, could regard it as worth mentioning. The same applies to the balustrade with the warning inscriptions which Josephus described in a more detailed manner. The most impressive of all the Herodian enclosing structures, the outer wall of the Haram and the porticoes on it, is beyond the cultic areas proper. Functionally there is a limited correspondence between the חיל of the Temple Scroll design and the Herodian enclosing structures, but in the Temple Scroll this is an embankment of 100 cubits in width and not an architectural feature. The חיל of *m. Middot* corresponds to the Herodian balustrade; the warning inscriptions restricted access to the 210 × 210 m square.

It is exactly that square which appears with numerical identity but functional difference as the middle court of the Temple Scroll and the Herodian court of Israel, in the latter twice: with a cubit of 0.56 m (the maximum cubit; 500 × 0.56 m = 280 m) and with a cubit of 0.42 m (the minimal cubit; 500 × 0.42 m = 210 m), thus clearly integrating two traditional concepts identical in numerical and symbolic value but differing in actual extent. For Herod this integration seems to have been very useful as he aimed to provide ample space for non-cultic, royal and public purposes. Herod's design, even in its uncompleted form, is a monumental demonstration of royal power and at the same time it was a strategic construction of great value as well as providing an effective means for the supervision of the Temple and its precincts. Herod enclosed the cultic areas within his massive building works and he secured their control through the Antonia fortress at the north-west, which was connected with the court of the gentiles by stairs and with the porticoes through access to their roofs. And at the southern wall he set his magnificent stoa.

NOTES

* I gratefully acknowledge the kindness of Mr Eric Lapp who helped to revise the English of this contribution.

1. See the contribution of H. Stegemann to this volume and the bibliographical notes there.

2. See in *Archaeology and History in the Dead Sea Scrolls. The New York University Conference in Memory of Yigael Yadin* (ed. L.H. Schiffman; Baltimore: American Schools of Oriental Research and Johns Hopkins University, in press).

3. F. García Martínez, 'La nueva Jerusalem y el Templo futuro de los Mss. de Qumran', *Salvación en la Palabra, Targum–Derash–Berith. Homenaje al prof. A. Diéz Macho* (ed. D. Muñoz Léon; Madrid: Ediciones Cristiandad, 1986), pp. 563-90. The significance of these fragments for the study of ancient Jewish metrology is evident, especially in connection with Temple Scroll and Herodian architectonic measures.

4. G.W. Ahlström, *Royal Administration and National Religion in Ancient Palestine* (Studies in the History of the Ancient Near East, 1; Leiden: Brill, 1982); E. Lévy (ed.), *Le système palatial en orient, en Grèce et à Rome. Actes du Colloque de Strasbourg 19-22 juin 1985* (Travaux du Centre de Recherche sur le Proche Orient et la Grèce Antiques, 9; Leiden: Brill, 1987); U. RütersWörden, *Die Beamten der israelitischen Königszeit* (BWANT 6/17 = 117; Stuttgart: Kohlhammer, 1985); E. Lipiński (ed.), *State and Temple Economy in the Ancient Near East: Proceedings of the International Conference organized by the Katholieke Universiteit Leuven, 10-14 April 1978* (Orientalia lovaniensia analecta, 5-6; 2 vols.; Leuven: Department Oriëntalistiek, 1979).

5. Y. Yadin, *The Temple Scroll*, I, pp. 237-39, 263 (Heb.: I, pp. 183-84, 204-205).

6. For the older periods see now H. Schulz, *Leviten im vorstaatlichen Israel und im Mittleren Osten* (München: Kaiser, 1987). For the period of the kingdom of Judah see G.W. Ahlström, *Royal Administration and National Religion* (note 4), and T. Polk, 'The Levites in the Davidic-Solomonic Empire', *Studia Biblica et Theologica* 9 (1979), pp. 3-22.

7. S.L. McKenzie, *The Chronicler's Use of the Deuteronomic History* (HSM 33; Atlanta: Scholars, 1985); S. Japhet, *The Ideology of the Book of Chronicles and its Place in Biblical Thought* (Frankfurt/New York: Lang, 1986); H.G.M. Williamson, *Israel in the Book of Chronicles* (Cambridge: Cambridge University Press, 1977).

8. T. Veijola, *Die ewige Dynastie. David und die Entstehung seiner Dynastie nach der deuteronomistischen Darstellung* (Annales Academiae Scientiarum Fennicae, B 193; Helsinki: Suomalainen tiedeakatemia, 1975); T. Veijola, *Das Königtum in der Beurteilung der deuteronomistischen Historiographie. Eine redaktionsgeschichtliche Untersuchung* (Annales Academiae Scientiarum Fennicae, B 198; Helsinki: Suomalainen tiedeakatemia, 1977); K.M. Beyse, *Serubbabel und die Königserwartung der Propheten Haggai und Sacharja* (Arbeiten zur Theologie, 1/48; Stuttgart: Calwer, 1972); J.D. Newsome, 'Towards a New Understanding of the Chronicler and His Purpose', *JBL* 94 (1975), pp. 201-17.

9. For a first orientation see J. Maier, *The Temple Scroll: An Introduction, Translation and Commentary* (JSOTS, 34; Sheffield: JSOT, 1985), pp. 124-28, and the bibliographical notes there; M. Hengel, J.H. Charlesworth, D. Mendels, 'The Polemical Character of "On Kingship" in the Temple Scroll. An Attempt at Dating 11QTemple', *JJS* 37 (1986), pp. 28-38.

10. In general see O. Camponovo, *Königtum, Königsherrschaft und Reich Gottes in den frühjüdischen Schriften* (Orbis biblicus et orientalis, 58; Fribourg/Göttingen: Éditions Universitaires/Vandenhoeck & Ruprecht, 1984); cf. also G.J. Brooke, *Exegesis at Qumran* (JSOTS, 29; Sheffield: JSOT, 1985), pp. 169-74; J. Maier, 'Psalm 1 im Licht antiker jüdischer Zeugnisse', *Altes Testament und christliche Verkündigung. Festschrift A.H.J. Gunneweg zum 65. Geburtstag* (ed. M. Oeming & A. Graupner; Stuttgart: Kohlhammer, 1987), pp. 353-65.

11. See E. Schürer, *The History of the Jewish People in the Age of Jesus Christ* (revised and edited by G. Vermes, F. Millar & M. Black; Vol. II; Edinburgh: T. & T. Clark, 1979), pp. 227-36.

12. *Ant.* 13.291.

13. *B. Qidd.* 66a.

14. See also the stimulating article by H. Raviv:

ח. רביב, יחסי כהונה והמלוכה ביהודה בראי ההיסטוריוגרפיה
המקראית, ספר יצחק אריה זליגמן: מחקרים במקרא
ובעולם העתיק, עורכים: יאיר זקוביץ ואלכסנדר רופא,
כר' ב' (ירושלים: א. רובינשטיין, 1983), עמ' 319-26

15. J. Simons, *Jerusalem in the Old Testament* (Leiden: Brill, 1952), pp. 396-97: 'a figure. . . which escaped control' (p. 397).

16. Cf. J. Simons, *Jerusalem in the Old Testament*, pp. 401-402, 421-22, who also assumed a pre-Herodian stoa but not of a length of 400 cubits nor inside the Herodian enclosure. But see A. Muehsam, *Coin and Temple* (Leiden: Brill, 1966), pp. 34-36. For the NT see Acts 3.1-11; 5.12; Jn 10.23.

17. For this 'short cubit' see Y. Beit-Arieh, 'Horvat 'Uzza', *Qadmoniot* 19 (1986), pp. 31-40.

18. *Jerusalem Revealed: Archaeology in the Holy City 1968-1974* (revised articles from *Qadmoniot*; Jerusalem: Israel Exploration Society & Shikmona, 1975); B. Mazar, *The Mountain of the Lord* (Garden City, N.Y.: Doubleday, 1975); M. Ben-Dov, *The Dig at the Temple Mount* (in Hebrew; Jerusalem: Keter, 1982).

19. J. Simons, *Jerusalem in the Old Testament*, pp. 421-22.

20. Cf. M. Ben-Dov, *The Dig at the Temple Mount*, p. 77; B. Bagatti, *Recherches sur le site du Temple de Jérusalem* (Jerusalem: Franciscan Press, n.d.), p. 11.

21. See for instance:

י. רופא, מקום מקדשנו—איתור בית־המקדש בדרומה של
רחבת הר־הבית, ניב המדרשיה 13 (1978/79), עמ' 88-166.

22. See note 21.

23.

א . אייבשיץ, חומת הר הבית בבניין הורדוס,
סיני 93 (1982/83), עמ' 204-193.

Figure 1   The Sanctuary according to the Temple Scroll

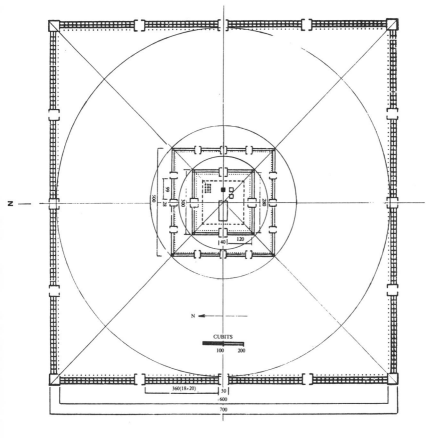

Figure 2   Temple Scroll design and Herodian Sanctuary
            (minimal variant: 1 cubit = 0.42m)

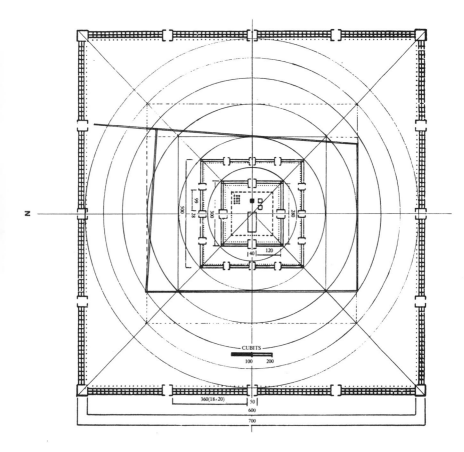

Figure 3a

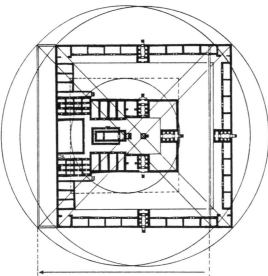

Figure 3b

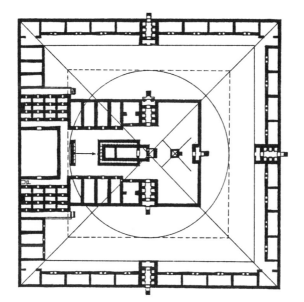

Figure 4

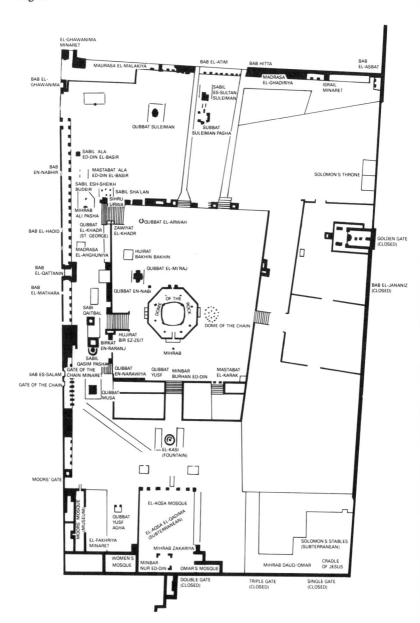

Figure 5a   Reconstruction of the southern part of Herod's enclosure (from *Qadmoniot* 5 [1971/72], by B. Lalor and B. Mazar)

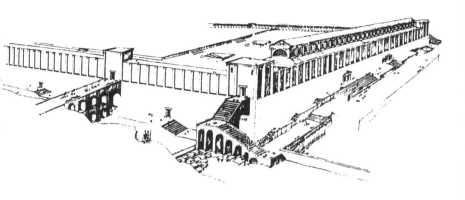

Figure 5b   Reconstruction of the stairs at Robinson's arch (from M. Ben-Dov, *The Dig at the Temple Mount* [Jerusalem, 1982], p. 92)

Figure 6a Herodian Jerusalem (from John Wilkinson, *Jerusalem as Jesus Knew It* (2nd edn, London, 1982), p. 62.

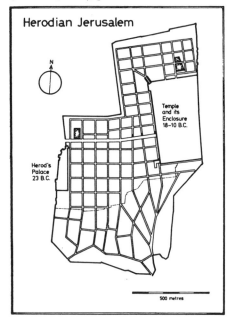

Figure 6b Plan of the reconstructed Temple area of Jesus' time (from Wilkinson, *ibid.*, p. 71).

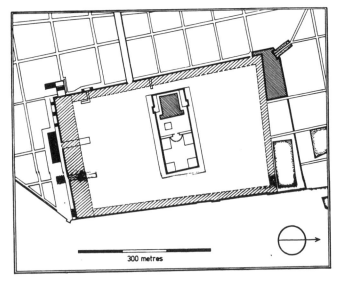

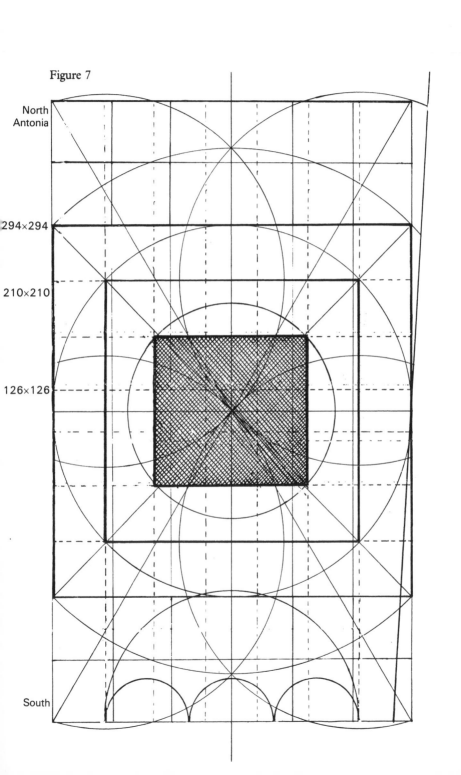

Figure 7

North
Antonia

294×294

210×210

126×126

South

Figure 8

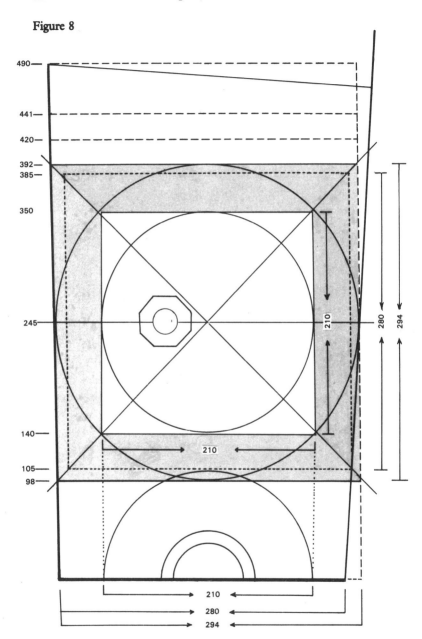

THE TEMPLE MEASUREMENTS
AND THE SOLAR CALENDAR

Margaret Barker

Borrowash

How was the solar calendar calculated? There is an elaborate system of gates in the astronomy section of *1 Enoch*, but no information as to how these gates were determined. With a lunar calendar it is possible to observe the moon in its various phases in order to reckon time, but how was the solar calendar established? It must have been done by observing the position of the sunrise and sunset, and this would have needed fixed markers by which solstices and equinoxes could be predicted. The measurements given for the Temple courts in 11QT suggest that the gatehouses served this purpose.

There is as yet no consensus as to how the measurements of the temple courts are to be interpreted, but in the calculations which follow, the results are broadly similar for whatever set one takes. The size of the angles thus obtained is not affected by the value we assume for the length of the cubit.

If we take the figures for the outer court, each wall consisted of 3 × 50 cubit gatehouses, separated by equal wall spaces of 360 cubits each. For 11QT 40.8 J. Maier reads 'in length (about) one thousand and si[x hundred] cubits'.[1] By trigonometry we can find the angle from the centre of the Temple complex to the outer corner of the NE and SE gates. These projected 7 cubits beyond the wall. Let O be the centre of the inner court, T the outer corner of the gatehouse and A the point where the line East from O and South from T intersect.

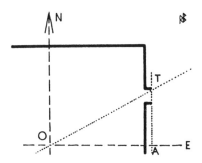

The distance OA is 800 cubits + 7 cubits projecting beyond the wall, i.e., 807 cubits. AT is 25 (half a gatehouse) + 360 (a wall space) + 50 (a gatehouse) i.e., 435 cubits. The tangent of angle α is therefore 435/807. Angle α is 28.32°.

If we make a similar calculation for the middle court, and use Maier's suggestion of 508 cubits for an overall outside wall length, the distance OA is 254 cubits + 4 cubits projecting beyond the wall, i.e., 258 cubits. AT is 14 (half a gatehouse) + 99 (a wall space) + 28 (a gatehouse) i.e., 141 cubits. The tangent of angle α is in this case 141/258. Angle α is 28.65°.

These are very similar readings, and given the uncertain nature of the figures, a remarkable correspondence. The gatehouse of the outer and middle courts and the centre point of the complex would have formed a straight line.

If the axis of the Temple was W-E, then the middle gate would be the point where the sun rose at the equinoxes. J. Morgenstern has demonstrated the importance of the autumn equinox in the temple cult,[2] and the people who preserved 11QT had sunrise prayer rituals.[3] It must be significant that the outer corners of the easterly gates (i.e., the NE corner of the northerly east gate, and the SE corner of the southerly east gate) mark the points where the sun rises at the winter and summer solstices. From the centre of the Temple complex the bearing of these gates would be:

NE gate (90−28.32) = 061.68°
          or (90−28.65) = 061.35°
SE gate (90+28.32) = 118.32°
          or (90+28.65) = 118.65°

At this latitude the sunrise at the summer solstice is approx 061° and at the winter solstice approx 117°.[4]

Were the Temple gates the means of calculating the solar calendar? From a central point, perhaps from the roof of the Temple, the solstices and equinoxes could be predicted and observed. Were these Temple gates perhaps the remote ancestors of the gates in the Astronomy Book of *1 Enoch*? The gate system there is confused, and the six gates would not have corresponded to the three easterly gates of the Temple. But in both *1 Enoch* and *2 Enoch* 13-14 there are gate systems to describe the movements of the sun, and they are different from each other. Since the Ethiopic *Enoch* differs considerably from the Aramaic in the astronomical sections, we may be seeing later developments of an earlier system in both the Ethiopic and the Slavonic versions.

1 Enoch does have *a* twelve-gate system which would correspond to the gates of the Temple. In chs. 34-36 and 76 Enoch sees the various winds and weathers issuing from twelve gates, three each in the north, the east, the west and the south. Further, the solar calendar is described as dividing the year into four quarters of ninety days, each marked by one intercalary day ruled by an angel. If the sun's movements were reckoned by the movement back and forth between the three Temple gates, we should have the four quarters determined, and the intercalary days would fall as the sun passed each gatehouse. The spring equinox occurs when the sun is at the 'great gate' (*1 Enoch* 72.6), presumably the name for the central eastern gate through which the sun's light could reach the Temple. *1 Enoch* 82.13 names the four angels of the intercalary days,[5] and Rev. 21.12 says that each of the twelve gates of the city not only has the name of a tribe of Israel, *but also an angel*.

Was the plan of 11QT calendrical? And did the whole Temple complex symbolise the cosmos, with the gates at the outer edges such as Enoch saw on his travels, and the Temple itself at the centre, representing the mountain garden of the throne of God?[6] Was it calculations such as these which enabled the wise to predict the times and the seasons?

NOTES

1. *The Temple Scroll: An Introduction, Translation & Commentary* (JSOTS, 34; Sheffield: JSOT, 1985), p. 37.

2. 'The Calendar of the Book of Jubilees: Its Origin and its Character', *VT* 5 (1955), pp. 34-76.

3. According to Josephus, *War* 2.128.

4. I am grateful to Mr Owen Roberts for supplying this information about the position of the sunrises. He regretted he had not the means to give a more accurate figure. Given that the temple measurements are far from certain in some places, and that the horizon would have been the top of the Mount of Olives, i.e., the sun would not have been visible until after the true sunrise, we cannot aspire to complete accuracy. The correspondence is still significant.

5. R.H. Charles, *The Book of Enoch or 1 Enoch* (Oxford: Clarendon, 1912), p. 177, comments as follows on the names of two of these angels: 'Milkiel from מלכיאל is simply an inversion of Helemmelek from אלימלך as Halévy has shown'. Since Helemmelek is the angel of the autumn equinox (1En 82.18), it would be interesting to know if the two names were once manifestations of the same figure, and the other form was the spring aspect of the angel of the eastern gate.

6. As I suggested in *The Older Testament* (London: SPCK, 1987), pp. 25, 127, 236, 239-41.

IS THE TEMPLE SCROLL
A SOURCE OF THE HERODIAN TEMPLE?*

Mathias Delcor

Paris

1. Introduction

The descriptions of the Herodian Temple according to Josephus[1] and the *Mishnah*[2] have never ceased posing problems for modern historians. On the one hand Josephus gives details that *m. Middot* does not mention; on the other hand the *Mishnah* describes many things about which Josephus says nothing at all. In addition, there are some flagrant contradictions between the diverse traditions and several textual obscurities.[3]

In attempting to elucidate these problems, historians, both for the texts of Josephus and of the *Mishnah*, have had at their disposal the biblical sources concerning the earlier temples of Solomon and of the restoration as well as contemporary sanctuaries of the Roman period which excavations have brought to light in Nabatea and in the Syrian region. To be convinced of this one need only glance at the most recent works of L.H. Vincent,[4] of Th.A. Busink,[5] and of A. Parrot[6] on the Herodian Temple. In 1954 Vincent devoted an important study to the Herodian Temple according to the *Mishnah*[7] and concluded it with a comparison of the evidence given by the *Mishnah* and by Josephus. An impartial study of the text, Vincent says, makes it evident that the redactor of *m. Middot* did not have at his disposal any fixed tradition and above all no architectural diagram. Rather, much of his information derives from a scriptural exegesis which rarely coheres; he borrows the rest from the personal memories of impressive authorities which indeed often conflict with one another.[8] Josephus, on the contrary, strives to describe a real building which in front of his very eyes became an archaeological ruin—this in spite of the exaggeration which here or there falsifies his opinion and his terminology.[9] For his part in 1980 Busink, over and above the very detailed study of Josephus and the *Mishnah*, devoted an important chapter to the temples in Nabatea and in Syria.[10]

Yadin asked himself whether there was not a relationship between the description of the sanctuary in Jerusalem according to the Temple Scroll and the Herodian Temple. An examination, even superficial, of the plans of the courts and of their structure suggested that there was not any resemblance in the conceptions implied by the two plans.[11] However, the Israeli scholar admitted that Josephus could have known the Temple Scroll, especially for its description of the courts or squares of the Temple of Solomon for which there is no correspondence in the biblical sources (*Ant.* 8.95-98).[12] Let us recall this important text:

> He also surrounded the temple with a parapet called *geison* in the native tongue and *thrinkos* (enclosing wall) by the Greeks, which he raised to a height of three cubits; it was to keep the multitude from entering the sacred precinct and to signify that entry was permitted only to the priests. Outside of this he built another sacred precinct (ἱερὸν) in the form of a quadrangle (ἐν τετραγώνου σχήματι)[13] and erected great and wide porticoes which were entered by high gates, each of which faced one of the four quarters and was closed by golden doors. Into this precinct all the people who were distinguished by purity and their observance of the laws might enter. But wonderful and surpassing all description, and even, one might say, all sight, was the (third) sacred precinct (ἱερόν) which he made outside of these, for he filled up with earth great valleys, into which because of their immense depth one could not without difficulty look down, and bringing them up to a height of four hundred cubits he made them level with the top of the mountain on which the temple was built; in this way the outer precinct, which was open to the sky, was on a level with the temple. And he surrounded it with double porticoes supported by high columns of native stone, and they had roofs of cedar which were smoothly finished in panels. And all the doors which he made for this sacred precinct were of silver.[14]

Yadin observed that there were resemblances between the square surrounding wall which was entered by the four gates which Josephus describes and the inner court of the Temple according to the Scroll. Apparently the description of the external court of

Josephus resembled that described in the Scroll. Yadin concluded from this: 'We may conjecture that in his description of Solomon's Temple Josephus drew upon the description of the Temple in our scroll, but also interpolated details from the Temple in his own day'.[15]

Josephus's first-hand experience of the Herodian Temple which he knew as a priest and the influence of the Temple Scroll from Qumran could explain the description given in the *Antiquities*. Before 11QT was ever known, Thackeray and Marcus, the translators of *Antiquities*, had suspected the influence of a plan of the Herodian Temple on the account of Josephus concerning the various courts of the Solomonic Temple: 'The following unscriptural account of the temple courts etc. is probably based on Josephus's knowledge of the temple of Herod'.[16] They refer to *Ant.* 15.398 and to *War* 5.184. As for the influence of the Temple Scroll on Josephus, it is not limited to ch. 8 of *Antiquities* alone; it must extend, in my opinion, to the plan of the Herodian Temple described by the Jewish historian.

2. *The Description of the Temple*

The description of the Temple, its structure, its furniture, its utensils, its ritual and festival calendar (11QT 13-29), and the preservation of the purity of the sanctuary and the city (11QT 47-51) take up most of the manuscript. That which concerns the construction of the Temple proper, for which the Scroll describes in great detail adjoining constructions, the courts and their portals (11QT 30-46), raises two essential questions: (1) What are the inspirational or foundational biblical texts and (2) has this description had any influence on the construction of the Herodian Temple?

a. *The Problem of Sources*
The author of the Scroll relies at one and the same time on the descriptions of the Israelite camp and the tent in the wilderness according to the Pentateuch and on the *torah* of Ezek. 40-48[17] where questions of the architecture of the sanctuary, of ritual and of law are all mixed together. There are indeed several resemblances between the Scroll and Ezekiel: both describe the courts more than the actual Temple. According to Ezekiel and the anonymous Qumran author the courts have a square plan. But while the Scroll's Temple has

three squares or courts, the sanctuary of Ezekiel only knows of two (Ezek. 40.17-27 and 40.28-37). According to the prophet the inner court is laid out as a horseshoe around the sanctuary proper and the altar forms the centre of the square formed by the outer court.

In the Temple Scroll the plan of the overall construction of the courts in relation to the sanctuary proper is completely different from that of Ezekiel because it is based on a very rigorous understanding of the purity of the sanctuary which was developed in the Essene world of Qumran. The three courts are concentric to underline and further preserve the sanctity of the geometric centre of this entire entity, the Temple surrounded on four sides by the first court. Without doubt the idea of square courts is borrowed from Ezekiel, but one must ask how the author of the Scroll could imagine three courts in place of two. There is room to believe that this triple division, which in the temple built by Herod the Great constituted the court of Israel, the court of the women and the court of the Gentiles, could have been inspired in part from the Bible: in 2 Chron. 20.5 under Jehoshaphat there is a new court; in 2 Kgs 21.5 under Manasseh the two courts of the house of the Lord are mentioned and in Jer. 36.10 it is in the upper court, as distinct from the lower court, that Baruch stands. But let me repeat, it is above all his demand for extreme purity with regard to the Temple which has pushed the Qumran author to compartmentalize in three zones the area arranged around the sanctuary of Jerusalem, becoming increasingly holy as one moves from the periphery towards the centre. Yadin asked why the Temple Scroll did not further follow the plan of the Temple according to the book of Ezekiel. The Temple of Ezekiel, he specified, would be built by God himself in the time to come, but that advocated by the author of the Scroll would be realized by the Israelites themselves. The plans of these two temples could not be identical on all points since the intentions of the respective builders differed.

b. *The Problem of the Influence of the Qumran Plan on that of Herod*

The description of the plan of the Temple according to the Scroll presents certain striking resemblances to that which Josephus gives for the Herodian Temple. The Qumran text describes three concentric courts, each a perfect square. The inner court measured

280 cubits on each side not including the thickness of the walls (11QT 36.2-7). The middle court has sides of 420 cubits: 'You shall make a second court around the inner court, width one hundred cubits and the length towards the east four hundred and eighty cubits and the same is the width and length in all its directions, to the south and to the west and to the north' (11QT 38.12-14). No woman is allowed to enter this court 'or a child until the day when it fulfils the prescription... as the [sum of] his redem[ption] for YHWH the half-shekel' (11QT 39.7-8). The outer court has sides of about 1,600 cubits each: 'And you shall make a t[hird] court... for their daughters and for the proselytes who are bor[n]... [the ar]ea around the middle court... in length (about) one thousand and si[x hundred] cubits from (outer) corner (building) on each side according to this measurement, to the east and south and to the west and to the north' (11QT 40.5-9).[18]

One notes that the technical term used by the anonymous Qumran author to designate the court is חצר as in the Hebrew Bible.[19] The term is to be found in 1 Kgs 6.36; 7.12; 8.64; Isa. 1.12 and above all in the *torah* of Ezekiel (Ezek. 40.14 + 38 times). This list is of special interest when it is recalled that these chapters of Ezekiel can be considered as the biblical source of the Temple Scroll. By contrast the term עזרה with the sense of 'enclosure' is found only six times in Ezekiel but is used in *m. Mid.* 2.6 and *m. Zebah* 5.8 to describe the Temple and three times in Chronicles (2 Chron. 4.9; 6.13). The term עזרה thus appears to be a late word; if it is not used by the author of the Scroll, it is because it is inspired predominately by Ezekiel and his preponderant usage.

For his part Josephus describes in the *Antiquities* the outer enclosure of the Herodian Temple, in fact a perfect square with each side measuring a stade[20] in length: τοῦτο δὲ ἦν τὸ πᾶν περίβολος, τεττάρων σταδίων τὸν κύκλον ἔχων, ἑκάστης γωνίας στάδιον μῆκος ἀπολαμβανούσης, 'Such was the whole enclosure, having a circumference of four stades, each side taking up the length of a stade' (*Ant.* 15.400).[21] This enclosure was made up of a wall whose construction Josephus anachronistically attributes to Solomon: '... the size and height of the structure, which was square (τετραγώνου), were immense, and the great size of the stones was seen along the front surface, while iron clamps on the inside assured that the joints would remain permanently united' (*Ant.* 15.399).

The square character of the enclosures specified by Josephus is perpetuated in rabbinic tradition: according to *m. Mid.* 2.1 each side of the temple esplanade, called 'the mountain of God', measured 500 cubits.[22] To try to harmonize the data supplied by Josephus and those of the rabbinic tradition is out of the question.[23] It is sufficient for our purposes to underline the square plan of the enclosure of the Herodian Temple in both places.

c. *Is it Necessary to Envisage the Influence of the Temple Scroll on the Architects of the Herodian Plan?*

A non-biblical tradition reported by Josephus concerns the square plan of the Temple as a symbol of its destruction: 'The Jews, after the demolition of Antonia, reduced the temple to a square, although they had it recorded in their oracles (ἐν τοῖς λογίοις) that the city and the sanctuary would be taken when the temple should become four-square (ἐπειδὰν τὸ ἱερὸν γένηται τετράγωνον)' (*War* 6.311).[24] Modern commentators remark that they do not know of this prediction; for example, this is the case with the French translators of the *Oeuvres complètes de Flavius Josephus*.[25] O. Michell and O. Bauernfeld declare that they do not know whether the expression τὰ λόγια describes a biblical text or a rabbinic tradition.[26] Thackeray, in his Loeb Classical Library translation, comments in relation to the words of Josephus: 'Authority unknown'. The term λόγιον is used only four times in the works of Josephus: *War* 6.311, 313; *Ant.* 3.127, 163. It means 'prediction', 'prophecy', 'oracle' in the two passages in *War*. In *Ant.* 3.127 and 163 λόγιον, 'oracle', is given as the Greek equivalent of the Hebrew חשן, transcribed ἐσσήν by Josephus. That was a kind of pocket carried on the chest of the high priest in which were kept the *Urim* and *Thummim*. It is significant that in *War* 6.312 Holy Scripture is designated as ἐν τοῖς ἱεροῖς γράμμασιν; as such it is not to be confused with λόγιον, 'oracle'. Thinking that no scriptural or rabbinic source could have been designated by this term, Yadin asks whether the passage of Josephus in which this motif occurs does not refer to the Temple Scroll.[27] Perhaps, he adds, Josephus uses this precision because he had knowledge of the Essene writings in general and of our scroll in particular. He was able to come to his idea recalling that at some point in the writings of the sect there was an allusion to the fact that before the Lord creates his temple, that edifice must be square as the Scroll indicates. Yadin even envisaged that there existed among the writings from Qumran a *pesher* concerning the squaring of the Temple from where Josephus's use of the word λόγιον 'oracle', derives, a term which certain translators render very imprecisely as 'prophetic books', as if it is a reference to something biblical.[28] The explanation that Yadin has given to the passage of Josephus on the origin of the squaring of the temple must apparently be retained until a better exegesis is found for ἐν τοῖς λογίοις.

However, temples with square plans did not exist solely in the imagination of the Essene author. There are parallels in the Syrian region in the Roman period, as, for example, the Temple of Bel at Palmyra. It was built at the beginning of the Christian era and consecrated in the year 32,[29] but the overall construction of this vast building took until the second century CE. In 1933 J. Cantineau wrote:

> The sanctuary of Bel comprises a temple proper, situated in the centre of a vast paved square court (about 200 m on each side), an altar for sacrifices, a basin for ablutions (and without doubt some other small monuments); this court was surrounded with a portico with columns, in pairs on the north, east and south sides, single and much higher on the west side; it was enclosed by a high wall forming a perimeter. It opened towards the west with a portico with three doors.[30]

K. Michalowski differs slightly from Cantineau over the measurement of the court. The sanctuary of Bel, he writes, is composed of two parts, an enormous square of 205 or 210 m and the chamber proper.[31] Since these studies the results of the excavations of the Temple of Bel have been magnificently published as a result of the care of H. Seyrig, R. Amy and E. Will.[32] These authors have given the definitive plan of the sanctuary, composed of a great enclosure with a square plan (perimeter) with porticoes.

Several examples of temples in the Nabatean region with square plans could also be cited. For example, in Hazneh the principal room measures 12 m on each side, and at Kasr Firaoun the chamber is a perfect square.[33] The court of the Nabatean Temple of Khirbet Tannur measures 15 m 68 × 15 m 47, nearly a perfect square.[34]

Thus if temples with square plans did not exist solely in the dreams of the Essene scribes but could have been visited in the neighbourhood surrounding Palestine at the turn of the era, one can envisage that the plan of the Herodian Temple was realized from such a perspective.

It must equally be stressed that the Temple constructed under the direction of Herod consisted of three courts just as in the Temple Scroll. That Temple consisted in fact of the court of Israel, the court of the women, and the court of the Gentiles.[35] There, however, are the limits of the resemblance, because in the Herodian Temple the courts are not concentric as in the Scroll, but, so it seems, the first two courts are juxtaposed, while the third, the biggest, surrounded the whole on all sides.

3. *The Temple Scroll and Josephus*

a. *Are the Courts Concentric according to Against Apion?*
In *Ag. Ap.* 2.102-104 Josephus describes briefly the various courts of the Temple destroyed by Titus. This work was composed after the *Antiquities* which were finished in 93 or 94 CE.

> Sciunt igitur omnes qui viderunt constructionem templi nostri, qualis fuerit, et intransgressibilem eius purificationis integritatem. Quattuor etenim habuit porticus in circuitu, et harum singulae propriam secundum legem habuere custodiam; in exteriorem itaque ingredi licebat omnibus etiam alienigenis; mulieres tantummodo menstruatae transire prohibebantur. In secunda vero porticu cuncti Iudaei ingrediabantur eorumque coniuges, cum essent ab omni pollutione mundae, in tertia masculi Iudaeorum mundi existentes atque purificati; in quarta autem sacerdotes stolis induti sacerdotalibus, in adytum uero soli principes sacerdotum propria stola circumamicti.

> All who ever saw our temple are aware of the general design of the building, and the inviolable barriers which preserved its sanctity. For it comprised four courts within its circumference, each with its special statutory restrictions. The outer court was open to all, foreigners included; women during their impurity were alone refused admission. To the second court all Jews were admitted and, when uncontaminated by any defilement, their wives; to the third male Jews, if clean and purified; to the fourth the priests robed in their priestly vestments. The sanctuary was entered only by the high-priests, clad in the raiment peculiar to themselves.[36]

In the sole witness of the text which is the Latin translation of *Against Apion* by Cassiodorus (485-580)[37] the use of the term 'porticus' must be noted; Blum renders it literally as 'portique' but, given the context, this must be understood as 'court' as Thackeray has done.[38] In fact, the term 'porticus' is used by Gregory of Tours in the sixth century to designate the court of a church.[39] Besides, 'in circuitu' is translated inexactly by Blum as 'concentriques', but it is necessary to understand it as 'in the enclosure', i.e. 'within the circumference'. 'Quattuor etenim habuit porticus in circuitu' must be translated as 'For it comprised four courts within its circumference'.[40] One must conclude that it is not a question of concentric courts in *Against Apion* as the translation of Blum, and even of Thackeray, might lead one to suppose.

b. *Some Common Architectural Characteristics*

Another datum, more of an architectural kind, puts the Herodian Temple in strict relation with the Jerusalem Temple planned at Qumran. According to 11QT 4.10 the height of the temple is sixty cubits. This is the same height that is given by Josephus for the Herodian Temple (*War* 5.215): 'Passing within one found oneself in the ground-floor of the sanctuary. This was sixty cubits in height, the same in length, and twenty cubits in breadth'. According to *Ant.* 15.391 the height of the Temple at this place is described as 120 cubits which corresponds to the height of the vestibule of the Solomonic Temple according to the book of Chronicles (2 Chron. 3.4) and according to Josephus (*Ant.* 8.65). The height of sixty cubits was borrowed by the Temple Scroll and subsequently by the Herodian Temple from the Second Temple for which the edict of Cyrus provided (Ezra 6.3).

It is specified in the Temple Scroll (46.5-8): 'And you shall make a terrace (רובד) round about outside the outer court (with a) width (of) fourteen cubits corresponding to all the gate openings and you shall make twelve steps for it, so that the Israelites may go up to it to come into my sanctuary'. It must be noted that the word רובד, which can be rendered either as 'terrace' or as 'perron', is not biblical but belongs to the vocabulary of the *Mishnah* (*m. Mid.* 3.6); it designates some structures of the Herodian Temple which are analogous to those of the Temple Scroll. Above all, the excavations carried out from 1968 to 1974 by Israeli archaeologists at the south and west of the actual enclosing wall of the Mosque of Omar have revealed the existence of a monumental staircase leading to the royal gateway, dating from the Herodian period,[41] which corresponds to the data of the Scroll.

11QT 46.9-10 contains the following prescription: 'And you shall make a fosse (ditch) around the sanctuary, one hundred cubits wide, so that it divides the holy sanctuary from the city'. Because of the size of the חיל, it cannot be a question of an outer wall but of a ditch[42] whose purpose was to protect the outer court and to prevent a sudden intrusion into the Temple which would thus run the risk of being defiled. In *m. Mid.* 2.3 it is also a question of a חיל, there of ten cubits, which is likewise situated in front of a wall, called there סורג. This use in both cases of the same term to designate the same object is not an isolated instance of common vocabulary. In fact, at least fifteen words in the Scroll which are not in the Hebrew Bible are to be found in the *Mishnah*: both use the same words for the rings and chains (טבעות) to which animals destined to be sacrificed are attached (11QT 34.6, 15), for the stoa or portico (פרור; 11QT 35.9; which admittedly also occurs once in 1 Chron. 26.18), for the laver (כיור; 11QT 31.10), for the turning stairway (מסבה; 11QT 30.5), for a technical term (מקרה) designating the platform (11QT 33.9), etc. These are most often architectural terms related to the Temple which in the *Mishnah* refer to the Herodian sanctuary.

c. The Problem of the Gold Curtain of the Temple Scroll and the Two Curtains in the Herodian Temple
11QT 7.13 contains the command: 'And you shall make a curtain of gold (פרוכת זהב)'. In relation to the biblical text of Exod. 26.31 the novelty is that the curtain must be woven of gold. Now, as M.R. Lehmann has recalled, *b. Yoma* 71b reads: 'The curtain is something about which no sort of gold is ever mentioned'.[43] For his part, Maimonides[44] describes 'two curtains that were furnished throughout the year for separating the sanctuary from the Holy of Holies'. He gives a list of the materials which are in the composition of the curtain and it does not include gold. Lehmann concludes justifiably that the Scroll differs from the *halakhah* concerning the curtains' materials but agrees with it concerning their number. In the Scroll it is a question of one of the two curtains which separated the Holy of Holies from the sanctuary, as in *m. Yoma* 5.1. Yadin found the only parallel to the gold curtain of the Scroll in the late *midrash Masseketh Kelim*.[45] There the פרוכת של זהב is mentioned.[46]

To those texts I must add that gold was used with other materials for the weaving of a golden veil by the seven young virgins drawn by lot for this task according to the *Protevangelium of James* 10.2:

The priest said: 'Cast me lots, who shall weave the gold, the amiant, the linen, the silk, the hyacinth-blue, the scarlet and the pure purple (τίς νήσει τὸν χρυσὸν καὶ τὸν ἀμίαντον καὶ τὴν βύσσον καὶ τὸ σιρικὸν καὶ τὸ υακίνθινον καὶ τὸ κόκκινον καὶ τὴν ἀληθινὴν πορφύραν).[47]

The editor of this text, E. de Strycker, comments on this passage: 'Several of these materials are cited in various texts of Exodus (chiefly 26.31, 35.25), the author adds of his own invention gold, amiant and silk'. In fact, the specifications furnished by the *Protevangelium of James* are not completely invented, but appear to agree in part at least with those of the Temple Scroll. They could reflect the situation of the Herodian Temple, even though Josephus says nothing about the material of which the inner curtain was made,[48] but by contrast specifies precisely that the outer curtain was woven with violet thread of linen, and of scarlet and purple.[49] With regard to the inner curtain Josephus is very brief: 'The innermost recess measured twenty cubits, and was screened in like manner from the outer portion by a veil (καταπέτασμα)' (*War* 5.219).[50] Perhaps there is reason to think that the Jewish historian does not describe it because of a sense of religious awe.[51] In the Temple Scroll the 'gold curtain' must be understood to be woven with gold thread, without doubt to match the three lined walls of the Holy of Holies, themselves panelled with gold-plated planks according to Exod. 26.29 and 1 Kgs 6.20.

In addition to the inner curtain, the Temple Scroll, in a badly preserved passage, seems to describe another curtain (11QT 7.14). Perhaps it is a question of the outer curtain which, according to Josephus, was wrought with marvellous skill (θαυμαστῶς μὲν εἰργασμένος) (*War* 5.212).[52] In fact, in the same line in the Scroll, [מ]עשה חוש[ב] can be read, a biblical expression as in Exod. 26.1, with the sense of 'skilled work'.[53]

The Temple Scroll thus knows of the existence of two curtains, the inner curtain clearly indicated and the outer curtain.[54] But, according to *m. Yoma* 5.1, two curtains (פרכות) separated the sanctuary from the Holy of Holies. They were one cubit apart. That passage in the *Mishnah* mentions the witness of R. Jose according to which there was only one curtain because Exod. 26.33 has the word curtain in the singular: 'And the veil shall separate for you the holy place from the most holy'. In the reconstruction of the ritual of the

Day of Atonement that did not prevent the rabbis from describing how the High Priest went forward across the היכל until he reached the space between the two curtains which separated the sanctuary from the Holy of Holies.

But without doubt Josephus' direct eye-witness account is to be preferred to that of the *mishnaic* tradition. As a priest Josephus also participated in the cult in the Temple. Now, according to Josephus, there was only one curtain separating the Holy of Holies from the outer sanctuary (*War* 5.219).[55] There was in addition in the Herodian Temple a second curtain hung at the entrance to the *naos*: 'Babylonian tapestry, with embroidery of blue and fine linen, of scarlet also and purple, wrought with marvellous skill. Nor was this mixture of materials without its mystic meaning: it typified the universe'.[56]

If the Temple Scroll really mentions two curtains, the inner one at the Holy of Holies and the outer one at the entrance to the *naos*, it could be thought that they were the origin of the presence of two curtains in the Herodian Temple as described by Josephus. It must be recalled that the Solomonic Temple did not require curtains but partitions and wooden shutters; the presence of curtains in the Solomonic sanctuary according to later sources actually describes realities that are contemporaneous with the redaction of those sources. Curtains only appeared with the Second Temple and it is the inner curtain (פרוכת) which is the more anciently attested in post-exilic literature. One cannot affirm with certainty, writes Légasse,[57] that a curtain had been hung at the entrance of the *naos* since the beginning of the Second Temple, but some indication of its existence in the pre-Herodian Temple could be suggested in 1 Macc. 1.22 (τὸ καταπέτασμα),[58] in the Letter of Aristeas 86, and in Josephus (*Ant.* 14.105-109). Thus it is not impossible that the Temple Scroll alludes to this outer curtain, called 'the work of a skilled artist'.

d. *Protection against Birds*

It is not impossible that 11QT 46.1-4, a passage with many lacunae, alludes to a scarecrow intended to protect the Temple from bird droppings.[59] The text reads: '. . . [shall n]ot [fly any] unclean [b]ird? over [my] san[ctuary]. . . roofs of the gate, [which belong to the] outer court'. Following Yadin the next lines could be reconstructed as:

וכול [עוף טמא לוא יוכל (?) ל]היות בתוך מקרשי לעו[לם]
ועד כול הימים אשר א[ני שוכ]ן בתוכם

'And no [unclean bird will be] in my temple for ev[er] and eternally all the days that I [dwe]ll in their midst'. In any case the Qumran text distinguishes, so it seems, between the excrement of clean and unclean birds. The crow (ערב), for example, is classified among the unclean birds in Lev. 11.13 whence the term in *m. Mid.* 4.6 כלה ערב, 'scarecrow' to designate the device placed to that effect above the Temple.

This scarecrow unquestionably existed in the Herodian Temple to which the *Mishnah* refers; this is confirmed by Josephus (*War* 5.224). But though the *Mishnah* says nothing of its form, Josephus speaks of gold spikes (χρυσέους ὀβελούς), sharpened and erected on the roof of the Temple 'to prevent birds polluting the roof'.

It is not possible, in my opinion, to follow Yadin and use the witness of *Aboth de Rabbi Nathan B* 30. There is no explicit mention of a scarecrow in that passage which reads: 'A fly was never seen in the slaughterhouse. Nor was an unclean reptile. Birds (העורף) never passed over it (the Temple)'.[60] This is merely a part of the description of the ten miracles worked in the Temple at Jerusalem.

The device of the Herodian Temple differed radically from that described by Eupolemus in the second century BCE.[61] There it is not a question of tapered spikes but of nets on which were hung small bells intended to frighten the birds and prevent them from perching on the Temple or nesting above the gates and porticoes (ἐπὶ τοὺς φαντώμασι τῶν πυλῶν καὶ στοῶν) or defiling the Temple with their droppings.[62]

However, Saul Lieberman[63] judges that Eupolemus' description has no historical value, seeing that it relies on the tradition of the LXX, principally 2 Chron. 4.12-13. If such is the case, one can hardly use the text of Eupolemus to establish what the scarecrow, which would have existed in the Temple since the second century BCE, would have looked like or how it would have worked. Whatever the case, it appears difficult to deny the existence of some kind of scarecrow in some shape at that period.

R. Hananel[64] maintains, however, that the Temple of Solomon had no kind of scarecrow. But he draws his conclusion from *Aboth de Rabbi Nathan B* which, in recounting the ten miracles worked in the Temple, mentions that no bird was ever seen over the Temple. But the text called upon by R. Hananel does not constitute any proof in favour of his affirmation because the matter reported by *Aboth de Rabbi Nathan* is to be taken as a miracle and is not to be used for assessing the effectiveness of any such scarecrow placed above the Temple. Besides, such miracles are recounted by pagan authors, for example, for the sanctuary of Olympus.[65]

What conclusion can be reached concerning the origin of the scarecrow of the Herodian Temple? Because of the fragmentary character of 11QT 46.1-3, it is difficult to say whether Herod's architects found their model in it. They could just as well have been inspired by devices consisting of spikes used in pagan temples for protecting them from eventual pollution from the excrement of birds.[66]

e. *The Extravagant Use of Gold for the Decoration of the Temple*
B. *Sukk.* 51b reads: 'Whoever has not seen the Temple during his life, has never seen a sumptuous building'. This refers to the Herodian Temple as the rest of the context makes clear. The king had wanted to surpass the Temple of Solomon in grandeur and magnificence. Gold, it is true, already had a large place in the interior decoration of the Solomonic Temple (1 Kgs 6.20-22; 7.48-50) according to oriental custom which did not spare the use of the yellow metal, as excavations in Mesopotamia and Egypt have shown.[67] Without doubt one does not have mere hyperbole in the description in 1 Kings 6, but rather description of the wealth of gold which was actually displayed.[68]

In the accounts of Josephus more than in the *Mishnah* the Herodian Temple glitters throughout with its gold, as J. Jeremias has written.[69] B. *Sukk.* 51b reports on this subject: 'In addition he (Herod) wanted to cover the temple with gold. The sages said to him: Let it be so, because it is more beautiful like that; it resembles the waves of the sea'. Late rabbinic tradition is in agreement with Josephus, the contemporary of the construction of the Temple by Herod and, as a priest, a privileged visitor to the sanctuary on the occasion of liturgical service.

> The exterior of the building wanted nothing that could astound either mind or eye. For, being covered on all sides with massive plates of gold, the sun was no sooner up than it radiated so fiery a flash that persons straining to look at it were compelled to avert

their eyes, as from the solar rays. To approaching strangers it
appeared from a distance like a snow-clad mountain; for all that
was not overlaid with gold was of purest white' (*War* 5.222-23).[70]

Elsewhere he specifies that the façade of the Temple of 100 cubits in
length was covered with gold plates, just like the door between the
vestibule and the sanctuary (*War* 5.207-10). Above the entrance
which led from the vestibule into the sanctuary there was a gold vine:
'The gate opening into the building was, as I said, completely
overlaid with gold, as was the whole wall around it. It had, moreover,
above it those golden vines, from which depended grape-clusters as
tall as a man' (*War* 5.210). According to *m. Mid.* 3.8 the priests
hooked there the bunches of gold grapes coming from gifts. Above
this gate there was a golden lamp[71] which reflected the rays of the
sun; it had been given by queen Helena of Adiabene (*b. Yoma*
37b).

Furthermore, in the vestibule some gold chains were hung from
the roof-beams (*m. Mid.* 3.8). On entering the Temple one had to
pass under some portals covered with gold and silver: 'Of the ten
gates nine were completely overlaid with gold and silver, as were also
their door-posts and lintels; but one, that outside the sanctuary was
of Corinthian bronze, and far exceeded in value those plated with
silver and set in gold' (*War* 5.201). The *Mishnah* agrees here with
Josephus: 'All the gates that were there had been changed [and
overlaid] with gold, save only the doors of the Nicanor Gate. . .' (*m.
Mid.* 2.3). Also, in the court of the women, according to *m. Sukk.* 5.2,
there were four gold candlesticks with four gold bowls on the top of
them. The walls of the Holy of Holies were also covered with gold
(*m. Mid.* 4.1; *m. Šeqal.* 4.4). According to this latter passage the gold
plating of the Holy of Holies came from the surplus after deductions
had been made from gifts. Above the Temple itself the scarecrow
made of sharp spikes was golden (*War* 5.224).

After the capture of the city and the Temple by the Romans, gold
was so abundant in Jerusalem that an immense supply of gold
swamped the whole province of Syria; it resulted, says Josephus, in
the standard of gold being depreciated to half its former value (*War*
6.317).

A complete comparison of the Herodian Temple with that of the
Qumran Scroll cannot be established; the Scroll is often too
fragmentary in relation to objects or buildings of gold. We can only

glean some indication in the parts of the manuscript that have
survived.

Column 3 describes certain cultic utensils in the making of which
precious materials, notably gold, should be used. All the vessels
(כול כלי) shall be made of pure gold (זהב טהור; 11QT 3.8), even the
cover (הכפרת; 11QT 3.9). Likewise the bowls used for the altar
service are of pure gold, even the fire holders (מחתות) used for
carrying fire inside (11QT 3.12).[72] The Qumran author adds: 'The
candelabrum [and all the utensils shall be made of pure go]ld' (11QT
3.13). This text is easily restored on the basis of Exod. 3.14 (LXX and
Sam.).

At column 9 the author returns at greater length to the construction
of the candelabrum or *menorah*. One can easily reconstruct the
missing parts of the manuscript by using the biblical text of Exod.
25.31 and 37.17-21. One very significant detail in 11QT 9.11 must be
underlined: the weight of the candelabrum and its accessories is
given as two talents of pure gold in total (כולה ככרים). By contrast,
according to MT Exod. 25.39 and 37.24, the candelabrum and its
accessories must weigh one talent of pure gold (ככר זהב טהור). The
LXX of Exod. 25.39 speaks of one talent for the accessories alone:
πάντα τὰ σκεύη ταῦτα τάλαντον χρυσίου καθαροῦ; this allows us to
suppose that the *menorah* proper must have another talent. Here we
may well have a viewpoint close to that of the Temple Scroll. *B.
Menah.* 88b notes that there were disputes among the *Tannaim*
concerning the weight of the candelabrum and its accessories. Rashi
closed the debate categorically: 'One talent of pure gold. . . Its weight
with its accessories shall be exactly one talent, neither more nor less.
The talent for secular use was of sixty minas, that for sacred use was
double, one hundred and twenty minas'.

By doubling the weight of the *menorah* and its accessories in
relation to the biblical text, the Qumran author seeks to make the
Temple furniture more sumptuous. He agrees on this, so it seems,
with Josephus when he speaks of the Herodian Temple in *Ag. Ap.*
1.198: 'Beside it stands a great edifice, containing an altar and a
lampstand, both made of gold, and weighing two talents—βωμός ἐστι
χαὶ λυχνίον, ἀμφότερα χρυσᾶ δύο τάλαντα τὴν ὁλκήν'.[73] This
phrase, it is true, is ambiguous because one does not know whether
the two talents represent the total weight of the altar and the
lampstand or whether each of these two objects weighs two talents.

In any case, on the basis of *Against Apion*, J. Jeremias understands the giant candelabrum with seven branches to weigh two talents.[74] In this way I reckon that the total weight of two talents would clearly be insufficient for the two objects.

When the author of the scroll envisages that the curtain in the Temple must be made of gold, that is, woven from gold thread, he cannot be distinguished from Herod the Great and his sumptuous taste for the new Temple at Jerusalem. It is the same with the gates of the different courts. In fact, the inner court 'shall be furnished with panelling of cedar wood overlaid with pure gold and its doors will be overlaid with fine gold' (11QT 36.10-11). Similarly in the middle court the swinging door of the gateway will be plated with gold (מצופו]ת ז[הב; 11QT 39.3). For the outer court the author of the Scroll writes: 'with jambs of cedar wood and overlaid with gold' (11QT 41.16-17).

4. *An Hypothesis*

The description of the Temple according to the Scroll presents some striking similarities concerning its plan, its architecture, even the weight in gold of certain objects of its furniture. In other respects Josephus seems to have known the Temple Scroll as Yadin has well shown.

Two questions are raised by these correspondences between the Temple Scroll and the Temple constructed by Herod the Great: (1) who built the Herodian Temple; (2) what was the role of the Temple Scroll in the Herodian project?

(1) It must be recalled at once that, according to Josephus, there was lively opposition to Herod's scheme, because people judged his enterprise fanciful, wondering whether he would allow sufficient resources to bring the reconstruction of the Temple to completion (*Ant.* 15.388). The Jewish historian informs us that the Temple was rebuilt in a very particular manner since a thousand priests clothed in linen worked there as carpenters or masons. It is well known that neither the Temple of Solomon (1 Kgs 5–6) nor that of Zerubbabel (Ezra 3–6) was built by priests. Schalit, the historian of Herod the Great, has underlined that the use of priests in this building work finds its explanation in the fact that they must carry out their work in parts of the Temple where lay Israelites were not admitted.[75] This is also the interpretation of J. Jeremias.[76]

But has enough been said? It is noteworthy that the priests were dressed in priestly robes (ἱερατικὰς στολάς), and not in work clothes,[77] as if they were performing a liturgy. Without doubt their clothes were linen. This mark of absolute purity fits in every way with the Essenes. If Essene priests cooperated on the construction of the new Temple, the lively opposition of the people to Herod's project is all the more understandable, even though Herod met the opposition with a speech in which he tried to persuade the people of the cogency of his plans: 'These were Herod's words, and most of the people were astonished by his speech, for it fell upon their ears as something quite unexpected. And while the unlikelihood of his realizing his hope did not disturb them, they were dismayed by the thought that he might tear down the whole edifice and not have sufficient means to bring his project (of rebuilding it) to completion. And this danger appeared to them to be very great, and the vast size of the undertaking seemed to make it difficult to carry out' (*Ant.* 15.388).

Also we might suppose that Herod would have depended on the part of the population which was favourably disposed towards him, namely, the Essenes. Had not one of them, Menaham, predicted the rise of Herod and his accession to the throne (*Ant.* 15.374) and did he not honour all the Essenes in a particular way (*Ant.* 15.378)? The Essenes had strongly censured the priesthood of Jerusalem who had polluted the Temple and refused to offer sacrifices there.[78] One could easily understand that it might have been to them that Herod had appealed for the rebuilding of the Temple. In relation to the presence of a thousand priests employed as masons and as carpenters, C. Daniel has supposed that it was above all Essene priests who were used to such work from the comment of Josephus about the Essenes (*War* 2.129) where he says that 'they are then dismissed by their superiors to the various crafts in which they are severally proficient and are strenuously employed until the fifth hour'. However, this text does not explicitly say that there were priests among them.

Yet we know that the cultic functions of the Jerusalem priests were limited to two weeks each year, and to the three annual pilgrimage festivals. Priests lived for ten or eleven months at home. They were obliged to pursue a profession where they resided, principally some form of manual trade. For example, we know about a Pharisaic priest who was a hewer of stone; R. Eliezer ben Zadok was engaged in the oil trade in Jerusalem, and another priest was a butcher there. The priest Eleazer ben Azariah was engaged in the breeding of cattle on a large scale. A large number of priests were scribes.[79] Members of the priesthood in Jerusalem thus had a trade because only very occasionally did they exercise their priestly role.

In spite of the silence of Josephus, it is possible to hold as credible the idea that some part was taken by the Essenes in the reconstruction of the Temple.

(2) There need be nothing surprising, then, about the Temple Scroll, in the hands of the Essene priests, exercising a certain influence on this reconstruction, even though this document refers to a temple which will exist until the day when God himself will build it (11QT 29.9-10).

Although the plan of the Temple, according to the views of the Qumran author, does not agree with that of the Herodian Temple perfectly in every detail, in particular in relation to the courts and the outbuildings, nothing prevents the thought that Essene priests who participated in the reconstruction had wanted to be able to make real something of those dreams that were the least utopian of all in their writings.

NOTES

* Translated by George J. Brooke.

1. *War* 5.184-227; *Ant.* 15.391-425; *Ag. Ap.* 2.102-111.

2. M. *Middot*.

3. J. Chamonard (*Oeuvres complètes de Josèphe* [ed. Th. Reinach; Paris: Leroux, 1900-26], Vol. III, p. 354) comments thus on a difficult passage of *Ant.* 15.398: 'We translate by guess-work; the text is desperately obscure'.

4. L.-H. Vincent, *Jérusalem de l'Ancien Testament: recherches d'archéologie et d'histoire* (Paris: Gabalda, 1956), Vols. II-III.

5. Th. A. Busink, *Der Tempel von Jerusalem von Salomo bis Herodes: eine archäologisch-historische Studie unter Berücksichtigung des Westsemitischem Tempelbaus* (Leiden: Brill, 1980), Vol. II, pp. 1016-1251.

6. A. Parrot, *Le Temple de Jérusalem* (Cahiers d'Archéologie Biblique, 5; Neuchâtel: Delachaux et Niestlé, 1954), pp. 58-77.

7. 'Le Temple hérodien d'après la Mišnah', *RB* 61 (1954), pp. 31-35, 398-418.

8. 'Le Temple hérodien d'après la Mišnah', p. 412.

9. 'Le Temple hérodien d'après la Mišnah', p. 417.

10. _Der Tempel von Jerusalem von Salomo bis Herodes_, Vol. II, pp. 1252-1358.

11. _The Temple Scroll_, pp. 196-97 (Heb.: I, pp. 151-52).

12. _The Temple Scroll_, I, p. 192 (Heb.: I, p. 148).

13. Note that τετραγώνος means quadrangular or square. Thus nothing hinders the translation: 'He built a sanctuary in the form of a square', as Yadin remarks.

14. _Josephus: In Ten Volumes_ (trans. H.St.J. Thackeray, R. Marcus, A. Wikgren, & L. Feldman; LCL; London: Heinemann; Cambridge, Mass.: Harvard University, 1926-1965), Vol. V, pp. 623-25. A French translation is available in _Oeuvres complètes de Josèphe_, Vol. II (_Antiquités_ Judaïques, Books 6-10), pp. 180-81.

15. _The Temple Scroll_, I, p. 194 (Heb.: I, p. 150).

16. H.St.J. Thackeray & R. Marcus, _Josephus V_, p. 622, n. c.

17. Cf. J. Maier, 'Die Hofanlagen im Tempelentwurf des Ezechiel im Licht der Tempelrolle', _Prophecy: Essays presented to Georg Fohrer on his 65th Birthday_ (ed. J.A. Emerton; BZAW, 150; Berlin: de Gruyter, 1980), pp. 55-67.

18. Generally quotations in English of the Temple Scroll are taken from J. Maier, _The Temple Scroll: An Introduction, Translation and Commentary_ (JSOTS, 34; Sheffield: JSOT, 1985). A French translation by A. Caquot is available in 'Le Rouleau du Temple de Qoumrân', _ETR_ 53 (1978), pp. 443-500; reprinted in _La Bible: Ecrits Intertestamentaires_ (ed. A. Dupont-Sommer,& M. Philonenko; Paris: Gallimard, 1987), pp. 61-132.

19. See the study of V. Hamp, 'חָצֵר, ḥāṣer', _TWAT_ 3, cols. 140-48; A. Hurvitz, _A Linguistic Study of the Relationship between the Priestly Source and the Book of Ezekiel: A New Approach to an Old Problem_ (CRB 20; Paris: Gabalda, 1982), pp. 79-81.

20. The stade was 185 metres, if Josephus had the Roman stade in mind, which is probable, since he writes in Rome and above all for Romans; cf. J. Simons, _Jerusalem in the Old Testament: Researches and Theories_ (Leiden: Brill, 1952), p. 395 n. 1.

21. Trans. R. Marcus & A. Wikgren, _Josephus VIII_, p. 193.

22. H. Danby, _The Mishnah_ (London: Oxford University Press, 1933), p. 591; O. Holtzmann, _Middot: Text, Übersetzung und Erklärung_ (Giessen: Töpelmann, 1913), pp. 58-59.

23. R. Marcus & A. Wikgren (_Josephus VIII_, p. 193) comment on _m. Mid._ 2.1 in relation to _Ant._ 15.400: 'If the "royal cubit" is meant, as is probable, this would make c. 850 feet for each side'.

24. The translation of ἐν τοῖς λογίοις 'dans leurs livres' in _Oeuvres complètes de Flavius Josèphe_, Vol. V, p. 199, is imprecise.

25. _Oeuvres complètes de Josèphe_, Vol. VI, p. 199.

26. _De bello judaico II_ (Darmstadt: Wissenschaftliche Buchgesellschaft, 1969), p. 190.

27. *The Temple Scroll,* I, pp. 197-98 (Heb.: I, pp. 152-53).

28. See e.g. G.A. Williamson, *Josephus: The Jewish War* (Harmondsworth: Penguin, 1984), p. 362.

29. See J. Cantineau, *Inventaire des Inscriptions de Palmyre: 9/1 Le sanctuaire de Bêl* (Beyrouth: Imprimerie catholique, 1933), pp. 6-7.

30. *Inventaire des Inscriptions de Palmyre: 9/1 Le sanctuaire de Bêl,* p. 4.

31. K. Michalowski, *Palmyra* (London: Pall Mall, 1970), pp. 17-19. The same dimensions are retained by J. Starcky & M. Gawlikowski, *Palmyre: édition nouvelle et augmentée de nouvelles découvertes* (Paris: Maisonneuve, 1985), p. 117.

32. *Le Temple de Bel à Palmyre* (Textes et Planches; Paris: Geuthner, 1975).

33. Th.A. Busink, *Der Tempel von Jerusalem von Salomo bis Herodes,* Vol. II, pp. 1262-94, lists a certain number of Nabatean temples of this type; cf. J. Starcky, 'Pétra et la Nabatène', *DBSup* 7, cols. 973-81.

34. N. Glueck, *Deities and Dolphins: The Story of the Nabateans* (London: Cassell, 1966), pp. 156, 621 (plan).

35. Cf. Josephus, *War* 5.184-206; Th.A. Busink, *Der Tempel von Jerusalem von Salomo bis Herodes,* Vol. II, pp. 1071-79.

36. Trans. H.St.J. Thackeray, *Josephus I,* pp. 333-35; slightly adjusted, as the following comments and n. 40 show.

37. I have used the edition by C. Boysen, *Corpus scriptorum ecclesiasticorum latinorum* (Vienna: Academia Litteratum Caesarea, 1898), Vol. XXXVII, pp. 94-95.

38. L. Blum, *Oeuvres complètes de Flavius Josèphe,* Vol. VII, p. 79.

39. Cf. A. Blaise, *Dictionnaire latin-français des auteurs chrétiens* (Strasbourg: 'Le Latin Chrétien', 1954), p. 635.

40. Thackeray's translation, 'it had four surrounding courts', does not render the Latin literally enough and takes no account of 'in circuitu'.

41. Cf. *Jerusalem Revealed: Archaeology in the Holy City 1968-1974* (ed. Y. Yadin; Jerusalem: Israel Exploration Society, 1975), pp. 27-30.

42. With Yadin, *The Temple Scroll,* I, p. 188 (Heb.: I, p. 145); against Caquot and Maier (see n. 18).

43. 'The Temple Scroll as a Source of Sectarian Halakah', *RevQ* 9 (1977-78), p. 581.

44. *Hilkhoth Keley hamiqdash* 7.16.

45. Cf. A. Jellinek, *Bet ha-Midrasch* (2nd edn, Jerusalem: Bamberger & Wahrmann, 1938), Vol. II, p. 89.

46. For the discussion see Yadin, *The Temple Scroll,* II, pp. 27-28 (Heb.: II, p. 21).

47. E. de Strycker, *La forme la plus ancienne du Protévangile de Jacques* (Brussels: Société des Bollandistes, 1961), p. 112. The English trans. is by A.J.B. Higgins (from the German of O. Cullmann) in *New Testament*

Apocrypha (ed. E. Hennecke, W. Schneemelcher, & R.McL. Wilson; London: SCM, 1963), I, p. 380.

48. Cf. *War* 5.219.

49. *War* 5.212-14.

50. Writings contemporary with the Second Temple are almost silent on the subject of the inner curtain; their attention is focussed on the large tapestry visible to all at the entrance to the Temple: cf. S. Légasse, 'Les voiles du Temple de Jérusalem', *RB* 87 (1980), pp. 560-89, and the studies of A. Pelletier cited by Légasse on p. 560.

51. On this see Th.A. Busink, *Der Tempel von Jerusalem von Salomo bis Herodes*, Vol. II, p. 1123.

52. In Josephus it is a question of the large outer tapestry at the entrance of the היכל. *M. Mid.* 4.1 completely ignores its existence. See S. Légasse, 'Les voiles du Temple de Jérusalem', pp. 578-79.

53. See E. Qimron, 'New Readings in the Temple Scroll', *IEJ* 28 (1978), p. 162.

54. Yadin, *The Temple Scroll*, II, p. 28 (Heb.: II, p. 21), comments: 'Perhaps there the other curtain is intended'.

55. Similarly, see Th.A. Busink, *Der Tempel von Jerusalem von Salomo bis Herodes*, Vol. II, p. 1126.

56. *War* 5.212 (trans. H.St.J. Thackeray). A recent French trans. is that by A. Pelletier, *Flavius Josèphe: Guerre des Juifs* (Paris: Les Belles Lettres, 1982), Vol. III, p. 138.

57. 'Les voiles du Temple de Jérusalem', p. 583.

58. F.M. Abel & J. Starcky (*Les Livres des Maccabées* [Paris: Editions du Cerf, 1961], p. 87) identify it with the outer curtain.

59. This allusion was recognized by Yadin, *The Temple Scroll*, I, pp. 271-72 (Heb.: I, pp. 211-12); J. Maier, *The Temple Scroll: An Introduction, Translation and Commentary*, pp. 12, 116; A. Caquot, 'Le Rouleau du Temple de Qoumrân', pp. 479-80.

60. *ARN B* 30; trans. J. Saldarini, *The Fathers according to Rabbi Nathan: A Translation and Commentary* (SJLA, 11; Leiden: Brill, 1975), p. 233.

61. Cf. Eusebius, *Praeparatio Evangelica* 9.198. Greek text with English trans. in C.R. Holladay, *Fragments from Hellenistic Authors. Vol. I: Historians* (SBLTT, 20; Chico: Scholars, 1983), pp. 310-11.

62. See my study, 'La description du Temple de Salomon selon Eupolémos et le problème de ses sources', in *Mémorial Jean Carmignac, RevQ* 13 (1988), pp. 251-71.

63. *Hellenism in Jewish Palestine* (New York: Jewish Theological Seminary of America, 1950), p. 173.

64. *B. Šabb.* 57b.

65. Cf. Pausanius 5.14.1 (ed. W.H.S. Jones & H.A. Ormerod; LCL; London: Heinemann; Cambridge, Mass.: Harvard University, 1966, p. 457).

66. See the references assembled by S. Lieberman, *Hellenism in Jewish Palestine*, pp. 174-75.

67. Cf. A. Parrot, *Le Temple de Jérusalem*, p. 28.

68. See the commentaries by Montgomery (ICC; Edinburgh: T. & T. Clark, 1951), pp. 140-60; J. Gray (OTL; 2nd edn, London: SCM, 1970), pp. 157-76; M. Noth (BKAT 9/1; Neukirchen-Vluyn: Neukirchener Verlag, 1968), pp. 95-129.

69. *Jerusalem zur Zeit Jesu* (2nd edn, Göttingen: Vandenhoeck & Ruprecht, 1958, Part 1, pp. 24-25); *Jerusalem in the Time of Jesus* (London: SCM, 1969), p. 24; *Jérusalem au temps de Jésus* (Paris: Éditions du Cerf, 1967), p. 41.

70. Trans. H.St.J. Thackeray, *Josephus III*, p. 269.

71. Jeremias (*Jerusalem in the Time of Jesus*, p. 24) speaks of a 'concave mirror' (*Hohlspiegel*), but the text of *B. Yoma* 37b reads היליני אמו עשתה נברשת which means 'his mother Helena made a golden lamp', because such is the meaning of נברשת and in biblical Aramaic of נברשתא (Dan. 5.5); cf. A.R. Millard, 'The Etymology of Nebrašta' Daniel 5, 5', *Maarav* 9 (1986-87), pp. 82-92. It is also the translation of L. Goldschmidt, *Der Babylonische Talmud* (Berlin: Calvary, 1901), Vol. II, p. 856.

72. See the disussion by Yadin, *The Temple Scroll*, II, p. 8 (Heb.: II, p. 5), 'Inside' does not allude to the Holy of Holies but to the sanctuary.

73. Trans. H.St.J. Thackeray, *Josephus I*, p. 243.

74. *Jerusalem in the Time of Jesus*, p. 24.

75. A. Schalit, *König Herodes. Der Mann und sein Werk* (Studia Judaica, 4; Berlin: de Gruyter, 1969), pp. 372-73.

76. *Jerusalem in the Time of Jesus*, p. 206.

77. Th. Reinach's suggested correction of ἱερατικὰς to ἐργατικὰς is not convincing (*Oeuvres complètes de Josèphe*, Vol. III, p. 353).

78. For this see C. Daniel, 'Nouveaux arguments en faveur de l'identification des Hérodiens et des Esséniens', *RevQ* 7 (1969-71), p. 399; see also his earlier articles that try to show that the Herodians are to be identified with the Essenes, 'Les 'Hérodiens' du Nouveau Testament sont-ils des Esséniens?', *RevQ* 6 (1967-69), pp. 30-53; 'Les Esséniens et 'ceux qui sont dans les maisons des rois' (*Matthieu* 11, 7-8 et *Luc* 7, 24-25)', *RevQ* 6 (1967-69), pp. 261-77.

79. These examples are gathered together by J. Jeremias, *Jerusalem in the Time of Jesus*, pp. 206-207.

DOES THE TEMPLE SCROLL DATE FROM THE FIRST OR SECOND CENTURY BCE?*

E.-M. Laperrousaz

Paris

The Temple Scroll can be considered to be one of the oldest works of the Essene community of Qumran, attributable therefore to Period I of the occupation of the site by the community of the Teacher of Righteousness. The editor of this document, Yigael Yadin, has categorized its script as Herodian; but a fragment of another exemplar of this text whose identification is disputed, to be found in the Rockefeller Museum in Jerusalem, is in a script considered as Hasmonean. Let us look at the several criteria used for dating.

1. *Script*

It is well known that precision in dating on the basis of palaeographic criteria is extremely relative, as is underlined by the specialists in the discipline. Before citing some of them, I shall reiterate two remarks that I have already had the opportunity to formulate elsewhere:

In the first place it is a matter of recalling a warning—which seems to be self-evident—which features in my book *Qoumrân*: 'It is advisable to be similarly cautious in the use of palaeographic evidence, because, obviously, scribes of different ages writing at the same time will generally appear to have worked at different times!'[1] Could any scholarly colleague not be in agreement with this remark? However, in practice, even those who would wish to be considered as subtle in the handling of these delicate matters do not actually take this into account.

Then let me dismantle another method which is unfortunately all too frequent. Following an error of method in the use of coin evidence and other objects discovered in the ruins, and sometimes following a simple error in the identification of this or that coin— an excusable error given the state of preservation of many of them—a chronology is constructed for the occupation of the sites. Then texts are interpreted in terms of this chronology. Lastly, when the use made of this evidence is contested, and also the chronology constructed on the basis of its use, such an objection is challenged as a misinterpretation of the texts. Thus, 'la boucle est bouclée'!

Let me add that often in this process the fact of not taking the former remark seriously plays a significant role.[2]

Now in support of the first of these remarks I will report the opinions published by four eminent colleagues concerning the use of palaeographic evidence in the dating of the Dead Sea scrolls.

In a work which appeared nearly ten years after the discovery of Qumran Cave 1 Millar Burrows, who was the Director of the American School of Oriental Research in Jerusalem at the time of the discovery of the first Dead Sea scrolls, as he himself has recalled in the same book, wrote:

> Several scholars have said that for dating the Dead Sea Scrolls in particular palaeography is of little use, because the material available for comparison is not sufficiently abundant, and what there is cannot be exactly dated. If what is meant is that we cannot assign a manuscript to a specific year or decade, this is true; we have quite adequate material, however, for determining the period to which a manuscript belongs within, say, a half or a quarter of a century.[3]

Two years later in an important article by Professor N. Avigad of the Hebrew University of Jerusalem one could read these lines:

> In the following we shall briefly discuss the suggested developments of some of the letters which were decisive for the relative dating as proposed. It should, however, be kept in mind that various scribes had different handwritings, and that scribes are naturally inclined to conservatism in the use of formal styles.[4]

Shortly afterwards in the work which 'reproduced with only slight development of their original form' the text of the lectures which he had given in London in December 1959,[5] Father R. de Vaux—then, at the same time, Director of the Dominican École biblique and of the French School of Archaeology in Jerusalem, and President of the

International Committee charged with the management of the Palestine Archaeological Museum (Rockefeller Foundation), and by right of the last two of these three offices co-Director of the Qumran excavations—arguing against C. Roth pointed out:

> The evidence of palaeography is equally hostile to Roth's theory. It is true that he refuses to take it into account, but he admits that it can supply an approximate date to within about one generation. That is sufficient for us.[6]

Lastly, in a note to an important article that appeared in *Revue Biblique*, J. Starcky has written, in relation to 'the history of the Essenes which the excavations and palaeography have revealed':

> It seems wise, when one fixes the date of a manuscript, to keep on both sides a margin of uncertainty of at least a quarter of a century. Even at Palmyra where we can set out numerous texts bearing a date, a similarly large margin has been shown to be necessary.[7]

We must always keep in mind these reservations when faced with any attempt at dating texts coming from the Qumran caves. Let me add that, obviously, the original *composition* of a text could precede, by more or less, the date of writing of the actual manuscript retrieved at Qumran, which might be only a copy of the original document.

2. *Language*

As far as the language of the author of the Temple Scroll is concerned let us note that Y. Yadin in Jerusalem as also A. Caquot in Paris, for example, have called attention to characteristics met only in Mishnaic Hebrew. Does not this precise observation invite us to attribute a later date than the period of John Hyrcanus to the composition of this document?

3. *Internal criteria*

As for internal criteria for dating offered by the account of the text itself, A. Caquot, in the Introduction to his French translation of the Temple Scroll,[8] has enumerated several, following Y. Yadin, the editor of the document. Those criteria are:

> (a) One point, however, must be particularly considered. Column 34 specifies that the young bull to be sacrificed must be attached by

the head to a ring, and for this reason the slaughter-house is built with chains coming down from the ceiling. Now an ancient rabbinic tradition, quoted several times, attributes the introduction of rings to John Hyrcanus who modified, so it is said, the rules for slaughter in the Jerusalem temple by prohibiting the use of the mallet. The Temple Scroll appears to reflect the innovation of this man who was high priest and king from 134 to 104,[9] unless it is admitted that John Hyrcanus was influenced by the teaching of the scroll.

(b) Other characteristics, less precise, corroborate the hypothesis that this detail makes conceivable; these characteristics are the following:

(1) The Temple Scroll shows great interest in the institution of the monarchy—much more marked than in the biblical text of Deuteronomy 17.14-20 which inspired it,

(2) and in military questions, with a perspective altogether worldly that profoundly distinguishes our text from the War Scroll. One can conclude that the Temple Scroll was conceived at a time when these two preoccupations were current. Is it necessary to recall that it was the father of John Hyrcanus, the high priest Simon, who instituted in 140 the hereditary plurality of the supreme religious and lay powers and that all his life John Hyrcanus himself followed an expansionist policy based on military strength? Is this not the spirit of a time which shows itself in what one could call the nationalism of the Temple Scroll, which revives the xenophobia of Deuteronomy?

(c) Let me cite a last point which itself suggests the opposition of the author to an innovation of John Hyrcanus. The Law of the King of the Temple Scroll stipulates that the king must be surrounded with a guard of 12,000 men for which each Israelite tribe must supply 1,000 men. It is very probable that this insistence on the national character of the royal guard is a reaction against an initiative of John Hyrcanus who, according to Flavius Josephus (*Antiquities* 13.249), 'became the first of the Judaeans to maintain foreign troops'.

With respect to these internal criteria for dating the Temple Scroll I can remark at the outset that if the author of this text is 'reacting against an initiative of John Hyrcanus', then this text must have been composed after this initiative—or at least the part of the text where this reaction features.

On the other hand I underline that if such and such a regulation or allusion figuring in our document reflects such and such a measure taken by such a person or is motivated by him, this measure only constitutes a *terminus a quo* for the dating of the Temple Scroll. This text, or at least the part of this text concerned with the event, must have been composed after the measure was taken; but later by how many days, or months or years? Between the two a longer or shorter time could have elapsed and this does not oblige us to date the composition of the Temple Scroll during the lifetime of John Hyrcanus, or of any other person to whom it would be suitable to attribute this measure.

Furthermore, it is not John Hyrcanus who was the first of the Hasmoneans to take the title king, but one of his sons, either Aristobulus I (104-103 BCE)—who held power for a very short time—or, more likely, Alexander Jannaeus (103-76 BCE). It was the latter who recreated to his benefit 'a realm as large as that of David and Solomon';[10] it was at the end of his reign that the 'high point of Hasmonean power' was attained.[11]

Lastly, as far as the maintenance of foreign troops is concerned, if John Hyrcanus was the first of the Hasmoneans—rather than of the Judaeans—who 'maintained foreign troops', one might say that he appears less active in this respect also than Alexander Jannaeus.[12]

4. *Archaeology*

The last criterion invoked in this debate is archaeology. In fact, as proof of his hypothesis for dating—during the reign of John Hyrcanus or a little earlier[13]—the Temple Scroll, Y. Yadin believed that he could invoke the date, established on the basis of the archaeological data, of the setting up of the sectarians at Qumran, a date which he would place in the second half of the second century BCE. Let us recall, however, that in my opinion, on the one hand the archaeological evidence found in the ruins of Qumran does not allow the dating with precision of the beginning of the setting up at this site of the Essene community of the Teacher of Righteousness; on the other hand there is nothing else that would confirm that this installation had already been established in the second century BCE in the time of John Hyrcanus. To be sure, in his preliminary reports of the excavations which he directed at Qumran, de Vaux believed that he was able to show that 14 or even 15 coins going back to John Hyrcanus had been discovered in the course of these excavations.

But, not only is this insufficient to prove that the site was occupied during that time, because it would be unwise to assert that the coins of this Jewish prince stopped being used after his death, particularly during the principality, or the reign, of his two sons Aristobulus I (104-103 BCE) and then Alexander Jannaeus (103-76 BCE); but also, what is more, in his last publications on Qumran de Vaux corrected this numismatic information, signifying that only one coin of John Hyrcanus had been identified with certainty.[14] We consider, therefore, that it was probably round about the year 100 BCE that this Essene installation was established at Qumran.[15]

5. *Conclusion*

For these various reasons I propose to place the composition of the Temple Scroll during the first quarter or the first third of the first century BCE.

Finally it seems to me useful to underline the following. In this year, 1987, we celebrate the fortieth anniversary of the discovery of the first Dead Sea scrolls. But, in truth, since the tenth anniversary of this discovery a chronological scheme of the life and works of the Essene community of Qumran, the community of the Teacher of Righteousness, has been defined in its essentials. That scheme is too often clung to today come what may—notably, against some of the results of the last archaeological excavations carried out at the site of Qumran-Feshkha, and the more precise conclusions drawn from the methodical study of the data, furnished by the excavation of the entire site.

NOTES

* Translated by George J. Brooke.

1. E.-M. Laperrousaz, *Qoumrân. L'établissement essénien des bords de la Mer Morte. Histoire et archéologie du site* (Paris: Picard, 1976), p. 98. Thus a scribe aged 60 writing in 100 BCE would appear—on the basis of the style of his script, his handwriting being the same as it was when he was, let's say, aged 20—to have written in 140 BCE!

2. E.-M. Laperrousaz, *Évolution, progrès des connaissances et interdisciplinarité* (Cahiers d'Histoire et de Philosophie des Sciences, 10; Paris: C.N.R.S., Centre de Documentation en Sciences Humaines, 1979), pp. 62-63.

3. M. Burrows, *The Dead Sea Scrolls* (London: Secker & Warburg, 1956), p. 85; French trans. by M. Glotz and M.-T. Franck, *Les Manuscrits de la Mer Morte* (Paris: Laffont, 1957), p. 107.

4. N. Avigad, 'The Palaeography of the Dead Sea Scrolls and Related Documents', *Aspects of the Dead Sea Scrolls* (ed. C. Rabin & Y. Yadin; Scripta Hierosolymitana, 4; Jerusalem: Magnes, 1958), p. 72.

5. R. de Vaux, *L'archéologie et les manuscrits de la Mer Morte* (The Schweich Lectures of the British Academy, 1959; London: Oxford University Press, 1961), p. viii; posthumous, supplemented, English trans. *Archaeology and the Dead Sea Scrolls* (London: Oxford University Press, 1973), p. ix.

6. R. de Vaux, *L'archéologie et les manuscrits de la Mer Morte*, p. 94; *Archaeology and the Dead Sea Scrolls*, p. 122.

7. J. Starcky, 'Les quatre étapes du messianisme à Qumrân', *RB* 70 (1963), p. 482 n. 3 (continued from p. 481).

8. A. Caquot, 'Le Rouleau du Temple de Qoumrân. Introduction, traduction et notes', *ETR* 53 (1978), p. 446.

9. I.e., BCE.

10. F.-M. Abel, *Histoire de la Palestine depuis la conquête d'Alexandre jusqu'à l'invasion arabe* (Études bibliques; Paris: Gabalda, 1952), I, p. 238; we cite a French historian but this opinion is confirmed in the works of many non-French specialists.

11. F.-M. Abel, *Histoire de la Palestine*, p. 238.

12. F.-M. Abel, *Histoire de la Palestine*, p. 231.

13. 'Not later than the third quarter of the second century BCE': *The Temple Scroll: The Hidden Law of the Dead Sea Sect* (London: Weidenfeld and Nicolson, 1985), p. 222.

14. Cf. R. de Vaux, *L'archéologie et les manuscrits de la Mer Morte*, p. 15; *Archaeology and the Dead Sea Scrolls*, p. 19.

15. Cf. E.-M. Laperrousaz, *Qoumrân*, pp. 28-33; *L'attente du Messie en Palestine à la veille et au début de l'ère chrétienne, à la lumière des documents récemment découverts* (Paris: Picard, 1982), p. 52; *Les Esséniens selon leur témoignage direct* (Religions et culture; Paris: Desclée, 1982), p. 44; most recently, see my article, 'Brèves remarques archéologiques concernant la chronologie des occupations esséniennes de Qoumrân', *RevQ* 12 (1986), pp. 199-212. In as much as they consider more especially the date of the Temple Scroll, see my articles, 'Note à propos de la datation du *Rouleau du Temple* et, plus généralement, des *Manuscrits de la Mer Morte*', *RevQ* 10 (1981), pp. 447-52; 'Notes sur l'évolution des conceptions de "Guerre Sainte" dans les *Manuscrits de la Mer Morte*', *RevQ* 12 (1986), pp. 271-78; 'Yigael Yadin, *The Temple Scroll*...', a review in *REJ* 145 (1986), pp. 400-404.

THE DATE OF COMPOSITION OF THE TEMPLE SCROLL

Barbara Thiering

University of Sydney

The date of composition of the Temple Scroll is one of the critical questions of Qumran research, as so many of the sectarian scrolls are related to it and apparently follow it.

The appropriate steps to be taken in determining the date of any Qumran document would appear to be, in order:

1. Discover the palaeographical dating of the earliest copy of the document.
2. Consider its unity and use of sources. If its final form is simply a compilation, look for its earliest stratum. If the finished work has an overall unity and structure, look for the time of the final form.
3. Group either the earliest stratum or the end product with other documents to which it is related, and consider their date.
4. Look for a time period into which the group of documents successfully fits.

Each of these questions will be dealt with in relation to the Temple Scroll.

1. Palaeographical Dating of the Earliest Copy

The main extant Temple Scroll is in two plainly Herodian hands (cols. 1-5, late; remaining columns middle Herodian). However, considerable weight has been given by some writers to a group of fragments called Rockefeller 43.366 (*The Temple Scroll*, III, plates 38, 40), said to belong to the Temple Scroll, which are in a different script designated middle Hasmonaean semiformal. They have been used to give a *terminus ad quem* of c. 90 BCE.[1]

This conclusion is open to challenge on several grounds, as others also have pointed out.[2]

a. There is no certainty that the fragments belong to the Temple Scroll. J. Strugnell has denied that they do in his letter of April 28 1981 published by B.Z. Wacholder;[3] and B.A. Levine has pointed out that the pieces in plate 40 twice use the name of Moses, which is not found, but in fact carefully avoided, in the main scroll.[4] The piece in plate 38 does correspond to 41.4-42.8*-11*, but this need only mean that it is a source or related work.

b. The end of the middle Hasmonaean period is c. 75 BCE, not 90 BCE.[5] Even if the work were part of the Temple Scroll, Cross's reminder that fifty years must be allowed clearly applies;[6] a date of 25 BCE is not impossible.

c. It should further be pointed out, in reference to this and other important documents, that the script in question is not an undoubtedly Hasmonaean one. It is another piece in the same class as 4Q Qoh(eleth), 4Q Pr(ières liturgiques), and, significantly, 1QS and 4QTestim, a group which exposes a weakness in Cross's typological analysis. These scripts were classed by him as Hasmonaean semiformal because of the appearance of letters which, on a simple evolutionary scale, would be archaic.[7] But the classification was thrown into doubt by the publication by J. Starcky of some Palmyrene inscriptions which were actually dated, 44 and 33 BCE, containing the same 'archaic' letter forms.[8] Palmyra, ancient Tadmor, between Upper Syria and the Euphrates, was a great city, the centre of a trading empire. Its scribes were renowned for their use of a prestigious script which had become a classical one, retaining archaic features well into the third century CE.[9] Some Palmyrene scribes were present in Jerusalem, as shown by inscriptions, one of them dated in the first half of the first century CE.[10] The Qumran scripts listed above, and also the Rockefeller fragment, contain letter forms that Palmyrene scribes used in the time of Herod the Great, *and they also use Jewish Herodian letter forms*.[11] An historical complication has occurred: a Herodian script has become mixed with a foreign script, reintroducing letters that would be archaic in the Jewish script but are not in the foreign script.

According to J. Strugnell, there is an unpublished group of 4Q

fragments which 'contain quotations from, or the text of, the Temple
Scroll, or at least one of its sources', and should be dated about 150
BCE.[12] As M. Hengel *et al.* agree, the possibility that they are sources
must be noted.[13] This material is too uncertain to be used as a means
of dating the scroll.

On the palaeographical evidence, there is in fact no objection to
the dating of the Temple Scroll in the reign of Herod the Great.

2. *Unity and Sources*

There are clearly independent sources used in the present work:
most obviously large parts of Deuteronomy. A.M. Wilson and L.
Wills have shown that the festival calendar (cols. 13–30) differs from
the rest by not using the divine fiction; and they argue also that the
Torah of the king was an independent unit.[14] They have claimed,
further, that there is a separate purity source in cols. 48–51, indicated
by the lack of the divine fiction; but P. Callaway has argued that the
whole purity section 45–51.10 is a thematic unity, and questions
whether there is such a sharp differentiation between sources as they
have maintained.[15]

It is plain that, whatever sources have been used, they have been
worked into a composition that has a coherent structure from start to
finish. J. Milgrom comments on the logical order of the plan.[16] The
single purpose of the Temple Scroll is to set out divine laws for the
building and organization of the temple and the conduct of the state
centring round the temple, with the whole dominated by the theme
of purity, both ritual and moral. It has a greater degree of unity than
any other of the major scrolls. Deuteronomy has not simply been
reproduced, but carefully worked in to serve the overall purpose,
even to the point of altering its order.

For that reason, it is possible to speak of a particular point when
the idea was conceived of preparing a document setting out plans for
a new temple and a state that would conform to the Deuteronomic
ideal. The date to be sought is that of the conception, which would
also be that of the final, or nearly final, form of the work.

3. *Other Documents in the Same Group*

There are obvious connections between the laws of the Temple Scroll
and those of 1QM, 1QS-1QSa and CD.

With 1QM it shares the exclusion of women and boys from the holier areas (1QM 7.3; 11QT 39.6); the Second Priest (1QM 2.2; 11QT 31.4); the organization into twelve priests, twelve Levites, and twelve lay (1QM 2.1-3; 11QT 57.11-13); the placement of latrines at an approved number of cubits away (1QM 7.6-7; 11QT 46.13).

With 1QS and 1QSa it excludes the physically afflicted from the holy precincts or highest privileges (1QSa 2.3-8; 11QT 45.12-17; 48.14-17); sets twenty years as the age of maturity (1QSa 1.8; 11QT 39.10-11); organizes in thousands, hundreds, fifties and tens (1QS 2.21-22; 1QSa 1.14-15; 1.29-2.1; 11QT 57.2-5; 58.4); sets the hierarchy as priests first, Levites second, laity third (1QS 2.19-21; 6.3-9; 1QSa 2.22-25; 11QT 57.18-21).

Many of these rules are also shared with CD (exclusion of the physically afflicted, 15.15-16; thousands, hundreds, fifties, tens, 13.1; priestly hierarchy, 14.3-5), and in addition the prohibition of sexual activity in the holy city (CD 12.1-2; 11QT 45.11-12); the ban on niece marriage (CD 5.7-11; 11QT 66.15-17); the law of monogamy (CD 5.1-2; 11QT 57.17-19), use of the term עיר המקדש (CD 12.1-2, 11QT *passim*). Levine,[17] Vermes,[18] and P. Davies[19] comment on the affinities between the Temple Scroll and CD.

These connections make it difficult to accept the view of Levine,[20] L. Schiffman,[21] and H. Stegemann[22] that the Temple Scroll is non-sectarian; rather, one must agree with Vermes's assessment that it belongs with the sectarian writings, above all the Damascus Document, and that it precedes both this and the War Scroll.[23] These works, and 1QS-1QSa, manifestly include the organization of the Temple Scroll in a phase that has developed the doctrine (eschatology, messianism) well beyond that of the Temple Scroll.

The date of composition of these related works will more appropriately be considered below.

There is another work with which the Temple Scroll shows a direct connection. This is the New Testament book of Revelation. It is not simply that both works have a plan for a foursquare New Jerusalem with three gates on each of the sides associated with the twelve tribes (11QT 39, 44; Rev. 21.10-21). It is also probable—and this appears not to have been so far observed—that the order of tribes in Revelation 7 shows dependence on the order in the Temple Scroll. If the Revelation 7 list is associated with the gates and read from the opposite corner, then six of the twelve names of tribes appear in the same place (see diagram). Of the remainder, two pairs, Judah and Issachar, and Zebulun and Reuben, are directly exchanged. Only Asher and Manasseh are independently placed. (There is no Dan in Rev. 7; Manasseh and Ephraim [Joseph] are counted independently). The order of tribes is not accounted for by the Old Testament in either source (cf. Num. 2.3-31). The book of Revelation could be seen to have a reason for starting from the western side, in the preference of Christians for the West. It is more likely that Revelation is consciously altering the Temple Scroll than that the correspondences are coincidental.

There are further points of correspondence, on organization and calendar. The heavenly temple of Revelation contains twenty-four elders dressed in white garments which have to be washed (4.4; 7.14); cf. the sets of twelve leaders (but with also twelve priests) of 11QT 57.11-13, and the rules for washing garments (11QT 45.8-9 *et passim*). There are 144,000 celibates, superior to others (Rev. 14.1-5). The list of produce in Rev. 6.6—wheat, barley, oil and wine—includes the names of the new pentecontad feasts of 11QT 18-21. The four horses of Rev. 6.1-8 have the colours of the four seasons (white, summer [cf. Jn 4.35]; red, autumn; black, winter; green (χλωρός, v. 8), spring); the solar calendar was divided into four clear seasons marked by the additional 31sts. The 1260 days of Rev. 11.3 and 12.6 may be accounted for in terms of the solar calendar.[24] The sets of seven throughout Revelation (churches, spirits, stars, trumpets, etc.) may be seen to reflect the importance of seven in the solar calendar.

11QT 39, 44

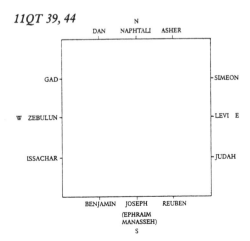

Rev. 7.5-8 with Rev. 21.10-13

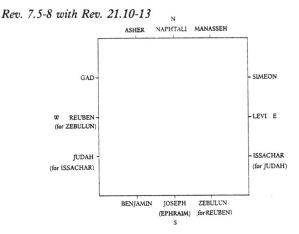

Equally strong links are found between Revelation and the other Qumran documents related to the Temple Scroll. With 1QM it expects a great final battle and the destruction of Satan; uses the image of light (sons of light; seven stars and seven lampstands, Rev. 1.20 *et passim*); the archangel Michael (1QM 9.15, 16; 17.6, 7; Rev. 12.7); the term Abaddon (Heb. 'destruction', 1QM frag. 9.3; Rev. 9.11); a pit for Satan (1QM 13.11; Rev. 20.3); washing garments (1QM 14.2; Rev. 7.14); the priestly colours (1QM 7.10-11; Rev. 17.4). Rev. 16.15 ('Blessed is he who. . . [keeps] his garments that he may not go naked and be seen exposed) reflects the rule of 1QS 7.12, 13-14. The messianic figure of Rev. 19.11-16, a military leader, is very similar to the Prince of the Congregation of 1QSb 5. Revelation and CD both refer to the mark on the foreheads of the elect (from Ezek. 9.4; CD 19.12; Rev. 13.16-17); both speak of a register of the names of the elect (CD 4.5-6; Rev. 13.8 *et passim*). There are of course striking differences also; but there are sufficient links to make it necessary to suppose that the book of Revelation knows the Qumran structures and is dealing with them in its own way.

4. *The Historical Setting of the*
Group of Documents Containing the Temple Scroll

M. Hengel, J.H. Charlesworth and D. Mendels have made the convincing point that the chapter on kingship (11QT 56.12–59.21) contains polemic against an actual Jewish king.[25] They go on to give reasons for identifying this king with Alexander Jannaeus: (1) his army and bodyguard should be Jewish. Alexander intensified the hiring of mercenaries (*Ant.* 13.374). (2) The king was bound by a council of thirty-six. Alexander committed many errors of judgment. (3) The king must be monogamous. Alexander had concubines (*Ant.* 13.380). (4) The queen must be 'from his father's house and clan' (57.16-17). This 'may refer to Alexandra, who belonged to his own family when he married her' (p. 34). (But this is to assume a disputed point, that Alexandra wife of Aristobulus was the same as Alexandra wife of Jannaeus,[26] and moreover the 11QT context (57.15-17) means that the queen must be Jewish rather than Gentile; further, the scroll would then be approving the king's action). (5) The defence system of Judaea must be maintained. Alexander had no defence system. (6) The king must not go to war with Egypt. Jannaeus provoked the Egyptians. (7) The king is to have no priestly functions. The Pharisees held, against Jannaeus, that the king should not be a priest. (8) The recommendation that traitors should be crucified parallels Jannaeus' use of this punishment. (But this is, again, to approve Jannaeus' action.)

There are more points of correspondence, and more specific ones, between the king whom the writers of the scroll have in mind, and Herod the Great (37–4 BCE). (1) The king must be Jewish, not a foreigner (56.14-15 [Deut. 17.15]). Herod's father was an Idumaean (*War.* 1.123). (2) Polygamy is forbidden (56.18 [Deut. 17.17]; 57.17). Herod had nine wives at the same time (*Ant.* 17.19). (3) Divorce is forbidden (57.18). Herod freely divorced his wives (*Ant.* 17.68, 78). (4) The king must not take a foreign wife (57.15-17, 19). Herod's wives included a Samaritan (*Ant.* 17.20). (5) Niece marriage is forbidden (66.15-17). One of Herod's wives was his niece (*Ant.* 17.19). (6) The king must observe the *Torah* and Jewish ways (59.1-15). 'Herod went still farther in departing from the native customs, and through foreign practices he gradually corrupted the ancient way of life' (*Ant.* 15.267). (7) He must not go to Egypt to v ar (56.16). Herod had a feud with Cleopatra in the early part of his reign (*Ant.* 15.48, 63, 98). (8) He must subordinate himself to a council (57.11-15). Herod was an autocrat who ignored his councillors (e.g. *Ant.* 15.284-288; 17.150-152). (9) He must be subordinate to the high priest (58.18-21). Herod arranged the murder or dismissal of several high priests (*Ant.* 15.173, 322; 17.164). (10) 'He shall not pervert justice and he shall not accept bribery' (57.19-20). Herod was accused of gross injustices and the extorting of bribes (*Ant.* 17.304-308).

The most prominent link of all is the fact that Herod planned and carried out the rebuilding of the temple (*Ant.* 15.380-425). According to Josephus he made a public speech announcing that the temple would be rebuilt, and would be restored to the true form originally set down by God (*Ant.* 15.381-387). Josephus also notes, immediately before the section on the temple, that Herod held 'all Essenes in honour' as a result of the predictions of Menahem (Manaemus) the Essene (*Ant.* 15.373-379). Menahem also accused him of forgetting piety and justice (376). These details offer the perfect setting for the writing of the Temple Scroll. The Essenes, accepting Herod's support but prepared to criticize him, saw their opportunity of having the temple rebuilt according to their specifications. Their priesthood would reign in the renewed temple, and the state would be run by them according to Deuteronomic law. They offered their plans in the form of a divine revelation. But Herod, recognizing the criticisms of himself and not prepared to tolerate a strict Essene priesthood that forbade divorce and marriage with relatives (cf. Mk 6.17-19, a later Herod killed the Baptist for this reason), rejected their plan. Herod's temple, fully described by Josephus (*Ant.* 15.391-420) did not follow the plan of the scroll.

This hypothesis would have been immediately obvious if it were not for the fact that the Temple Scroll manifestly precedes 1QM, 1QS and CD, and at least the latter two of these have long been held to come from the time of Essene origins before 100 BCE. Is it quite certain that they do come from that time?

The Date of Composition of 1QM, 1QS and CD
There is no difficulty in placing the composition of the successive phases of 1QM in the period after Herod the Great, when the abolition of the native kingship and the imposition of direct Roman rule led to the rise of zealotry. The regular Herodian script of 1QM, without idiosyncrasies, allows a date of copying in the first century CE. A zealot-Essene coalition in phase two of the occupation of Qumran is suggested by the history of the region throughout the first century CE, and by the Qumran documents found at Masada. The destruction of the Qumran buildings is to be attributed to the campaign of Vespasian in 68 CE against zealots in the Jericho region.[27]

As has been noted above, the palaeographical classification of 1QS must be modified in the light of the dated Palmyrene scripts. It is an idiosyncratic script, combining Palmyrene and Herodian features. 1QS, 1QSa and 1QSb may therefore be placed in the same period as 1QM; the link is already indicated by common organisational terms.

CD remains as the main difficulty. It or its earliest form have been placed before 100 BCE by most writers.[28] The first reason given is the palaeographical dating of the earliest fragment of the work, set by Milik at 75–50 BCE.[29] There is considerable confusion about the siglum of this fragment,[30] but when it is tracked down it is found to be a semicursive.[31] The semicursive scripts are the most difficult of all to date, as Cross agrees:

> (The semicursive) is an unstable type, in which much mixing of traditions occurs, and hence a source of 'infection' of both formal and cursive styles.
>
> The semicursive scripts, since they mix cursive and formal typological elements, provide extra, if interwoven and complex, criteria for dating. Since the script has a certain integrity in its tradition, an inner typology can be constructed; this is no simple task, owing, as we have noted, to the variety within the tradition.[32]

In the light of this uncertainty, it is impossible to build a case on the palaeographical dating of the CD fragment.

The other main reason is the phrase concerning the three hundred and ninety years in CD 1.5-6. While it is recognized that the figures come from Ezek. 4.5, the phrase is universally translated '390 years after he gave them into the hand of Nebuchadnezzar king of Babylon', and taken to give a date somewhere in the second century BCE for the founding of the Plant-root, with the Teacher of Righteousness twenty years later.[33]

It may first be remarked that the attempt to treat th⸱ phrase as secondary on metrical grounds[34] can scarcely succeed, since the poetry of Qumran, as evidenced in the Hodayot, is characterized by marked irregularity of metre, with a tendency for the parallelistic structure to break down into prose.[35]

The key questions are the meaning of לתיתו (1.6) and of 'Nebuchadnezzar king of Babylon'.

לתיתו has been taken as meaning 'after he gave', and the date of Nebuchadnezzar's attack on Jerusalem (587 BCE) then gives a starting-point for the 390 years. But I. Rabinowitz has pointed out that ל 'never occurs in Hebrew in the temporal meaning "after", "from the time that" and it never has this meaning in the scrolls. לתיתו quite clearly means "at (the time of) His giving" or "to (the time of) His giving" or "as of His giving"'.[36]

In the light of the Qumran treatment of the term 'Babylon', evidenced in the *pesharim*, the possibility must always be considered, when the word 'Babylon' appears, that it is a pseudonym for Rome. Such a usage is fully demonstrated in contemporary literature: 'Babylon' is used as a pseudonym for Rome in 1 Pet. 5.13 and in Revelation 18 (cf. 17.9). The process by which Old Testament Chaldaeans have become Kittim (Romans) would then simply have been carried to its logical conclusion.

If these points were taken into account, the meaning of the sentence would be:

> In the Period of Wrath, the three hundred and ninety years for his giving them into the hand of the ruler of Rome, he visited them. .

The 390 years, drawn from Ezek. 4.5, would then be seen as a *prophecy* of the duration of the Roman oppression. The writer, suffering under that oppression, and calling it the Period of Wrath, has turned to Ezekiel to discover how long it will last.

The question would then arise: when did the Roman oppression begin? Of the two possible dates, 63 BCE (the arrival of Pompey) and 6 CE (the abolition of the native kingship, the imposition of direct Roman rule under procurators, the census of Quirinius that led to the zealot uprising), the latter is far more likely to have been called the 'Period of Wrath'.

On such an interpretation, the Plant-root of CD 1.7 was formed in 6 CE, and had zealot connections. It would be necessary to suppose a coalition of Essenes and Zealots—a supposition already suggested, as noted above, by the finding of Qumran documents on Masada, and by the history of the region in the first century CE. This supposition would at once remove one of the difficulties of the view that the Teacher of Righteousness, who came twenty years after the Plant-root, was a founder of the Essenes in the second century BCE. If this had been the case, no account of the Essenes would have been complete without a mention of this figure, faith in whom would give salvation (1QpHab 8.1-3), and who was the subject about whom the Old Testament prophets spoke. Yet Josephus and Philo never mention him. If, however, the Plant-root were a breakaway movement from the classical Essenes occupying Qumran in its second phase, at the turn of the era, then the Teacher was not a member of the classical Essenes, but could have preserved some of their traditions. The supposition would also remove the other great difficulty, that the *pesharim*, written in the Herodian period for the first time (as only one copy of each was found) claim that scripture was fulfilled by the Teacher; yet, on the view that the Teacher lived in the second century BCE, they are speaking of events over a hundred years before their time. Such a genre of literature prefers to find the fulfilment of scripture in the author's own time, not a hundred years before.

There would then be an exact date available for the Teacher of Righteousness: 26 CE, twenty years after the formation of the Plant-root in 6 CE. The possibility would then arise that he was to be identified with John the Baptist, who in significant respects (place of working; baptisms to bring repentant Jews into a renewed covenant of Abraham; message of a coming fiery judgment; priestly birth; asceticism; rhetorical gifts) was very like the Teacher. The Teacher's name means, by a play on words, 'he who rains down righteousness', that is, 'he who baptizes with righteousness'.[37]

There are, of course, further consequences of such a theory: that the party in schism from the Teacher, who 'flouted the Law', were the followers of Jesus. This question has been dealt with elsewhere,[38] and is not, in detail, relevant to the present argument.

The foregoing reassessments of the dates of the works related to and following the Temple Scroll make it easy to follow the indications of the scroll itself and place its composition in the time of Herod the Great.

An Overall Chronology and History

It is possible to go further than this, by drawing on other related works: the *Apocalypse of Enoch*, Daniel, *Jubilees*, the *Testament of Levi*, parts of other scrolls, and the New Testament. An overall chronology becomes available, one which gives a precise date and a further reason for the writing of the Temple Scroll, and one which also promises to account for the setting of the Christian era and for some of the major events in the New Testament. It may here be set out in summary form.

(1) *238 BCE. The Apocalypse of Enoch.* The first stage was in 238 BCE, when a community following the solar calendar, called the Plant of Righteousness, drew up a scheme of world history. Their central concern was a Restoration of the Zadokite high priesthood and of the Davidic kingship to the temple and the throne. In the Apocalypse of Weeks of *1 Enoch* 93.3-10, 91.12-17 they claimed that history since creation had been divided into even periods of 490 years ('weeks', here called world-weeks), with the great events of Israelite history occurring at each peak. Their own formation had come at the significant seventh. This pattern enabled them to predict that the Restoration would come at the eighth, the year 3920 Anno Mundi. The writers, who naturally placed the destruction of the first temple at one of the peaks, were operating on the false date for that event that is found in Dan. 9.24-27, 728 BCE. Their own formation was 490 years after that, in 238 BCE. Their scheme, on which all subsequent adjustments were built, was:

World week	Anno Mundi	BCE–CE	Event
0	0	3668 BCE	Creation
1	490	3178	Birth of Enoch
2	980	2688	The Flood
3	1470	2198	Election of Abraham
4	1960	1708	Giving of the Law on Mt Sinai
5	2450	1218	Building of the first temple
6	2940	728	Destruction of the first temple
7	3430	238	Formation of 'the Elect, from the eternal Plant of Righteousness'
8	3920	253 CE	The Restoration and building of 'the temple of the kingdom of the Great One'.
	(4000)	(333 CE)	(Nothing stated, but a great event presumably to be expected)
9	4410	743	Righteous judgment over the whole earth
10	4900	1233	The Last Judgment; a new heaven and earth.

(2) *168 BCE. Adjustment in Daniel and Jubilees. The 3½ Years Intercalation.* At the time of the desolation of the temple by Antiochus Epiphanes (168 BCE) the solarists, now called or associated with Hasidim or Hasidaeans, allied with the Maccabees (1 Macc. 2.42). The association gave them reason to hope that their Restoration would come at the end of the war of liberation. The chronology had

consequently to be adjusted, with results set out in Daniel 9 and the book of *Jubilees*. The date of 728 BCE for the fall of Jerusalem was still preserved.

World-week	Jubilee week	Year-week	Anno Mundi	BCE–CE	Event
0			0	4088 BCE	Creation (420 years earlier)
1			490		
2			980		
3			1470		
4			1960		
5			2450	1638	Entry into Canaan (Jub. 50.4) (Exodus events and all subsequent peaks one world-week later)
6			2940	1148	
			(3360)	(728)	(Destruction of the first temple)
7			3430	658	Decree of Cyrus, 70 years after the destruction (Dan. 9.2, 25)[39] 'The going forth of the word to restore and build Jerusalem'.
	1	7	3479	609	Arrival of Ezra. Dan. 9.25: 'to the coming of an anointed one, a prince, there shall be seven weeks'. (Ezra a descendant of Zadok, Ezra 7.1-5)
		69	3913	175	Accession of Antiochus Epiphanes (1 Macc. 1.10). Dan. 9.25: 'For sixty-two weeks it shall be built again... but in a troubled time'.
			3918	170	Murder of the high priest Onias III (2 Macc. 4.27-38). Dan. 9.26: 'After the sixty-two weeks, an anointed one shall be cut off'.
8	10	70	3920	168	Desolation of the temple by Antiochus Eiphanes. Dan. 9.24, 26: 'Seventy weeks of years are decreed concerning... your holy city;... the people of the prince who is to come shall destroy the city and the sanctuary... desolations are decreed'. Dan. 9.27: '(The prince who is to come)... shall make a strong covenant with many for one week'. 175-168 BCE. Cf. 1 Macc. 1.11: 'Lawless men came forth from Israel... saying, "Let us go and make a covenant with the Gentiles"'.
		70½	3920 (see below)	164, March	End of 3½ years from September 168, used as an intercalation. Dan. 9.27: "For the half of a week

			(construct) he shall cause sacrifice and offering to cease.
	(4000)	(88)	(Great event expected)
9	4410	323 CE	
10	4900	813 CE	Last Judgment

Dan. 9.27 speaks of 'the half of a week' (חצי השבוע) in which sacrifice and offering cease. The construct form permits it to be understood as following the 'one week' of v. 27a, 175–168. The three and a half years plainly refer to the period from 168 to 165 when there were no sacrifices in the temple. So also do the 1290 days of Dan. 12.11 ('From the time that the continual burnt offering is taken away, and the abomination that makes desolate is set up, there shall be a thousand two hundred and ninety days'). The subsequent chronology indicates that the opportunity was taken at this time to introduce an intercalation of three and a half years, commemorating the period when there had been no festivals, so no religious time. The year date remained the same at the end of the three and a half years as it had been at the beginning. The three years were for the actual period of desolation, and the half year was for the purpose of changing the observance of the New Year from September to March; the 'half-week' was from September 168 to March 164.[40]

It further becomes apparent that not all who followed the solar chronology accepted the intercalation of three and a half years, which honoured the Jerusalem temple. One party, probably with a Diaspora orientation, preserved the unaltered datings. Their chronology is reflected in the New Testament. From this time on there were two occurrences of the same year, for the two different parties.

(3) *The Final Form of the Chronology.* On the chronology as it was held from the time of Daniel and *Jubilees*, a great event should have happened in either September 88 or March 84, the year 4000 AM. When these years passed without any appropriate crisis, the solar prophets were driven to check their figures. The error concerning the date of the fall of Jerusalem must then have been discovered. It was corrected, as can be seen indirectly from the *Testament of Levi*, to 581 BCE, near to the true date. There was then another adjustment, preserving the principles of the original prophecy, whose purpose had been to predict a Restoration to power by the solarists at the

eighth world-week, 3920 AM. This revision remained unchanged, and gave the basis for the Christian era.

World-week	Jubilee-week	Year-week	Anno Mundi	BCE–CE	Event
0			0	3941 BCE	Creation (147 years later, to account for the correction from 728 to 581)
1			490		
2			980		
3			1470		
4			1960		
5			2450		
6			2940		
			3360	581	Destruction of the first temple
7			3430	511	Decree of Cyrus, 70 years later SCHEME OF JUBILEES AND HIGH PRIESTS OF TLEVI 16-18:
	1		3479	462	'High priest . . . for *salvation* of world' Joshua (Zech. 3.1)
	2		3528	413	'High priest. . .conceived in sorrow. . .'
	3		3577	364	'High priest. . .taken hold of by sorrow'. Johanan? (*Ant.* 11: 298-301)
	4		3626	315	'High priest in pain. . .all Israel shall hate each one his neighbour'. Samaritan schism.
	5		3675	266	'High priest taken hold of by darkness'
	6		3724	217	'Likewise'.
				Sep. Mar.	
	7		3773	168 164	'Such pollution as I cannot express'. Desolation of the temple by Antiochus
		1	3780	161	
		2	3787	154	
		3	3794	147	
		4	3801	140	
		5	3808	133 129	'They shall return to their desolate country, and renew the house of the Lord'. The solarists expelled to Qumran on the accession of John Hyrcanus (135/4-104 BCE).
		6	3815	126	
8		7	3822	119 115	'Priests who are idolaters, adulterers, etc.' Sadducees supported by Hyrcanus.[41]
				(88 84)	(Correction of dating. New chronology of TLevi drawn up)
9			3871		
			3900	41 37	Beginning of the final millennium of world history. Herod the Great,

					who favoured the Essenes, rose to power between 41 and 37 (*War* 1.242-354); he would have been seen at first as inaugurating the final millennium.
		3910	31		The earthquake at Qumran. The Essenes would have been permitted by Herod to resettle in Jerusalem. The year 3920 for the Restoration and the true high priest (TLevi 18) was now approaching, the Herod announced the rebuilding of the temple. The Temple Scroll was written to prepare for the Restoration, which seemed to be about to come at the predicted date.
8	10	3920	21	17	The long prophesied year of the Restoration. The temple rebuilt by Herod,[42] but the Temple Scroll plan rejected. Adjustment was made by allowing a zero jubilee from creation. There was still a Last Jubilee (11QMelch 7); the Restoration would come in 29 and 33 CE.
		3940	1BCE 4CE		Those who also counted in generations of forty years (1QM 2; CD 20.15; Acts 7) now allowed a zero generation from creation, to cancel the Herodian millennium and declare a new one. This, in its Diaspora version (1 BCE) became the Christian millennium.
		3941	1CE 5CE		Year 1 of the revised millennium.
			6CE		The zealot uprising. The Period of Wrath. Formation of the Plantroot.
			26CE		Appearance of the Teacher of Righteousness.
	1	3969	29CE 33CE		End of the Last Jubilee. 29 CE, the 15th year of Tiberius, the first year of Jesus' ministry (Lk. 3.1); 33 may be the year of the crucifixion. Jesus announced a jubilee year at the outset of his ministry (Lk. 4.19, cf. 11QMelch 6-7). March 31 CE was the end of year 46 of the jubilee, pro-temple version; cf. Jn 2.20. Does 'the Hour' (Jn 2.4; 17.1; Mk 14.41) mean the Restoration?

			Was Jesus' crucifixion connected with its non-appearance?
			(Jesus was a descendant of David.)
		37CE	March of Vitellius across southern Judaea, against Aretas, in support of Herod the tetrarch (*Ant.* 18.109-126). 1QpHab written, on the armies of the Kittim marching across the land; and a non-fulfilment (1QpHab 3.1; 7.7). The Qumran community flee to Damascus under the protection of Aretas (cf. 2 Cor. 11.32). CD written justifying the exile to Damascus. Are they the Jews in Damascus (Acts 9.23)?
	4000	60CE 64CE	Significant event of the year 4000 expected if zero jubilee and generation not allowed. 60 CE Paul's shipwreck.[43] Cf. Acts 27.20 with Mk 13.24. 64 CE the persecution of Christians by Nero; had they demonstrated in expectation?
	4010	70CE 74CE	70 CE the fall of Jerusalem. 74 CE the suicide of zealots on Masada. (Date corrected)[44]
9	4410	470CE	
10	4900	960CE	Last Judgment if no zero generation allowed.
		1000CE	Last Judgment if zero generation allowed.

In discussing the date of composition of the Temple Scroll, it has become necessary and possible to raise matters of far wider importance. The fact that the Temple Scroll fits so well into the period of Herod the Great raises the probability that the works following it, 1QM, 1QS and CD, belong after the time of Herod and in the first century CE. This has been seen to follow once the palaeographical data have been more closely examined, and once the passage in CD 1.5-6 is read consistently with the *pesharim*. Then, by drawing on works related to the sectarian scrolls that give chronological information, a further consequence emerges in the foregoing scheme, which would bring the Christian events into continuity with Qumran history. It need scarcely be emphasized that the consequences for our understanding of Christian history would be major. The hypothesis is here presented in as succinct a form as possible; a fuller treatment will be found in *Redating the Teacher of Righteousness* (1979), *The Gospels and Qumran: A New Hypothesis* (1981) and *The Qumran Origins of the Christian Church* (1983).[45]

NOTES

1. M. Hengel, J.H. Charlesworth & D. Mendels, 'The Polemical Character of "On Kingship" in the Temple Scroll: An Attempt at Dating 11Q Temple', *JJS* 37 (1986), pp. 28-38 (p. 29).

2. G. Vermes in Schürer, *The History of the Jewish People in the Age of Jesus Christ (175 BC–AD 135) by Emil Schürer*, III.1 (Revised and edited by G. Vermes, F. Millar & M. Goodman; Edinburgh: T. & T. Clark, 1986); p. 407 n. 3; B.A. Levine, 'The Temple Scroll: Aspects of its Historical Provenance and Literary Character', *BASOR* 232 (1978), p. 6.

3. B.Z. Wacholder, *The Dawn of Qumran: The Sectarian Torah and the Teacher of Righteousness* (HUCM, 8; Cincinnati: Hebrew Union College, 1983), pp. 205-6, 278.

4. Levine, *BASOR* 232, p. 6: 'It is inconceivable that the Scroll contained any passages naming Moses. I therefore suggest that fragment no. 1 be detached from the group numbered Rockefeller 43.366 and given a different catalogue designation'.

5. F.M. Cross, 'The Oldest Manuscript from Qumran', *JBL* 74 (1955), pp. 147-72 (p. 164); letter of Strugnell, note 3 above.

6. F.M. Cross, 'The Development of the Jewish Scripts', in G.E. Wright (ed.), *The Bible and the Ancient Near East* (London: Routledge & Kegan Paul, 1961), p. 136. The inflexible use of palaeographical datings is strongly criticized by E.-M. Laperrousaz, 'Note à propos de la Datation du Rouleau du Temple et, plus généralement, des Manuscrits de la Mer Morte', *RQ* 10 (1979-81), pp. 447-52.

7. Cross, 'The Development. . .', pp. 158-160.

8. J. Starcky, 'Inscriptions archaïques de Palmyre', *Studi Orientalistici in onore di Giorgio Levi della Vida* II (Rome: Istituto per l'Oriente, 1956), pp. 509-28; also J. Starcky, *Palmyre* (Paris: Maisonneuve, 1952); Du Mesnil du Buisson, *Inventaire des Inscriptions Palmyréniennes de Doura-Europos* (Paris: Geuthner, 1939) No. 1.

9. J. Cantineau, *Grammaire du Palmyrien Epigraphique* (Cairo: Imprimerie de l'Institut Français d'Archaeologie Orientale, 1935).

10. J.-B. Frey, *Corpus Inscriptionum Iudaicarum* II (Rome: Pontificio Istituto di Archeologia Cristiana, 1952), no. 1388, cf. also no. 1222.

11. The Palmyrene letter forms in Rock. 43.366 are: broad *bet* with rounded right to left base; high joining *gimel*; reversed-'k' *he*; *ḥet* with low

cross bar; *lamed* with a small hook; medial *mem* with a curved cross bar drawn before the oblique; *'ayn* and *qof* with very short legs; *ṣade* with a horizontal-'t' right arm; *taw* joining low on the left side.

It uses a Herodian or late Hasmonaean *dalet*, *tet*, *kaf* (medial and final); final *mem*; *nun* (medial and final); *pe*; *resh*; *shin*.

The absence of final *pe* and *ṣade* is a feature shared with Herodian semiformals and with Palmyrene.

One letter deserves special mention: the *'alef* is unlike any in the formal series, being drawn in two joined half-loops: ⌒ᴗא The lower loop can come near to being closed. This is related to the *'alef* of Mur. 72, with a completely closed lower loop, whose connections with the Palmyrene and Nabataean scripts of the first century BCE have been commented on by J. Starcky (*DJD* II, pp. 172-73), By pointing out the Nabataean-Palmyrene connections of many letter forms in Mur. 72, Starcky has modified Milik's estimate of 125-75 BCE to the first half of the first century BCE (p. 173).

For the discussion of 1QS as a Herodian-Palmyrene script, see my *Redating the Teacher of Righteousness* (1979), ch. 4.

12. Letter cited in note 3, p. 206.

13. Hengel, Charlesworth, Mendels, 'The Polemical Character. . . .', p. 30.

14. A.M. Wilson and L. Wills, 'Literary Sources of the Temple Scroll', *HTR* 75 (1982), pp. 275-88.

15. P. Callaway, 'Source Criticism of the Temple Scroll: the Purity Laws', *RevQ* 12 (1985-87), pp. 213-22.

16. J. Milgrom, 'The Temple Scroll', *BA* 41 (1978), pp. 105-20 (p. 108).

17. Levine, 'The Temple Scroll. . . ', p. 12.

18. Vermes in Schürer III.1, pp. 412-13.

19. P.R. Davies, 'The Temple Scroll and the Damascus Document', in the present volume.

20. Levine, 'The Temple Scroll. . . ', p. 7.

21. L.H. Schiffman, *Sectarian Law in the Dead Sea Scrolls, Courts, Testimony and the Penal Code* (BJS, 33; Chico, CA: Scholars Press, 1983), pp. 13-14.

22. H. Stegemann, 'Die Bedeutung der Qumranfunde für die Erforschung der Apokalyptik', *Apocalypticism in the Mediterranean World and the Near East* (ed. D. Hellholm; Tübingen: Mohr, 1983), p. 516.

23. Vermes in Schürer III.1, pp. 412-17.

24. See note 40.

25. Hengel, Charlesworth, Mendels, 'The Polemical Character. . . ', p. 31.

26. *Ant.* 13.320, see note in Loeb edition.

27. *War* 4.450, 476.

28. Vermes in Schürer III.1, p. 396; P.R. Davies, *The Damascus Covenant* (JSOTS, 25; Sheffield JSOT, 1983), p. 203.

29. J.T. Milik, *Ten Years of Discovery in the Wilderness of Judaea* (London: SCM, 1959), p. 58.

30. Milik in *Ten Years*: 'As far as the Damascus Document is concerned, the oldest copy we have was written c. 75-50 BC. It is a fairly extensively preserved manuscript, abbreviated provisionally 4QD^b'. Milik in 'Milki-ṣedeq et Milki-reša', *JJS* 23 (1972), pp. 95-144, p. 135: '4QD^a (4Q266)... the manuscript which dates from the first third of the first century BC'. In an attached footnote he says: 'cited in my book under the siglum 4QD^b and dated from the years 75-50 BC'.

A piece is published in J.T. Milik, 'Fragment d'une source du Psautier (4QPs 89) et fragments des Jubilés, du Document de Damas, d'un Phylactère dans la grotte 4 de Qumran', *RB* 73 (1966), pp. 94-106. The same information is given concerning the change of siglum (footnote 4, p. 103: I have several times cited this important manuscript in my previous publications, under the siglum 4QD^b. I have identified remains, sometimes minute, of 33 columns of the scroll, which contained 38'). On p. 103 it is given the number 4Q266, although in the same article it is called 4Q226, presumably a typographical error. That it is the same early piece is shown by Milik's remarks on its inclusion in the work of a school of scribes of three successive generations, beginning 175-125 BCE.

31. Milik, 'Fragment d'une source...', pp. 102-103. Note the *he* with reversed 'k' shape, the N-shaped *ḥet*, the round-shouldered *resh*, the *shin* with right arms made in one continuous stroke, the D-shaped *samekh*.

32. Cross, 'The Development...', pp. 146, 182.

33. Recently maintained in M.A. Knibb, *The Qumran Community* (Cambridge: Cambridge University Press, 1987), pp. 19-20.

34. Davies, *The Damascus Covenant*, pp. 62-63.

35. See B. Thiering, 'The Poetic Forms of the Hodayot', *JSS* 8 (1963), pp. 189-209.

36. I. Rabinowitz, 'A Reconsideration of "Damascus" and "390 Years" in the "Damascus" ("Zadokite") Fragments', *JBL* 73 (1954), pp. 11-35, (p. 14 n. 8b).

37. G. Jeremias, *Der Lehrer der Gerechtigkeit* (SUNT, 2; Göttingen: Vandenhoeck & Ruprecht, 1963), p. 313.

38. See note 45.

39. Vermes (Schürer III.1, p. 248) assumes that the anointed one is Cyrus, and consequently begins the period from the fall of Jerusalem, not from the decree of Cyrus. This disregards the plain sense of v. 25.

40. Dan. 12.11 (1290 days) advocates a New Year changed from Tabernacles to Passover. Dan. 12.12 ('Blessed is he who waits and comes to the thousand three hundred and thirty-five days') supports a party changing from Tabernacles to Pentecost.

Dan. 12.11

1092	three years (364 × 3)
16	the 31st at the seventh month (the four extra 31sts were counted with the following month, Jub. 6.23) + days 1-15 of the seventh month (New Year, Atonement, Tabernacles).
182	16/VII to 15/I inclusive, i.e. the half year from the day after Tabernacles to the date after Passover.

1290

Dan. 12.12

1092	
243	15/VII Tabernacles to 15/III Pentecost, inclusive.

1335

The 1260 days of Rev. 11.3 and 12.6 may be accounted for as three years, 1092 days, + 168 days from one of the equinox feasts to the beginning of the alternative equinox month, i.e. it also advocates a calendar rather than a festival beginning. The 168 days may be: 14/I to 30/VI inclusive: or 15/I to 31/VI inclusive; or 15/VII to 31/XII inclusive.

Note: The solar calendar was not utopian, as has sometimes been claimed. It would work if two and a half weeks (17½ days) were intercalated every fourteen years, to make up for the thirty hours (1¼ days) by which the 364 day year fell short of the actual 365¼ day solar year. The half week (a familiar concept for solarists, cf. Dan. 9.27) would mean that in alternating quartodecimal periods the dates fell on different days; for instance, the 31st was on a Tuesday at 6 a.m. in the normative day position, but after inserting two and a half weeks would begin on a Friday evening at 6 p.m., coinciding with the sabbath.

41. This setting for the 490 years of *Testament of Levi* has been independently arrived at by R.T. Beckwith ('The Significance of the Calendar for Interpreting Essene Chronology and Eschatology', *RevQ* 10 [1979-81], pp. 167-202). He agrees that the beginning was the return from exile, also that the inexpressible pollution was the desolation of the temple. But he places the fifth and seventh weeks of the end of the passage within the seventh jubilee. This is not justified by the text; these weeks are in the eighth jubilee.

42. Two different dates are given by Josephus: in Herod's eighteenth year (20-19; *Ant*. 15.380); and his fifteenth year (23-22; *War* 1.401). The completion of the temple building itself is said to have taken a year and five months (*Ant*. 15.421).

43. Schürer I (revised), p. 467; Robert Jewett, *Dating Paul's Life* (London: SCM, 1979), p. 43 and note 164.

44. Schürer I (revised), pp. 512, and 515 n. 139.

45. Australian and New Zealand Studies in Theology and Religion; Sydney: Theological Explorations.

PART II

COMPOSITION AND STATUS

THE LITERARY COMPOSITION OF THE TEMPLE SCROLL AND ITS STATUS AT QUMRAN

Hartmut Stegemann

University of Göttingen

Treatment of the Temple Scroll is similar to the treatment of an old Egyptian mummy. To begin with there is much decay and a thick layer of dust and the person who formerly used the bones remains quite strange to us. But the scarab replacing the heart in the mummified body, being inscribed with all the good deeds and intentions of that person, is still in place and can be read not only by some judging God but also by our scientific eyes. Likewise, beyond the dust and decay of the scroll itself the Temple Scroll's scarab, or heart, is the way its composer or author has used literary sources in its composition and in so doing disclosed his own purposes and interests.

The main part of this paper will discuss some aspects of those sources of the Temple Scroll and the way they have been redacted. This main part will be followed by some brief reflections on the status of the Temple Scroll at Qumran. But first of all I wish to consider two basic problems which have precedence over the questions of sources and composition, namely the material evidence of what we call 'the Temple Scroll' and the historical circumstances of the final composition of its text.

1. The Material Evidence of 'the Temple Scroll'

The main manuscript of the Temple Scroll came into the hands of the late Professor Yigael Yadin in Jerusalem on 8 June, 1967. About ten years later, in the autumn of 1977, he published its full text[1]—the best edition yet of any of the Qumran finds and a reliable basis for all further scientific research on Temple Scroll questions. To distinguish this scroll from others I call it 'Yadin's Temple Scroll'.

Yadin's Temple Scroll was discovered in the home of Mr Kando at Bethlehem; but there are good arguments to suppose it was found initially by Bedouin in Qumran's Cave 11 in the year 1956.[2] The text of this scroll was written about the end of the first century BCE or the beginning of the first century CE.[3] As yet it is the longest scroll surviving from any of the Qumran caves, but less than half of the text of the original manuscript is represented in what has survived. Most of its 66 columns as published by Yadin probably originally had 22 written lines each; columns 49 to 60 probably had 28 lines each. The scroll is extensively damaged: the upper third of every column is lost by decay, as is most of the middle third of every column from the beginning of the scroll to column 40; every line represented by the fragments of columns 1 to 15 is destroyed except for some letters or a few words, less than half the original lines still being readable, and for the rest there are many more gaps or breaks which are difficult to restore. But with the help of key words, biblical parallels, and the good order of contents according to Yadin's arrangements of fragments and columns it is still possible to know something about the destroyed passages of this scroll and even to restore their text partially.

Yadin's Temple Scroll was in part already damaged by its former readers in antiquity, mainly at its beginning and end, but also in the bottom parts of some other columns. Repairs dating to the first half of the first century CE are clearly visible.[4] The first and the last sheet of the scroll with about four columns each were cut off and replaced by new sheets. The four columns at the beginning of the scroll were rewritten by another scribe in five columns; as he reached the end of his rewritten text at the top of his new column 5, he filled up the rest of that column with the same text that comes again in the following column 6—a curious method of restoration, eagerly recognized by Yigael Yadin who used the fragmentary doublets for the mutual restoration of the two columns.

On the other hand the repair sheet at the end of the scroll remained uninscribed. Yadin thought it was only a very small sheet for one further column of text which ended in the lost area of lines 1 to 5 in column 67.[5] The breadth of this final repair sheet is now only about 20 centimetres, while the breadth of all the other sheets of this scroll, with three or four columns each, is between 37 and 61 centimetres. In my opinion, however, there was also a long repair sheet at the end of the scroll, prepared for a text of four more columns, but never inscribed. At some time afterwards, most of it was cut off and used for some other purpose, the remaining edge thus becoming some kind of handle sheet at the end of the scroll.[6] The proper assessment of this matter is naturally important for the correct answer to the question whether the original text of the Temple Scroll ended shortly after Yadin's column 66, as he himself thought, or continued for about four more columns, now lost, which in my opinion is the better supposition. I shall discuss this matter in greater detail when considering the scroll's sources.[7]

Besides Yadin's Temple Scroll there is one other scroll with the same text, also from Cave 11 of Qumran, but rather fragmentary. Most of its fragments are printed on plates 35* to 40* of the supplement of Yadin's edition and were used by him to restore some gaps in his scroll. The text of this version corresponds with columns 15 to 51, the broader middle part, of Yadin's Temple Scroll. The contents of these fragments were described by their future editor, Jan van der Ploeg, in a paper he read at the Louvain Qumran Symposium, 1976—without any knowledge of Yadin's parallel text;[8] the publication of Yadin's edition has shown that the textual evidence of both manuscripts is essentially the same. In addition to the completion of gaps in Yadin's Temple Scroll, there are two indisputable points associated with the fragments of van der Ploeg's Temple Scroll: without any doubt it comes from Qumran's Cave 11, and, as van der Ploeg recognized,[9] it was written by the same scribe who also wrote 1QpHab, a specifically Qumranic text composed about the middle of the first century BCE, the 1Q copy of its text being contemporary with its composition. Therefore, van der Ploeg's Temple Scroll is about half a century older than Yadin's, and was definitely written by a member of the Qumran community, not by somebody else. From this we know that the Temple Scroll was not only brought to the Qumran settlement of that community and stored up in one of their libraries, but was also used by its members and was well known to at least some of them.

Apart from these two copies of the Temple Scroll, Yadin's and van der Ploeg's, there are no other copies of this text known to us, neither from the Qumran caves nor from any other evidence. The three 4Q fragments with the Rockefeller Museum's photo-number 43.366, presented on the supplementary plates of Yadin's edition of the Temple Scroll and written in the second half of the second century BCE,[10] do not come from another copy of the Temple Scroll, but from 'a Pentateuch with frequent non-biblical additions', 4Q 364 and 365, as stated correctly by its future editor, John Strugnell, in a letter to Ben Zion Wacholder of 28 April 1981, which the latter cited in his book *The Dawn of Qumran*.[11] The different numbers, 4Q 364 and 365, are caused by the fact that this large scroll of the whole Pentateuch was written by two different scribes intermittently, the fragments from each scribe being listed under a separate number; but there is good evidence that they come from the same scroll.

In the same letter to Ben Zion Wacholder John Strugnell wrote: 'There is one group of 4Q fragments not yet published, which contain quotations from, or the text of, the Temple Scroll, or at least one of its sources: it is in a hand (which) would be difficult to date much later than 150 B.C'.[12] The true nature of this text can be discussed only after its publication by Émile Puech. He kindly showed me the poor fragments of this scroll which he dates to the end of the second century BCE. This scroll is probably a copy of an expanded text of Deuteronomy, evidently differing from the extant text of the Temple Scroll. Therefore, not a single copy of the Temple Scroll exists from Qumran's main library in Cave 4, but only two copies from Cave 11, those of van der Ploeg and Yadin. As there are about ten or more copies from the different caves of the books favoured by the Qumran community, such as Deuteronomy, Isaiah, the biblical Psalms, the book of *Jubilees*, *Serek ha-yahad*, the *Hodayot*, or the War Scroll, we can deduce that the Temple Scroll was not one of the favoured books of the Qumran community, but only known to some of its members and perhaps used for some specific purposes.

I shall return to this topic in the final part of my paper. Our next step will be to ask for the historical circumstances of the final composition of the Temple Scroll's text.

2. *The Historical Circumstances of the Final Composition of the Temple Scroll's Text*

The first to discuss the historical circumstances of the final composition of the Temple Scroll's text was the late Professor Yigael Yadin himself. He correctly stated that the Temple Scroll is a *sēper tôrāh sensu stricto*—not simply a collection of materials for some particular area of religious life. He also stated correctly that this book was composed as an 'additional' *Torah* to the five books of the Mosaic *Torah*, our Pentateuch, as a given authority and on the same level of religious value:[13] indeed, the Temple Scroll was not intended to supersede the canonical books of the Pentateuch and the other books of the Hebrew scriptures as well, as Ben Zion Wacholder claims,[14] nor is it some kind of commentary on given authoritative texts, but a sixth book of the *Torah*, supplementing the Pentateuch and with the same level of authority. But who composed this 'supplementary *Torah*'?

From the beginning of his research into the Temple Scroll, Yadin was convinced that it was composed as a 'sectarian' *Torah* in the Qumran community. Moreover, in a second stage of his research he became convinced that the famous 'Teacher of Righteousness' himself, whom he supposed to have been a man named Zadok, was the historical author of this composition.[15] Yadin argued his case from many different angles: from the language of the Temple Scroll to hints regarding its authority and authorship in specifically Qumran texts like the Damascus Document, the *Pesharim*, or 4Q Catena[a]. And as Professor Yadin continues to be the main authority in all Temple Scroll questions, most scholars share his opinions without hesitation.

However, all the arguments adduced by Yadin to support his theory of the historical origin of the Temple Scroll's composition are weak or evidently mistaken.[16] This is also the case with Ben Zion Wacholder, who took his basic ideas from Yadin, dating only the activity of the Teacher of Righteousness and the composition of the Temple Scroll half a century earlier than Yadin. On the contrary, in my opinion there is no specific connection at all between the Qumran community and the composition of the Temple Scroll; it must have been composed quite independently of that specific group of Second Temple Judaism. I cannot discuss here in great detail my opposing arguments, but I will briefly sum up the main results of my own investigations.[17]

In fact, there is not one mention of the Temple Scroll's existence in any of the other Qumranic writings, neither in the published ones nor in the unpublished. There is not one quotation from the Temple Scroll in the many Qumran scrolls which otherwise, time and time again, cite all the books of the Pentateuch as their unique law. This is often called תורת מושה in the specifically Qumranic texts, while the Temple Scroll itself avoids the aspect of the human authority of Moses as far as possible, attributing its commandments directly to God himself, independent of any human mediator. Furthermore, there are clear differences between the Temple Scroll and the specifically Qumranic texts in matters of *halakhah*, style, terminology, and other linguistic and literary traits. There is also a quite different approach to the temple buildings in the Temple Scroll on the one hand—more than one third of its contents being dedicated to this subject -, and in the specifically Qumranic texts on the other—where there is no interest at all in the architectural features of the Jerusalem temple. We find much polemic against the illegitimate priesthood offering sacrifices there, against people who participate in their cult, or against specific cultic customs, but the building itself or its courts, etc., are never criticized as being at variance with God's commandments, nor is there any hint in all the specific Qumranic texts of any intention to change that building or its broader architectural features. Last but not least, only two copies of the Temple Scroll's text were found in the Qumran caves, both of them in Cave 11, not one in the main library of Cave 4.

The result of these statements is unequivocal in my opinion: whatever the status of the Temple Scroll at Qumran was, it was never something like 'the specific law of the Qumran community', nor is it possible any longer to place the composition of the Temple Scroll within that specific group. The Temple Scroll must have come there from outside as a composition either contemporary or earlier than the settlement at Qumran. But where was its true place in the history of Judaism?

The *terminus ante quem* of the composition of the Temple Scroll is definitively provided by the palaeographic evidence of its oldest copy, van der Ploeg's Temple Scroll, written about the middle of the first century BCE. On the other hand, a *terminus a quo* for its composition is provided by the final sections of the Statutes of the King of Yadin's Temple Scroll, which clearly reflect the situation of the exile in the sixth century BCE as a given fact. Therefore we have about half a millennium to work with for placing the composition of the Temple

Scroll in history: from the end of the sixth century to the middle of the first century BCE. And there is no clear external evidence to shorten this period of time to one of the centuries in question. For the moment I have just three arguments towards such a limitation:

1. It is difficult to imagine that a supplementary sixth book of the *Torah* could have been compiled and acknowledged by at least some Jewish authorities much later than in the fourth century BCE. I cannot imagine this in the time after Ben Sira, or in the time of the historical existence of the Qumran community from the second third of the second century BCE onwards. On the other hand, the five books of Moses, the Pentateuch as we know it from our Bibles, were a given authority to the composer of the Temple Scroll's text, together with some other books like the books of Samuel and the books of Kings, and some prophets like the book of Ezekiel. These factors may favour a date for the composition of the Temple Scroll between the end of the fifth and the end of the third century BCE—the earlier in this period the better, because of the assumption that such a supplementary sixth book of the *Torah* should be acknowledged as authoritative during the Second Temple period.

2. The language of the Temple Scroll, particularly on its redactional level, if compared with all other witnesses of Hebrew literature from the Second Temple period, mostly corresponds to the language of the books of Chronicles. And, as recognized by Jacob Milgrom,[18] the role of the Levites in both compositions, Chronicles and the Temple Scroll, is to some extent similar against other sources from Qumran or elsewhere. These findings also lead us to the fourth or third century BCE.

3. My third argument for reducing the span of time of the composition of the Temple Scroll concerns the traditions, or even literary sources, used by its author. Obviously, the composition of a text cannot be older than the youngest source, tradition, or way of thinking used by its author. Evidently, such arguments can only limit the *terminus a quo* of a specific composition, not its *terminus ad quem*; for traditional-minded people may use the same things in the same manner through centuries. But all limitations of the *terminus a quo* are helpful for bringing us nearer the precise point in history of any literary composition. For example, if Professor Johann Maier[19] is right to assume that the concept of the temple, its courts, or other architectural features in the Temple Scroll are deeply influenced by

specific peculiarities of Persian architecture on the one hand, but the text of the Temple Scroll, or even before that its 'temple source', were evidently composed by a Jew, one needs at least one century of Persian influence on Jewish minds to allow such an influence to contribute to the shape of the architectural features of their most holy place. Only from the end of the fifth century BCE onwards is it possible to conceive of such a possibility in Judaism. Or, if the author of the Temple Scroll used expanded *Torah* scrolls for the composition of his own text, at first such expansions had to develop for the given Pentateuch: the upshot of my research in this field is that the earliest date for the composition of the Temple Scroll must have been at least one century after the final redaction of the Pentateuch in the form we know it in our Bibles. The problem is that we do not know the exact date of this final redaction; was it performed already in Mesopotamia during the exile of the sixth century BCE, or in the time of Ezra about the middle of the fifth or in the beginning of the fourth century BCE, or still later? Because of this, our result remains a relative one; we would date the composition of the Temple Scroll at least one century after the final redaction of the books of the Pentateuch, whenever that was. Most Christian Old Testament scholars tend to date the final redaction of the Pentateuch 'about 400 BCE' or still later in the fourth or third century BCE. When all the so-called 'paraphrases' of books of the Pentateuch and the expanded *Torah* scrolls from the Qumran caves have been edited and published, and after some further research into the history of the text of the Pentateuch to be done by Frank M. Cross and others, one may incline to the supposition that it took some centuries to develop all these different treatments of the given books of the Pentateuch, and as a result date its final redaction earlier than is usually the case today. But this is a view anticipating further editions of Qumran texts, already known to me, and further research to be done in the next century, and so is highly speculative.

The following can be stated without such speculation:

1. Yadin's theory that the Temple Scroll was composed only in the second century BCE within the Qumran community, perhaps by its Teacher of Righteousness personally, is definitely wrong; the Temple Scroll was brought into existence quite independently of those specific circumstances.

2. The best place in history for the composition of the Temple

Scroll is close to the composition of the biblical books of the Chronicles, in the fourth century BCE or about that time. The earliest discussable date is the second half of the fifth century BCE, the latest possibility in the third century BCE—but not too late in it, as the Temple Scroll is still free from Hellenistic influence, and also is not a polemic against Hellenism. Any more precise dating of its composition is dependent on further research.

If we ask who the author of the Temple Scroll was, we can only answer vaguely that he must have been a member of one of the priestly families serving at the temple in Jerusalem. When the Pentateuch as we know it from our Bibles gained some kind of 'canonical' dignity at this temple, outlawing many other priestly traditions or even highly esteemed sources of priestly knowledge, he gathered a bulk of such materials and compiled them as a sixth, supplementary, book of the *Torah*, regarded by himself and by his followers to be as holy as the books of the Pentateuch. In this way he created the only real Hexateuch which ever existed, known to us now by the two later copies of its sixth book from Qumran's cave 11.[20] But the author had no such community in mind or in view when he wrote his supplementary *Torah*, but rather the whole of Israel with its twelve tribes, settling in the Holy Land God had given to them, surrounding his most holy dwelling place on earth, the temple of Jerusalem. The spirit of this composition is still quite far away from the second century BCE with its elite groups within Judaism like the Essene Qumran community, or the Pharisees, claiming to be the holy remnant of the true Israel and isolating themselves from those parts of Israel which had in their opinion gone wrong. The spirit of the Temple Scroll is not yet separatistic, but includes the whole of Israel as a homogeneous entity.[21] Considering the Temple Scroll's conceptualization of all Israel, it is difficult to understand why Yigael Yadin should have thought that the scroll was of Qumranic origin. He must have been totally preoccupied by the technical fact that his scroll came from one of the Qumran caves and, by the assumption that as its contents were not identical with the biblical books, it must be regarded as specifically Qumranic. But, as is well known, not more than about 20% of all scrolls from the Qumran caves belong to this specific group, while about 80% are copies of biblical books or of other literature not originating from the Qumran community, but just part of their libraries. The Temple Scroll clearly belongs in this latter category.

3. *The Sources of the Temple Scroll and their Redactional Composition*

The text represented by the Temple Scroll was not written by a single author independently of any sources; rather, to a great extent it is a composite text, taking over literary sources, combining them, and adding here and there some redactional elements.

Yigael Yadin has stated in his edition at several places that the author of the Temple Scroll used older traditions or given materials, but he did not discuss problems like oral or written tradition, the proportion of such materials in the scroll, or even the possibility of extensive literary sources being used as components of the final text. In Yadin's opinion a single author gathered together many different materials from his tradition, arranged them in a more or less systematic way, and characterized the whole text with his own leading ideas and interests. Yadin barely noticed the difficulties of this view visible in the extant textual evidence of the Temple Scroll itself.

The breakthrough to a more adequate valuation of the textual complexity of the Temple Scroll was provided by Andrew M. Wilson and Lawrence Wills, with many helpful suggestions from John Strugnell.[22] Starting from the division of the Temple Scroll into five different sections on the basis of their contents, they conclude that at least the bodies, or main parts, of these sections were at the same time literary sources, independent documents, which the author utilized in the composition of his final book. Basically, in my opinion, Wilson and Wills have detected the make-up of this text correctly. I shall not repeat, therefore, their line of argument and the technical points used by them to detect those sources; but I shall discuss the larger literary units in the Temple Scroll and the questions of the sources involved, always starting from observations of Wilson and Wills and adding some further comments which could be helpful.

A. *The Introduction of the Temple Scroll*

The first main section of the Temple Scroll, describing the architectural features of the temple buildings, etc., started in the lost upper part of Yadin's column 3. In front of this, little more than two columns, about 50 lines of text, were covered by a literary introduction to the whole composition, which is now lost except for some lines of column 2. The textual remains of column 1 are so poor that even

Yadin could not decipher one single letter clearly.[23] As a result the principal information on the purpose of the whole composition is gone. What remains of column 2 is a long repetition of Exod. 34.10-16, the text of Deut. 7.25-26 being imbedded between verses 13 and 14 of the Exodus text.

These final and concluding passages of the introduction to the Temple Scroll only state that in the land of Israel there will be no foreigners at all with their bad influences; this is enriched by the passage from Deuteronomy 7 with its command to destroy completely all the idols of the earlier inhabitants of this holy land without using them for any further purpose. This is just one of the basic ideas behind the composition of the whole Temple Scroll and one cannot really deduce from it the reason for the writing of such a supplementary *Torah*. Therefore, one can only suppose that in the lost parts of the introduction some further hint from the Pentateuch itself or from other traditional authorities may have been used to explain why the commandments already written in the Pentateuch had to be supplemented with further *tôrôt* compiled in a sixth book.

The only idea picked up later from what remains of the introduction reflects the way in which the Pentateuch's Exodus 34 is followed by Exodus 35-40, the establishment and equipment of the אהל מועד according to the corresponding commandments of Exodus 25-31. As the Temple Scroll has the tendency to supplement the evidence of the Pentateuch from the former and latter prophets, one may suppose that in the lost passages there was some reflection setting out how the temple to be built in Jerusalem was to be identified in some way with the אהל מועד of the desert time, both concepts being basically identical. As far as one can judge from the evidence and suppose from the parallel introductions of other such compositions, like Deuteronomy, there existed no source for this part of the Temple Scroll other than biblical material which would have been freely adopted by the final redactor, or author, as an introduction to his new composition.

B. *The Source Describing the Temple, its Courts, and Access to this Holy Area*

The first main source of the Temple Scroll starts in the top of column 3 of Yadin's manuscript and continues to the end of column 47.

Imbedded in this source is another one, from 13.8 to 30.2, the so-called 'Festival Calendar', to be discussed in the next section.

This part of the Temple Scroll is one of the two principal parts of the whole composition. It describes the areas of holiness of the land of Israel from the temple in the middle, starting with its central features, to the borders. Much of this description is done in a rather technical way which demonstrates that there is some debate behind it; old controversies are solved by specific declarations.

This part of the Temple Scroll is no re-working of one specific section of the Bible, but all its ingredients are gathered together from biblical passages, mainly from the cultic instructions of the Pentateuch, from the description of the temple of Solomon in 1 Kings 6–8, from the ideas of Ezekiel 40–48, and from some other sources related to the temple and to the areas of holiness for Israel.[24] This compilation was not initiated by the author of the Temple Scroll, but by some predecessor; starting from the observations of Wilson and Wills,[25] my reasons for thinking this are as follows.

In general the Temple Scroll has the tendency to formulate the commandments given by God himself in the first person, 'I command', often changing the biblical *Vorlage*, 'God commands', in this way. Usually these commandments are addressed to some representatives of Israel or to Israel as a collective in the second person *singular*, 'You My People'. These changes to the biblical *Vorlage* and the formulation of new materials are significant for the Temple Scroll as a whole as well as for some of its sources; they are also important for appreciating the redactional parts of its text. But there are some significant exceptions to this tendency. In the still extant materials of columns 3 to 47 (excluding columns 13.8–30.2) God speaks thirty times in the first person, but four times instead of this in the third person, in columns 34, 35, and 39.[26] The second person singular address is attested from columns 3 to 46; but there are also 3 occurrences of the second person plural address in columns 33 to 37, and 9 occurrences of this style in column 47.[27] Furthermore, in columns 30 to 46 there are many formulations in the *yihyeh qôṭēl* style—the future tense of the verb היה with a following participle -, a style which is otherwise quite rare in the Temple Scroll.[28] Twice, in columns 37 and 39, areas of holiness are called מושבות, 'dwelling places', while in the redactional parts, and from column 47 onwards, ערים, 'towns', is used instead of this.[29] All this evidence combined indicates that columns 30 to 47 of the Temple Scroll include materials which are formulated in part in dissimilarity to the common style of the Temple Scroll. Wilson and Wills thought that these materials could have been incorporated into the Temple Scroll in a secondary stage of literary development.[30] But this would be difficult as there are too many elements involved which are basic for the temple concept in this scroll and, therefore, cannot be added like 'further elements' in a secondary stage.

The literary problems become still more complicated by the observation, not made by Wilson and Wills, or anybody else, that precisely in this part of the Temple Scroll are found many matters which were taken over into the final composition from expanded *Torah* scrolls like that of John Strugnell, 4Q 364 and 365. The large fragment of this scroll with two columns of text not represented in our biblical Pentateuch, which was used by Yadin to complete the text of his scroll in columns 38 and 41,[31] is only one impressive example of this. These materials were taken over into an already existing description of the temple, its courts, etc., without changing their traditional style, God speaking in the third person to second person plural addressees; this style corresponds to the style of the expanded *Torah* scrolls.

I cannot discuss here the problems of this source of the Temple Scroll in detail. The results of my analysis are as follows. In the first place, there existed as a separate book an architectural description of the temple, its courts, etc., according to God's will, in which were gathered and combined all the relevant materials from the Pentateuch, 1 Kings 6–8, Ezekiel 40–48, and some other sources known and unknown to us. This book was already written with divine commandments in the first person singular style and with second person singular addressees. This book may have been composed about the fifth century BCE. In a second stage this book was partly revised with the inclusion of further materials from expanded *Torah* scrolls, some of which may have replaced some elements of the first version. In a third stage this revised book was taken over by the author of the Temple Scroll as one of the constituent parts of his composition. Personally, he preferred to conform with the style of the first book; but he did not change the stylistic evidence of his *Vorlage*.

It is difficult to discover whether he added further materials to the book he used. Wilson and Wills thought that column 47, the restriction on the bringing of animal hides into the Holy City, might be a redactional transition from the contents of columns 3 to 46 to the following purity laws;[32] but the subject of this column 47 is a highly specific topic, not really the kind of phrases commonly used for literary transitions. In any case, I agree with Johann Maier,[33] and with Wilson and Wills,[34] that the prescriptions of column 47 do not open the following purity laws, but belong to the preceding section of the Temple Scroll on the temple complex. The literary transition to the next section of the Temple Scroll, those purity laws, may have been in the seven lines lost by decay in the top part of the following column 48.

C. *The So-called 'Festival Calendar'*

In discussing the contents of columns 3 to 47 of the Temple Scroll, we have neglected columns 13.8 to 30.2, the so-called 'festival calendar'. This section is mainly based on Numbers 28–29, and Leviticus 23,[35] with the incorporation of many other biblical passages and some non-biblical evidence.

For the most part those materials form a separate literary source which existed as an independent document before its inclusion by the author of the Temple Scroll. This is evident from the fact that, against the dominant style of the Temple Scroll, God is always mentioned in the third person (24 times) and people are addressed in the second person plural.[36] The only exception is the final or concluding part of this composition, columns 29.2–30.2, where God is in the first person singular (19 times) directly speaking to his people. This part may be a redactional addition, as Wilson and Wills supposed,[37] or may have been added to the main body of this document at an earlier stage; whatever the case it was clearly composed by someone other than the author of the main part of the 'festival calendar'. Indeed, there are some further observations of Wilson and Wills which demonstrate that at least 13.8 to 29.2 was an independent source: against the broader context of columns 3 to 47, we find in 13.8 to 29.2, alongside the traditional *wᵉqāṭal* forms, many *wᵉyiqṭôl* forms which are very rare in the broader context.[38] Still more impressive is the finding that besides the adverb אחר, 'afterwards', often used in all parts of the Temple Scroll, only in this section is ואחר used, at least seven times; generally in the Bible this is found in the laws of the *Priesterschrift*, in this section of the Temple Scroll it is often in the same syntactic position as אחר is elsewhere.[39] Such linguistic observations establish much better than arguments from the contents that there is indeed an independent literary source behind the composition we have in the manuscript now in our hands.

Again, I cannot discuss this 'festival calendar', its specific feasts, its calendric system, or other components of its text in broader detail. But two points are worth mentioning. Firstly, this 'festival calendar' is not outlawing the parallel biblical evidence, but mainly completing it, often unifying divergent elements from the different biblical sources. Secondly, the principal purpose of this composition is not to establish a complete list of all feasts, but to list the offerings on the altar for all the given feasts.[40] Therefore, it would be more appropriate to call it a 'list of offerings' rather than a 'festival calendar'.

D. *The Purity Laws*

In columns 48 to 51.10 of the Temple Scroll there is a small collection of purity laws. Except perhaps for its final section (51.5-10) which may be redactional,[41] this collection of legal material forms another independent literary source. Against the broader context, but corresponding to the findings in the 'festival calendar', God is mentioned here in the third person, not speaking directly, and usually people are addressed in the second person plural.[42] Also here again are many $w^e yiqt\hat{o}l$ forms besides the commonly used $w^e q\bar{a}tal$ forms.[43] This collection of purity laws starts from a combination of Lev. 11.20ff. with Deut. 14.20, and it continues with further materials from Deuteronomy 14 and from Leviticus. Because of this start one might suppose that this section of purity laws belongs together with the other materials corresponding to Deuteronomy 12–26 in the following columns of the Temple Scroll. But the observations of Wilson and Wills clearly demonstrate that at least columns 48 to 51.5 were composed quite independently from those parts now following in the Temple Scroll.[44] As most of the law code of Deuteronomy 12–26, except for ch. 14, is used in different ways in the following parts of the Temple Scroll, the final redactor or author of the Temple Scroll may have left out material from that chapter to avoid duplicates, since he had already replaced such material with

the purity laws of columns 48 to 51.5 which were available to him as
a separate source. He did not have to compose this set of purity laws
by gathering its elements from the tradition and combining them; he
simply had to make use of this small law code as a given entity.

E. *The Laws of Polity*

The second main section of the Temple Scroll after the Temple
section in columns 3 to 47 and its enrichment by the 'festival
calendar' or 'list of offerings' and the purity laws, is the 'laws of
polity' from column 51.11 to the end of the whole composition,
except for the 'Torah of the King' in columns 57 to 59 which will be
discussed later.

At first glance this section of the Temple Scroll seems to be
redactional, i.e. composed by the author of the Temple Scroll himself.
God always speaks in the first person singular; a few exceptions to
this rule are variously explicable. The recipient of the commandments
is addressed mostly in the second person singular, rarely in the
plural—a little disturbing, but understandable in each case.[45] There
are many *w^eyiqṭôl* forms, and the places of holiness, or settlement of
the Israelites, are always called עָרִים, 'towns'.[46] Most of the
characteristics found in the—perhaps—redactional parts of columns
3 to 51, and also in some traditional parts of the temple source from
columns 3 to 47, are obvious here, and there is very little that does
not agree with this. The contents of this section are taken mostly
from the law code, Deuteronomy 12–26; its elements are combined
with other evidence from the Pentateuch and from the former and
latter prophets which is the same phenomenon as observed often in
the scroll's earlier sections. Therefore, it might be concluded that this
section is completely redactional, composed by the Temple Scroll's
author, who gathered together here some materials which were of
specific interest to him.[47] This section's formal and stylistic
differences from specific parts of the Temple Scroll might then result
simply from the fact that this part is clearly redactional while in the
sections before many differing sources were involved.

But this theory would certainly be incorrect. There are two
principal objections to it. Firstly, although some passages from
Deuteronomy are arranged in an order differing from the biblical
sequence, this section of the Temple Scroll really looks like a re-
working of the whole law code, Deuteronomy 12–26. Deuteronomy

12 is missing, but this may be replaced by the way columns 3 to 47 tell everything about the one place of God's service, the temple at Jerusalem. Deuteronomy 14 is missing, but this may be replaced by the purity laws of columns 48 to 51. Deuteronomy 23–26 are missing, but this may be explained by the lost ends of both extant manuscripts, both van der Ploeg's and Yadin's.[48] Therefore the final section of the Temple Scroll is mainly a complete rendering of the law code, Deuteronomy 12 to 26, with modifications, while all the other parts of the Temple Scroll do not follow a biblical book in this manner, but arrange their materials in a much more systematic way. This finding strongly differs from those characteristic elements of redaction, or authorship, which can be observed in the earlier columns.

Secondly, there are many rubrics in this section of the Temple Scroll, which repeat the text of Deut. 12–26 word for word, with only a few slight changes here or there. This is not the case elsewhere in the Temple Scroll where usually passages from different parts of the Pentateuch, together with other authorities, are assembled and reproduced in a new manner. In that way and through being organized by specific topics like the architectural features of the temple, those earlier passages supply the given Pentateuch, but they do not simply repeat it. However, straightforward repetition is the case in many passages of the Temple Scroll from column 51 onwards:[49] the law code of Deut. 12–26 is repeated with the implication being that the version given in the Temple Scroll is the better one and so outlaws the corresponding passages in the biblical Deuteronomy. As a result, the final section of the Temple Scroll is not only supplementary to the given Pentateuch, but a new law code replacing an essential part of it. This particular piece of evidence, even though it is restricted to the final section of the Temple Scroll, may have been what suggested the idea to Yigael Yadin, Ben Zion Wacholder, and others, that the Temple Scroll was composed as a new *Torah* for some Israelites, outlawing the Law of Moses at least in part.[50]

To my mind, the best explanation for the evidence of the last main section of the Temple Scroll is quite different from the suppositions mentioned above. The final section of the Temple Scroll, from column 51 to the lost end, may be nothing other than a copy of an expanded and modified text of the biblical law code, Deut. 12–26, such as is known in the as yet unpublished 4Q manuscript to be edited by Émile Puech,[51] or from so-called 'paraphrases' of the biblical book of Deuteronomy. The biblical law code of Deut. 12-26 was already much more systematically arranged than other collections of laws in the Pentateuch and so it proved to be a good basis for further systematization based on the given law in post-exilic Judaism: the topics of this law code were arranged in better and better ways, and combined with corresponding laws from other books of the Pentateuch, or even from the prophets. In this way 'modern' and expanded versions of the law code, Deut. 12-26, came into existence and were used as religious guides in many areas of *halakhah* from the sixth century exile onwards. In my opinion, the final section of the Temple Scroll, from column 51 to the end, is nothing other than a copy of such an 'expanded' text of Deut. 12-26, perhaps here or there augmented by the final redactor,[52] who may have removed from this source the passages corresponding to Deut. 12 and 14, as these were already dealt with in the earlier sections of his Temple Scroll composition. For him, the expanded version of Deut. 12-26 was something like a 'new text' compared with its biblical ancestor, just like Deuteronomy in its time was 'new' compared with its sources of Genesis to Numbers, or the Gospel of Matthew was 'new' compared with its ancestor Mark, even if many passages were taken over with only slight modification. Just as we have the Decalogue of Deuteronomy 5 in our 'canon' alongside that of Exodus 20, or the parables of Matthew 13 as well as those of Mark 4, partly the same, partly different and augmented, so the author of the Temple Scroll took into his new book an expanded version of the law code Deut. 12-26, not to outlaw its ancestor but to supplement it. Even if in this way his new Hexateuch had some duplication which the Pentateuch already had in itself, he had been shown the way to proceed by the Pentateuch itself and he would not have found his approach disturbing.

The first main source of the Temple Scroll provided its author with prescriptions for the Temple, its courts, and everything needed to guarantee the holiness of that place and its surroundings. The second, and concluding, main source of this composition provided its author with many *halakhot* of much value for every pious Jew who wanted to live in the Holy Land, or even in the holy city of Jerusalem, according to the will of the real owner of that land and its central city, God himself. On the one hand, this supplementary source helpfully combined many commandments from the tradition, including the books of the Pentateuch, in a harmonizing way; on the other hand, it conveniently added some new *halakhot* to the given authorities, and so was much more 'modern', or up to date, than the biblical books themselves. These may have been the main reasons why this source was included as a whole in the Temple Scroll. It was not a source composed by the Temple Scroll's author himself, but was well known to him and just as helpful to him and his readers as later on the *Mishnah*, the *Talmudim*, etc., would be for Jews of other times and circumstances.

F. *The Torah of the King*

A fifth source for the Temple Scroll was perhaps the specific *Torah* of the King in columns 57.1 to 59, which Yadin called the 'Statutes of the King'. Linguistically and stylistically it does not differ very much from its context, the laws of polity from column 51 onwards. Technically it is nothing but an addition to the king's law of Deut. 17.14-20 which had been reproduced just before in columns 56 and 57 with little variation from the biblical text. While in the concluding passage in column 59 God speaks in the first person singular 24 times, he is mentioned in the opening passage of the addition once (57.8) in the third person and never addresses the king or other people in the second person singular or plural. When compared with its context, these are minor stylistic differences. But the *Torah* of the King as a whole gives the impression of being a text composed independently from its present context, as Wilson and Wills eagerly remarked,[53] even if only on form-critical grounds. But as there was no real king in Israel in the first 400 years after the exile, there was time enough, and much reason, to speculate about the king, his duties, and the reason for his existence; such speculation would have been done quite independently of other *halakhic* or cultic contexts. To judge from the contents of this *Torah* of the King, its regulations are designed to prevent things that were troublesome with the kings of Judah or Israel in the past. For example, unlike David and Solomon the king is not to be married to many women, but may have one wife only as long as she lives; this wife must come from the royal family, i.e. from Israel, and never from abroad so that the risk of foreign gods can be avoided. Or again, the king is no longer involved in cultic affairs, but is clearly subordinated to the priests in general and to the high priest in particular; the king himself is reduced to being a military leader, and to some extent, also a judge, but nothing else. These are strong limitations when compared with the past and the motivation for them is not some bad experience with existing Jewish kings such as, later on, with the Hasmoneans,[54] but evaluations of the kings of the past as viewed by the so-called Deuteronomistic tradition.[55] Because the role of the kings in Israel had been a massive problem in the past, one can understand both why a specific *Torah* of the King should be composed and also why it should be incorporated into a supplementary *Torah*, supplementing especially the old king's law of Deut. 17.14-20.

G. *Concluding Remarks*

Why were those five sources taken up, combined, and made into a sixth book of the *Torah*? From the evidence given there are two principal reasons for this.

Firstly, many supplementary items could be included in the *Torah* in this way: matters concerning the temple, its courts, its areas of holiness, etc., and also many other materials basic for religious life. Early in post-exilic Judaism, about the time of Ezra the scribe, or even through Ezra himself as tradition states, the *Torah* became the basis for all cultic affairs and the whole of religious life. In relation to the temple in particular the Mosaic *Torah* treats only the מועד אהל of the desert time, not the temple at Jerusalem. According to God's will, his dwelling places on earth had to be mainly of the same plan, etc.; so there was good reason to combine God's advice to David, Solomon, Ezekiel and others, with the advice he had already given to Moses and to add the result of these combined witnesses to the Pentateuch as the given main authority. The rebuilt temple in Jerusalem was the first central institution of post-exilic Judaism, before the *Torah* occupied that place later on.[56] The giving of a more complete law of Moses is the first reason why the Temple Scroll constitutes a *Torah* which is supplementary to the given Pentateuch.

Secondly, many of the older *torot*, or *halakhot*, are up-dated in the Temple Scroll. The differences between many of the traditional commandments of God are noticed and sorted out by being combined in new ways, as has been noted already by Yigael Yadin and elaborated upon in more detail by Jacob Milgrom, Gershon Brin, and others.[57] Many up-datings of this kind were made by priestly families serving at the temple in Jerusalem after the exile. The expanded *Torah* scrolls from the Qumran caves, and other materials, show us the way those priests lived with the given Pentateuch, supplementing and up-dating its text according to the needs of current cultic practice and of the religious life of their time. When one day the shorter Pentateuch, as we know it from our Bibles, without those supplements and up-datings, became quasi-canonical, the supplementary and up-dated will of God was gathered and combined with the five separately existing sources as a sixth, supplementary book of the *Torah*, which thus became complete and sufficient for all the religious purposes of that time.

These are the reasons behind the Temple Scroll's composition, the reasons for establishing a new and complete law code in about the fourth century BCE.

4. The Status of the Temple Scroll at Qumran

As demonstrated above, the Temple Scroll was composed quite independently of the Qumran community. It was in its final form about two centuries before the Qumran community came into existence, and the Teacher of Righteousness wrote his *Hodayot*. For the members of the Qumran community the Temple Scroll was one of the many traditional texts which they knew, like the books of *Enoch*, or the book of *Jubilees*, like Sirach or Daniel, like the non-biblical psalms and prayers, like the War Scroll, or many other traditional books or collections. Many scrolls of this kind may have come to their libraries as new members joined and had their literary possessions deposited there. Who read all these books? Many of them may have been on the shelves in those libraries, covered by dust, like in our libraries, read by nobody any longer.

The Temple Scroll fared little better with that small group of the large Essene movement living at Qumran than some of these other non-Qumran works. Nobody cited it as an authority; none of the books written at Qumran mentioned its existence; no copy of it was to be found in the main library of the group, hidden in Qumran's Cave 4. But one copy of this book, van der Ploeg's Temple Scroll found in Cave 11, two kilometres north of the Qumran settlement, was written about the middle of the first century BCE by a member of this Qumran community; and another copy, Yadin's Temple Scroll written half a century later, was used by one person—or by several people—in such an intensive manner that it had to be repaired a few years later. There is good evidence, then, that this text was indeed known and used by some members of the Qumran community, but there is nothing concrete to indicate how members of the group took some profit from it, or to show how they valued it. We can only speculate on these topics.

In my opinion, there may have been some members of the Qumran community who had scholarly interests. They never intended to build the temple in Jerusalem perfectly according to God's will with their own hands; but it may have been interesting for them to study a text which had once gathered the scattered biblical notions on this topic and which presented an overall plan for such a purpose. Those members of the Qumran community who used this text were obedient to the *halakhah* of their own group, but it may have been interesting for them to study how their ancestors had solved some of the riddles of the *Torah*, to see how they had combined divergent traditions, or to learn how they had answered specific questions concerning the religious life in their own time.

In that way the Temple Scroll may have had a status at Qumran similar to that of traditional books in our libraries. Members of the Qumran community may have read it like a modern Protestant reads the *Summa Theologiae* of Thomas Aquinas, like a modern Roman Catholic reads something written by Martin Luther, or like a modern Jew studies Rambam: very interesting religious books, but not immediately basic for modern faith or *halakhah*. All traces of influence on the Temple Scroll from events, persons, or traditions contemporaneous with the existence of the Qumran community, as claimed by Yadin, and many others, to be still discernible in the Statutes of the King[58] and at many other places, are merely fantastic and without any basis in the text. If there is any indirect polemic in the Temple Scroll, it is aimed not against conditions in the second century BCE, but against conditions at least two centuries earlier, and then mainly against all the many imperfections of the kingdoms of Judah and Israel which lead to the exile.[59] To preserve Israel from a second exile, to establish everything in Israel according to God's everlasting will, as revealed to the patriarchs and Moses and confirmed by the rebuilding of the temple in Jerusalem with its cult flourishing once again, and to demonstrate to everybody in Israel the right *halakhah* by which to walk according to God's covenant on Mount Sinai—this is the message of the Temple Scroll, from its sources to its final redaction. It contains nothing specifically designed for the Qumran community or its time. It leads the whole of Israel to the everlasting will of its God by including the pattern of the temple in Jerusalem and an up-dated version of the law-code of Deut. 12–26 in the most holy book of Israel, ספר התורה.

NOTES

1. *Megillat ham-Miqdaš* (3 Vols.; Jerusalem: The Israel Exploration Society and the Shrine of the Book, 1977); English trans., *The Temple Scroll* (3 Vols.; Jerusalem: The Israel Exploration Society and the Shrine of the Book, 1983).

2. *The Temple Scroll*, I, pp. 1-5 (Heb.: I, pp. 1-4); Y. Yadin, *The Temple Scroll: The Hidden Law of the Dead Sea Sect* (London: Weidenfeld and Nicolson, 1985), pp. 8-55; H. Shanks, 'Intrigue and the Scroll. Behind the Scenes of Israel's Acquisition of the Temple Scroll', *Biblical Archaeology Review* 13 (1987), pp. 23-27.

3. *The Temple Scroll*, I, p. 18 (Heb.: I, p. 16).

4. *The Temple Scroll*, I, p. 12 (Heb.: I, p. 10).

5. *The Temple Scroll*, II, pp. 300-301 (Heb.: II, pp. 211-12).

6. When the Temple Scroll was opened, this small handle sheet was found to be its very end. This is clearly demonstrated by the narrow distances between the traces of each turn of the scroll, shortened to 2.7 cm at the left edge of the sheet.

7. See pp. 139-41.

8. 'Une *halakha* inédite de Qumrân', *Qumrân: Sa piété, sa théologie et son milieu* (ed. M. Delcor; BETL, 46; Paris: Duculot, Leuven: Leuven University Press, 1978), pp. 107-13; see especially the P.S. on pp. 112-13. A few further fragments of this scroll will be published in the future.

9. 'Une *halakha* inédite de Qumrân', p. 107.

10. *The Temple Scroll*, IIIa, plates 38* and 40*. Yadin dated this scroll in 'the last quarter of the second century B.C.E.' (*The Temple Scroll*, I, p. 20 [Heb.: I, pp. 16-18).

11. *The Dawn of Qumran* (HUCM, 8; Cincinnati: Hebrew Union College, 1983), pp. 206, 278 n. 169.

12. *The Dawn of Qumran*, p. 206.

13. *The Temple Scroll*, I, pp. 390-92 (Heb.: I, pp. 298-300).

14. *The Dawn of Qumran*, p. 30.

15. *The Temple Scroll*, I, pp. 394-95 (Heb.: I, p. 302); Y. Yadin, *The Temple Scroll: The Hidden Law of the Dead Sea Sect*, pp. 226-28.

16. H. Stegemann, 'The Origins of the Temple Scroll', *IOSOT Congress Volume Jerusalem* (VTSup, 40; Leiden: Brill, 1988), pp. 235-56; H. Stegemann, 'Die "Mitte der Schrift" aus der Sicht der Gemeinde von Qumran', *Mitte der Schrift? Ein jüdisch-christliches Gespräch* (ed. M. Klopfenstein, U. Luz, S. Talmon, & E. Tov; Judaica et Christiana, 11; Bern: Lang, 1987), pp. 160-61, 175-76.

17. Further references are given in my article 'The Origins of the Temple Scroll'; see n. 16.

18. 'Studies in the Temple Scroll', *JBL* 97 (1978), pp. 501-506.

19. J. Maier, 'The Temple Scroll and Tendencies in the Cultic Architecture of the Second Commonwealth', *Archaeology and History in the Dead Sea Scrolls. The New York University Conference in Memory of Yigael Yadin* (ed. L.H. Schiffman; Sheffield: ASOR and JSOT Press, in press); J. Maier, 'The Architectural History of the Jerusalem Temple in the Light of the Temple Scroll', in the present volume, pp. 23-62.

20. H. Stegemann, 'The Origins of the Temple Scroll' (see n. 16), pp. 252-55.

21. H. Stegemann, 'The Institutions of Israel in the Temple Scroll', *Proceedings of the Symposium Forty Years of Research in the Dead Sea Scrolls* (ed. D. Dimant, A. Kasher, & U. Rappaport; Jerusalem: Yad Izhak Ben Zvi, 1989), in press.

22. 'Literary Sources of the *Temple Scroll*', *HTR* 75 (1982), pp. 275-88.

23. *The Temple Scroll*, III, plate 16.

24. In my opinion the biblical books of 1 and 2 Chronicles were not yet known to the author of the Temple Scroll, or used by him as literary sources. Correspondences between the Temple Scroll on the one hand and 1 and 2 Chronicles on the other only indicate corresponding *traditions* used by both of them.

25. 'Literary Sources', pp. 276-80, 284-87.

26. 11QT 34.14; 35.7; 39.8.

27. 11QT 33.8; 35.8; 37.8; 47.14-18.

28. 'Literary Sources', pp. 284-86.

29. 11QT 37.8, 9; 39.9 versus 47.3, 8, 15, 16, 17; 48.14, 15, etc.

30. 'Literary Sources', p. 284.

31. *The Temple Scroll*, IIIa, plate 38*, Fragm. 5. Cf. *The Temple Scroll* II, pp. 160-64, 172-78 (Heb.: II, pp. 113-16, 121-25); see also above, pp. 125f.

32. 'Literary Sources', p. 277.

33. *Die Tempelrolle vom Toten Meer* (Uni-Taschenbücher, 829; München: Reinhardt, 1978), p. 18; English trans. *The Temple Scroll: An Introduction, Translation & Commentary* (JSOTS, 34; Sheffield: JSOT, 1985), p. 13.

34. 'Literary Sources', p. 278.

35. Commonly Numbers 28–29 is regarded as the main biblical base-text of this 'festival calendar'. But B. Levine, 'A Further Look at the Mo'adim of the Temple Scroll', *Archaeology and History* (above, n. 19), in press, demonstrates that the most important base-text is Leviticus 23.

36. 'Literary Sources', pp. 279-80.

37. 'Literary Sources', p. 275.

38. 'Literary Sources', p. 285.

39. 'Literary Sources', p. 287 n. 11.

40. This is also the reason behind the placement of this list in the literary composition of the Temple Scroll immediately after the description of the altar for burnt-offerings (11QT 11–13.7).

41. 'Literary Sources', p. 281.

42. 'Literary Sources', p. 280.

43. 'Literary Sources', p. 285.

44. 'Literary Sources', pp. 275, 280-81, 285.

45. 'Literary Sources', pp. 281-83.

46. 'Literary Sources', pp. 285, 287 n. 11.

47. This is the way Y. Yadin discussed those materials: *The Temple Scroll* I, pp. 277-343 (Heb.: I, pp. 215-63); Y. Yadin, *The Temple Scroll: The Hidden Law of the Dead Sea Sect*, pp. 170-91.

48. Cf. above, pp. 123-25.

49. This difference becomes most obvious if 11QT 51.11–66.17 is compared with 11QT 13.8-30.2 in relation to the biblical materials behind both compositions.

50. This estimation caused Ben Zion Wacholder, *The Dawn of Qumran* (see n. 11 above), pp. 1-32 (and *passim*), to change Yadin's designation 'The Temple Scroll' to his new designation '11Q Torah', insinuating at the same time that this book as a whole was composed to replace the Pentateuch in a way similar to that of the book of *Jubilees* whose author re-wrote Genesis and the beginning of Exodus, replacing the biblical version of these books at the same time with the aid of a 'new revelation'.

51. See above, p. 126.

52. Mainly the insertion of the 'Statutes of the King' (11QT 57.1-59.21) into the present context may result from the final redactor of this scroll.

53. 'Literary Sources', pp. 283, 287-88.

54. This aspect was introduced by Y. Yadin and is again stressed by M. Hengel, J.H. Charlesworth, & D. Mendels, 'The Polemical Character of "On Kingship" in the Temple Scroll: An Attempt at Dating 11Q Temple', *JJS* 37 (1986), pp. 28-38.

55. For detailed argumentation see H. Stegemann, 'The Institutions of Israel in the Temple Scroll' (above, n. 21), in press.

56. The first time we meet the *Torat Moshe* as the *main* institution of Israel is with the new movements of the second third of the second century BCE,

the Essene community, or the Pharisees, at the same time. In the wisdom book of Ben Sira, written about the beginning of the second century BCE, we still meet the temple of Jerusalem, represented by its High Priest, as the central institution (Sir. 50.1-24).

57. J. Milgrom, 'Studies in the Temple Scroll', pp. 501-23; 'Further Studies in the Temple Scroll', *JQR* 71 (1980-81), pp. 1-17, 89-106; see also his contribution to this volume. G. Brin, 'The Bible as Reflected in the Temple Scroll', *Shnaton* 4 (1979-80), pp. 182-225.

58. See above, pp. 141f., with note 54.

59. Basically Ben Zion Wacholder has also grasped the idea that the Temple Scroll was composed to avoid some of the bad experiences Israel had during the time from Mount Sinai to the exile of the sixth century BCE; see his *The Dawn of Qumran*, pp. 30-31. The main problem of his theories is that he thinks that the Temple Scroll was written by the Qumranic Teacher of Righteousness in the second century BCE, and so it is also concerned with specific problems of the later Second Temple period. But truly the Temple Scroll is only concerned with the restoration of the whole of Israel soon after the disaster of the exile, a restoration that is to be based on the Pentateuch supplemented with this further book.

EXTENDING DIVINE REVELATION: MICRO-COMPOSITIONAL STRATEGIES IN THE TEMPLE SCROLL

Phillip R. Callaway

Jonesboro

Introduction

One of the most enduring discoveries in the history of biblical studies is the recognition that God's laws and the history of Israel were recorded by human beings at various times and preserved in distinctive forms by equally diverse sociological groups. This formulation might lead one to think that these persons functioned only in a passive manner as scribes and antiquarians. This depiction robs many of these individuals of their intensive involvement in the interpretation of God's activity with Israel for their contemporaries and for their posterity. It is noteworthy that the biblical prophets are often associated with the pronouncement of a new message from God, while the act of law-giving is usually traced back to the ancient divine revelation given to Moses on Sinai.[1] Nevertheless, just as prophetic messages witness God's continued concern with Israel and Judaea in their histories, the proliferation of similar but often divergent law-codes incontrovertibly demonstrates that the Israelite-Judaean legalists were not concerned simply with transcribing received traditions verbatim.[2] Rather, the central task was often to make this tradition meaningful by unpacking what was latent in it. This unpacking or extending of divine revelation could involve the modification of known legislation or even the creation of newer laws by means of simple compositional strategies (used however consciously or unconsciously), as was done in the creation of the Covenant Code (Exod. 20.22–23.33), the Deuteronomic Code (Deut. 12–26), the

Holiness Code (Lev. 17-26), and the Priestly Code (Exod. 25-31; 34.29-Lev. 16; sections of Numbers).

In his *From Bible to Mishna* (Manchester: Manchester University Press, 1976), J. Weingreen illustrated well how the deuteronomic legislator could reshape older laws in order to understand God's word better. He also cited the non-canonical Temple Scroll as an analogous attempt to extend the traditional, divine revelation.[3] Discussing the complex relationship of the laws of the Temple Scroll to those in the classical law-codes, Yigael Yadin made the following statement:

> The editing of the scroll took several forms: drafting the text in the first person with the object of establishing that it is God Himself who is the speaker; merging commands that concern the same subject; unifying duplicate commands, modifying and adding to the commands in order to clarify their halakhic meaning; appending whole new sections.[4]

Yadin also notes the wholesale appropriation of several chapters from pentateuchal law. Thus the literary activity of the author of the Temple Scroll encompasses the gamut of compositional strategies, including verbatim and near verbatim quotations of biblical laws, varying degrees of conflation, and the production of additional, newer legislation.[5]

Before addressing specific passages in the Temple Scroll, it is necessary to explain the expression 'micro-compositional' strategies. 'Micro-compositional' signifies the author's interfacing and reacting to the legal traditions that he had inherited. This expression is used intentionally in order to contrast with the 'macro-compositional' explanation of Andrew Wilson and Lawrence Wills, who developed a hypothesis on the written sources that were strung together to form the Temple Scroll.[6] According to this hypothesis, several documents, none of which was identical with a block of the Hebrew Bible, were involved: a Temple Source (cols. 2-13, 30-46), a Calendar Source (cols. 13-29), a Purity Source (cols. 48-51.5a), a Deuteronomic Source (cols. 51-56.21; 60-66.17), and perhaps a King's Law independent of the Deuteronomic Source (cols. 56.12-59.21). The redactor created not only the transitional passages in 29.2-30.2, 51.5b-10, and probably col. 47 as well, but was also responsible for combining these older sources to form the extant Temple Scroll. One cannot deny the distinct possibility, indeed the likelihood, that some documents and even oral traditions served as sources of information and inspiration for the creation of the Temple Scroll, but close analysis reveals that it was not simply a matter of cutting and pasting sources together and the composition of a few redactional seams. Not one of the relatively extensive documents postulated by Wilson and Wills is extant outside of the context of the Temple Scroll.[7] The latter is the product of imaginative, exegetical reflection informed by the classical traditions, even in its final section where much of Deuteronomy is used.

In contrast to 'macro-compositional' postulations, which are often highly theoretical and difficult to control, because the hypothetical documents are apparently not extant, 'micro-compositional' analysis reduces speculation by comparing the individual laws of the Temple Scroll with thematically related laws in the Bible. A by-product of this approach is that the results can be controlled and checked against empirical data, thereby providing solid insights for subsequent 'micro- and macro-compositional' analyses of the Temple Scroll. This approach will be illustrated by examples from the laws for festivals, for purity, for the king, and concerning the rebellious and treasonous.

1. *First-fruits Festivals*

In general, the list of festivals in the Temple Scroll corresponds to those given in Leviticus 23 and Numbers 28–29. A major innovation appears however in the number and calculation of dates for its non-biblical first-fruits festivals in cols. 18.10–23.9. The series of first-fruits festivals commences with the waving of the sheaf, which is already mandated in Lev. 23.10-14 and Num. 28.26-31. Then 18.10–19.9 prescribes for the Feast of Weeks or new wheat festival that should fall seven sabbaths or fifty days after the waving of the sheaf (Lev. 23.15-16). Thus the system for calculating this first-fruit festival in reference to the previous one at an interval of fifty days is biblical. Following the new wheat festival, a non-biblical new wine festival is introduced that should be observed also after an interval of seven weeks, seven sabbaths, and fifty days. According to the same biblical principle, the new oil festival was created to be celebrated fifty days later.

Explicit prescriptions for new wine and new oil festivals are lacking in biblical legislation, but many passages do refer to the trio 'grain (דגן), wine (תירוש), and oil (יצהר)'.[8] This language is also found in col. 43. The Bible does not prescribe that the new wine and new oil festivals be celebrated at an interval of fifty days; nevertheless, Deut. 11.14 and Hos. 2.10-11 refer to these crops in their respective harvest seasons. A positive picture is painted in Deuteronomy:

> he (God) will give the rain for your land in its season, the early rain and the latter rain, that you may gather in your grain and your wine and your oil (Deut. 11.14).

In the book of Hosea the same imagery is used in God's indictment of Israel:

> She did not know that it was I who gave her the grain, the wine, and the oil,... therefore I will take back my grain in its time, and my wine in its season (Hos. 2.10-11).

Faced with the undeniable reality of new wine and new oil, the author of the Temple Scroll has simply formulated explicit laws corresponding to the other harvest seasons. After transcribing the laws for the sheaf and the new wheat, both of which may be subsumed under the rubric 'grain', he combined the biblical principle for calculating the date for observing the new wheat festival with two other obvious first-fruits festivals. Still, the precise date for the commencement of the calculation of the series of first-fruits festivals was a matter of debate.[9]

2. Purity Laws

This method of extrapolating additional laws based on the principle of analogy is also used extensively in cols. 45–51.5a, which constitute the purity laws to be applied once the Israelites enter and settle in the Promised Land. These laws fall rather easily into two groups: cols. 45.1–47.18 deal with the issues of impurity and purity within the temple-complex and the city of the temple; 48.1–51.5a treat the same subjects outside of this area. As a whole these laws represent a movement from within the temple itself, where absolute holiness is expected, outward to the land, where special facilities are to be erected for those bearing diverse impurities. Col. 45.1-7 begins with instructions concerning the avoidance of contaminated persons, garments, and vessels with cultically pure ones. The temple and its city assume the nimbus and sanctity of the biblical 'camp' mentioned in Deuteronomy 23, Numbers 5, and Leviticus 13.[10] In fact, the verb חנה is used in 45.5 to refer to the activity of the priestly courses. This is followed by the prohibition of those with nocturnal emissions from entering the entire temple-complex (45.7-10). This law reflects the influence of Deut. 23.11, which requires such a person to remain outside of the camp (מחוץ למחנה) until he has been purified. The same applies to those who may have had sexual intercourse (45.11-12; cf. Lev. 15.18-19). Blind persons are prohibited from ever entering the city of the temple (45.13-14; cf. Lev. 21.18), for it is God's abode among the Israelites. In 45.15-18 instructions are given for the purification of those with discharges and for lepers. The seven-day sequestration of lepers and those with discharges is strikingly reminiscent of Leviticus 13 (vv. 4, 21, 26, 31, 33, 50), where the priest is instructed to lock up the non-chronic leper. Lev. 13.46 gives the rationale for this procedure: 'He (the leper) shall remain unclean as long as he has the disease; he is unclean; he shall dwell alone in a habitation outside of the camp (ישב מחוץ למחנה מושבו)'. Clearly, the concept of the 'camp' has been transferred to the city of the temple in this document.

After presenting three laws commanding the construction of three non-biblical structures in col. 46, e.g. a device to protect the temple from the droppings of birds (46.1-4), a terrace with steps to facilitate access to the outer court (46.5-8), and an embankment one hundred cubits wide (46.9-12), the author returns to the biblical sources for laws on toilets and the quarantines for lepers and those with discharges. As is well known, Deut. 23.13-14 preserves the sole biblical injunction on this subject. Like those with nocturnal emissions and lepers, the persons needing to take care of toilet matters must exit the 'camp' of God's presence in order to reach the יד. In 46.13 instructions are given to build a מקום יד (cf. the Greek: τόπος) outside of the city (of the temple) to the north-west, again underscoring the equation of the temple-city with the biblical 'camp'. Yet the Temple Scroll adds that this structure should have houses, flowing water, and pits, in other words, a more or less developed sewerage system. The injunction to erect an area for toilets is indeed biblical, but the additional non-biblical information derives from practical thinking about the matter. 46.16-18 then commands the construction of three מקומות to the east of the city—one for lepers, one for those with discharges, and one for those contaminated by an emission of semen. This stipulation is related to Num. 5.2 that demands the exclusion of lepers, those with discharges, and those who have been contaminated by contact with the dead from the camp, the seat of the deity. The necessity of building facilities for these types of persons is apparently founded upon Lev. 13.46, which requires housing for lepers outside of the camp. It should not go unnoticed that the laws of col. 46, the biblical and non-biblical alike, are introduced identically by the command ועשיתה. Furthermore, all of the laws in cols. 45–46 are concerned with the city of the temple, which is understood in light of the 'camp' in Lev. 13.46, Num. 5.2, and Deut. 23.12-14.

The preservation of the camp's purity continues into col. 47, which commands that wine, oil, and foodstuffs that may be brought into the city of the temple must be pure. This means that such products may enter this restricted area only in the skins of animals sacrificed at the temple, where the deity is present (47.4, 9, 11, 13, 15-16, 18). Since col. 47 no longer commands the construction of buildings for various types of defiled persons, the formulation ועשיתה is not needed. Instead, it uses the expression כול with different objects to refer to potential cases of impurity (47.5-7, 9-17).[11]

Leaving the subject of the purity of the temple-city, the author quotes Deut. 14.18, 21 and Lev. 11.21-22 on animals that the Israelites may and may not eat in col. 48.3-7 and prohibitions from Lev. 21.5 and 19.28 on certain markings on the sin in 48.8-10. Both of these quotations conclude with reference to the holiness of God's people, after which the following prohibition appears: 'You shall not defile your land'. This sentence marks a transition and serves as an apt title for the subsequent laws. In 48.11-14 the Israelites are commanded not to bury their dead indiscriminately as the other nations do. Rather, cemeteries should be established in a ratio of one cemetery per four cities. Yadin suggested that this law may have been modelled stylistically on the biblical law concerning cities of refuge, but this is not at all clear.[12] The Hebrew Scriptures apparently preserve no such law for cemeteries. In terms of the obvious impurity of the dead, which is the subject of several biblical laws, the construction of cemeteries could easily have been deduced from Num. 5.2. This biblical passage requires that those contaminated by the dead remain outside of the camp. The style of the law on cemeteries in col. 48 is, however, nearly identical with that of col. 46.5, 9, 13, and 16, where the verb עשה is used to refer to the act of constructing. Similarly, 48.14-17 enjoin the construction of 'places' for those defiled by virtue of a discharge, for women during menstruation and after childbirth, and for lepers. This is manifestly a law for the land, which is analogous to other laws bearing upon the various categories of defiled persons who might eventually enter the city of the temple. The new component is the mention of women in their impurity—based on Lev. 12.1-5. These women should be construed as broadly analogous to certain types of contaminated men and, therefore, they too required special, separate quarters. Yadin points out that *Mishnah Niddah* 7.4 discusses housing for unclean women and notes that this is practiced by the Samaritans and the Falashas.[13]

In col. 49, the author turns his attention to the problem of a man who dies in a house as well as the objects and persons who could potentially be contaminated thereby. This topic is of particular interest, because these persons and objects could enter the city of the temple by mistake (cf. 47.4-5). Although not altogether identical in formulation, this column depends on Num. 19.11-22 and Lev. 11.32-34. The theme of contamination by corpse contamination continues in 50.4-9, but in the latter case it concerns contact with a corpse on an open field. Johann Maier describes the subsequent law in 50.10-19 as a 'surprisingly extensive section. . . constructed by analogy with the regulations for those unclean by virtue of contact with a corpse and deals with the birth of a dead child'.[14] Recognizing that this section is non-biblical, he suggests comparing it with col. 49. The author's logic is quite lucid: the dead fetus stands in the same relationship to the woman as a house does to its furnishings (cf. 48.11-14; Num. 5.2).

Therefore, the Temple Scroll's purity section preserves several laws that are not explicit in biblical law, but which can be derived by a simple principle of analogy. Based on the pentateuchal notion of the 'camp' (Deut. 23; Num. 5; Lev. 13), several categories of persons are barred from entering the city of the temple and must be quarantined until their purification is complete (cf. Lev. 13.46). The Bible preserves stipulations for the toilet and the housing for lepers, although they are not as extensive as those of the Temple Scroll. The requirement to erect quarters for those with bodily discharges was

created on the analogy of the law for lepers. Anticipating the issues
found in cols. 48–50, col. 47 contains purity laws for products and
materials that might find their way into the holy city. The
requirement to establish cemeteries in 48.11-14 was also conceived
on the principle of analogy: the dead are impure and require
sequestration. The indirect biblical basis for this was Num. 5.2. The
next law (48.14-17) commanding the construction of quarters for
impure women is also an analogous case based on Lev. 12.1-5 and
15.19-30. Finally, 50.10-19 (concerning the stillborn fetus) was
deduced analogously from col. 49, which itself depends on the laws
on corpse contamination in Num. 19.11-22 and Lev. 11.32-34. The
author of these laws had created a web of analogies that are not
explicitly found in the biblical text, but which can be derived quite
easily without violating the spirit and letter of the biblical bases.

3. *Law for the King*

Wilson and Wills have suggested that the King's Law in 56.12–59.21
may have existed as an independent source before its incorporation
into the proto-Temple Scroll.[15] In its extant form, this law belongs to
their Deuteronomic Source that stretches from cols. 51 to 66. In
these columns several chapters from the book of Deuteronomy are
quoted. Consecutive but not always verbatim copying of the
deuteronomic text commences with 55.15-21, which contains Deut.
17.2-5. In 56.12-21 one finds a modified version of the biblical law of
the king (Deut. 17.14-18). 56.20-21 are obviously based on Deut.
17.18, but there are two major modifications of that verse. The king
is not permitted to copy the law for himself. This privilege goes to the
priests. Furthermore, Deuteronomy refers to a 'copy of this law',
while the Temple Scroll speaks only of 'this law'. One would expect
to find Deut. 17.19-20 at the top of col. 57, which is badly damaged.[16]
These two verses would have required approximately five lines of
space.

   In any case, 57.1 opens with the words 'and this is the law', which
was most likely used to introduce the following supplements to the
biblical law of the king. These columns deal with several subtopics
related to the subject of kingship—mustering the troops (57.2-5),
selecting the royal guard (57.5-11), the composition of the council
made up of leaders from the people, the priests, and the Levites

(57.11-15), the marriage law for the king (57.15-19), and the monarch's behavior in matters of others' property (57.19-21). Yadin noted allusions to Lev. 27.3, Num. 31.3, and Exod. 18.21 in this column, but Kaufman is undoubtedly correct in characterizing it as original composition.[17] Nevertheless, in several lines the words והיתה עמו from Deut. 17.19 are unmistakably echoed—e.g. לחיות עמו in 57.6, והיו עמו in 57.9, and עמו in 57.12-13. In spite of this echoing, that which the king is to keep with him differs radically. Deuteronomy speaks of a copy of the law (17.14-18), which the king is supposed to read. In contrast, the Temple Scroll is concerned with the guard of 12,000, who are required to be present at all times. The biblical phrase from Deut. 17.20 'that his heart may not be lifted up above his brethren, and that he may not turn aside from the commandment' is reflected in 57.14-15, which say: 'and he shall not raise up his heart above them (i.e. the thirty-six members of the council) and he shall do nothing without their advice'.

In Deut. 17.19-20 the issue is the king's obedience to the תורה. In spite of appropriating some of the language of the biblical passage in 57.11-15, these lines present an innovation concerned not with general deviation from the Law but rather with particular decision-making without the approval of the trustees and executors of the Law—the leaders of the people, the priests, and the Levites. In the final subsection of this column, 57.15-19, the king is instructed that his wife 'shall be with him all of her days' (57.18). This is again an allusion to the phrases והיתה and כל־ימי חייו of Deut. 17.19. In the context of the Temple Scroll, they refer to the wife; in the Bible, to the Law. In light of this exegetical/compositional pattern that emerges in col. 57, it is clear that its author has extended the biblical law of the king, using smatterings of biblical phraseology in order to reinterpret the king's lawbook in quite a novel way as the royal guard, the royal council, and the queen. In fact, these three institutions serve to insure that the king is never violated or defiled and that he may not disobey God's precepts. This is precisely the purpose of the king's reading of the law in Deut. 17.19-20.

On the surface col. 58 also seems to have no connection to the biblical law of the king. In essence, it deals with varying degrees of military aggression toward Israel, appropriate responses, the division of spoils, and an Israelite war of aggression. Yadin recognized allusions to Num. 31.27, 1 Sam. 30.24-25, and Num. 27.21.[18]

Thematically, 58.1-15 takes up the roles of the commanders mentioned in 57.2-5. Moreover, the prepositional phrase עמו is used in 58.5-8 and 16, thereby continuing the pattern established in col. 57. As noted above, this echoes the language of Deut. 17.19. The twin themes of chariots and horses in 58.7ff. recalls the word סוס in 56.15-17, which ultimately derives from Deut. 17.16. The echoing of earlier themes is continued in 57.12-15, where the topic of the division of spoils ties in with the themes 'commanders, warriors, and the council composed of people, priests, and Levites' adumbrated already in 57.3-15. Column 58 is indeed original composition, but the resumptive repetition of language found in the biblical law of the king as well as of certain themes in col. 57 contributes to the feeling that a rather skilful legalist and literary craftsman is at work, weaving a web of interrelated *halakhot* that are dependent ultimately on Deut. 17.14-20. In that sense, these new prescriptions only make explicit what was already latent in that law.

With its potential curses and blessings on the people and the king, col. 59 concludes the law of the king. Yadin, Kaufman, and Brin indicate that it is a pastiche alluding to Zech. 7.13; Jer. 11.11; 21.12; Ezek. 39.23; 2 Kgs 21.14; Deut. 28.29; Judg. 2.18; Jer. 15.21.[19] Kaufman designates it as fine conflation.[20] As long as this designation does not deflect from its originality, this characterization seems appropriate. This column reflects a sophisticated organization of ideas about a particular theme—the obedience/disobedience of the people and the king. 59.2-13, which deal with the Israelites, disrupts the thematic cohesion of 56.12-58.21. In spite of this, a connection with the theme of kingship is made in 59.13-21. These lines speak of the potential curses and blessings on the king and his posterity. The influence of Deut. 17.19-20 on the language of several lines is undeniable, e.g. כבול דברי התורה הזואת (59.10), ממצוותי (59.14, 16), בחוקותי (59.16), כסא אבותיו (59.14-15), and כסא מלכות (59.17). Furthermore, 59.21 forms an obvious paraphrase of Deut. 17.20b:

> so that he may continue long in his kingdom, he and his children, in Israel (Deut. 17.20b).

> and his days shall be many over his kingdom, he and his sons after him (11QT 59.21).

Therefore, except for 59.2-13, which deals with potential curses and blessings on the people, 56.12-58.21 and 59.13-21 form a thematic unity. These columns evidence the imagination of a biblical legalist who was definitely guided by the classical laws which he had before him in written form and perhaps by equally ancient laws that may not have been recorded before the composition of the Temple Scroll. The biblical law of the king serves as a launching-pad for his masterful extension of divine revelation concerning the institutions surrounding the ruler. He began by writing a modified version of Deut. 17.14-18. Then he presented non-biblical laws on the royal guard, the council, and the queen, which function as concrete examples of the general concept תורה. Even this highly original composition alludes to 17.19-20. When he introduces the themes of war and the division of spoils, he again reiterates phraseology from 17.16, 19. Finally, as noted above, the theme of col. 59 derives from Deut. 17.19-20. This is clearest in the negative formulation of 59.13-15 and the positive language of 59.16-21.

4. *Laws of Rebellion*

One final example should suffice to demonstrate the interface between the author of the scroll and the ideological, often textual, framework out of which he was working. In 64.2-6 the biblical law of the stubborn and rebellious offspring is quoted (Deut. 21.18-21). Following this section, 64.6-13 contain two applications of a single law. Yadin noted the dependence of these lines on Lev. 19.16a and Deut. 21.22-23.[21] In an excellent compositional analysis of col. 64, Moshe Bernstein also pointed out the additional influence of Deut. 17.6 and Exod. 22.27 on these two laws.[22] 64.6-9 preserve the law of the איש רכיל, who commits a treasonous act against his/God's people by delivering them up to foreigners and doing evil in their midst. The source of the expression איש רכיל is Lev. 19.16a, where it refers to a 'slanderer'.[23] The subsequent law in 64.9-13 is introduced by the words 'if a man has committed a crime punishable by death'. Along with its sanction in 64.11-13, these words derive from Deut. 21.22-23. This person, who is guilty of a capital crime, is described as fleeing to the foreign nations, thereby cursing God's people the Israelites. Bernstein notes the dependence of 64.8, where the necessary number of witnesses is mandated, on Deut. 17.6-7.[24] He also suggests that cursing God's people the Israelites derives from Exod. 22.27: 'You shall not revile God, nor curse a ruler of your people'.[25] In both laws the criminal activities of the איש רכיל and the capital offender are expressed in original non-pentateuchal language.

The author's dependence on Exod. 22.27, Lev. 19.16, Deut. 17.6 and 21.22-23 has been demonstrated adequately, but the two laws of 64.6-13 exhibit a closer structural relationship to the foregoing law of the 'stubborn and rebellious offspring' than has been recognized until now. In terms of their form, each of these laws is introduced in a similar manner—in 64.2 by כי יהיה לאיש, in 64.6-7 by כי יהיה איש, and in 64.9 by כי יהיה באיש. Furthermore, all three deal with the problem of rebellious behavior in the land. They differ only slightly regarding the object of the rebellion. Deut. 21.18-21 (in 64.2-6) is concerned with rebellion against one's parents and indirectly against one's city and the Israelites. 64.6-13 involve treacherous/treasonous activity against God and his people. In addition, each of these three laws sanctions the death penalty—the first by stoning, the other two by hanging. The second law is in part dependent on the law of the איש רכיל in Lev. 19.16, but the latter recommends no punishment at all. The punishment for the second and third laws in col. 64 are culled from Deut. 21.22-23. All three of these laws have an interesting peculiarity in common: the nature of the punishable behavior is consistently expressed in nebulous language. Even the biblical law is puzzling. What sort of behavior toward one's parents would have warranted the death penalty?[26] Deut. 21.18-21 describes this inappropriate behavior as 'stubborn', 'rebellious', 'gluttonous', and 'drunken'. 64.6-13 speaks of 'delivering my (God's) people', 'doing evil', 'fleeing to the foreign nations', and 'cursing my people'. All of these characterizations require further clarification and concretization of the capital offense, if they are to be effectively applied.

In any case, the structural dependence of 64.6-9 and 9-13 on 64.2-6 is patent. The influence of Lev. 19.16, Deut. 17.6-7, and 21.22-23 is also unmistakable. These laws fit nicely into the overall thematic pattern established from col. 55.8 on. They deal with rebellion in the forms of idolatry, false prophecy, the necessity of a judicial system to deal with rebellion, the potential rebellion of the king implied in the curse of col. 59, and again false prophecy. Column 61, which preserves laws for combat inside and outside of the Holy Land, is also probably related in a general way to the potentially treasonous activities of 64.6-13.

Concluding Remarks

The preceding discussion demonstrates that the Temple Scroll was composed by a creative legalist, who exploited divine revelation in recognizable, logical ways in order to allow its hidden meanings to surface. The Bible's legal traditions, in particular those in Exodus, Leviticus, Numbers, and Deuteronomy, served him as an authoritative source of precedent law. They also functioned as points of reference for the exegetical creation of analogous non-biblical laws. These newer prescriptions have sometimes been characterized as original composition, which can be said about the Temple Scroll as a whole, but the sources of inspiration for this non-canonical legislation can be detected in known biblical traditions combined with practical reflection on matters of Israelite life in the Holy Land.

NOTES

1. E.g. 1 Kgs 2.3; 2 Kgs 14.6; 23.2; 2 Chron. 23.18; 24.6, 9; 25.4; 30.16; 33.8; 34.14; 35.6, 12; Ezra 3.2; 6.18; 7.6; Neh. 8.1, 14; 9.14; 10.30; 13.1; Mal. 3.22; Dan. 9.11, 13.

2. Michael Fishbane, 'Revelation and Tradition: Aspects of Inner-Biblical Exegesis', *JBL* 99 (1980), pp. 343-61.

3. J. Weingreen, *From Bible to Mishna* (Manchester: Manchester University Press, 1976), pp. 148-50.

4. Yigael Yadin, *The Temple Scroll*, I, p. 71 (Heb.: I, p. 60).

5. Stephen A. Kaufman, 'The Temple Scroll and Higher Criticism', *HUCA* 53 (1982), pp. 29-43; Gershon Brin, 'The Bible as Reflected in the Temple Scroll', *Shnaton* 4 (1980), pp. 182-225; Yadin, *The Temple Scroll*, I, pp. 45-88 (Heb.: I, pp. 38-73).

6. Andrew M. Wilson and Lawrence Wills, 'Literary Sources of the Temple Scroll', *HTR* 75 (1982), pp. 275-88.

7. Perhaps some of the so-called expanded תורה documents do correspond to some of the innovative non-biblical laws of the Temple Scroll. These fragments are still unpublished and have not yet been used to demonstrate this possibility.

8. E.g. Num. 18.12; Deut. 7.13; 11.14; 12.17; 14.23; 18.4; 28.51; 2 Chron. 31.5; 32.28; Neh. 5.11; 10.40; 13.5, 12; Jer. 31.12; Joel 1.10; 2.19, 24; Hos. 2.11, 24; Hag. 1.11.

9. Yadin, *The Temple Scroll*, I, pp. 119-22 (Heb.: I, pp. 95-99); Joseph M. Baumgarten, 'The Calendars of the Book of Jubilees and the Temple Scroll', *VT* 37 (1987), pp. 71-78; Marvin A. Sweeney, 'Sefirah at Qumran: Aspects of

counting formulas for the first-fruits festivals in the Temple Scroll', *BASOR* 251 (1983), pp. 61-66; Z. Ben Shachar, 'The Day after the Sabbath', *Beth Mikra* 24 (1979), pp. 227-28.

10. Yadin, *The Temple Scroll*, I, pp. 278-82 (Heb.: I, pp. 215-19).

11. Some examples: כול טהרת המקרש מכול דבר, לכול טמאת, כול אשר, כול אוכל, וכול מושקת, כול עור, כול צורכיהמה

12. Yadin, *The Temple Scroll*, I, pp. 395-96 (Heb.: I, pp. 302-303).

13. Yadin, *The Temple Scroll*, I, p. 307 (Heb.: I, p. 238).

14. Johann Maier, *The Temple Scroll* (JSOTS, 34; Sheffield: JSOT, 1985), p. 120.

15. Wilson and Wills, 'Literary Sources', pp. 287-88.

16. Yadin discussed the possibility that Deut. 17.19-20 originally stood at the head of col. 57. It is just as possible, based on the use of Deut. 21.22-23 in the innovative laws of 64.6-13 rather than immediately following Deut. 21.18-21 in 64.2-6, that it did not.

17. Yadin, *The Temple Scroll*, I, p. 66 (Heb.: I, pp. 56-57); Kaufman, 'The Temple Scroll', p. 34 n. 16; Brin, 'The Bible', pp. 196-200.

18. Yadin, *The Temple Scroll*, I, p. 67 (Heb.: I, p. 57).

19. Yadin, *The Temple Scroll*, II, pp. 265-70 (Heb.: II, pp. 186-90); Kaufman, 'The Temple Scroll', pp. 38-39; Brin, 'The Bible', pp. 196-200.

20. See n. 19.

21. Yadin, *The Temple Scroll*, I, p. 69 (Heb.: I, p. 59).

22. Moshe Bernstein, 'Midrash Halakhah at Qumran? 11Q Temple 64.6-13 and Deuteronomy 21.22-23', *Gesher* 7 (1979), pp. 145-66.

23. Bernstein, 'Midrash Halakhah', p. 148. While there is no ostensible sanction against the biblical 'slanderer', in the Temple Scroll he is a capital offender, even if it is less than unambiguous what his crimes were.

24. Bernstein, 'Midrash Halakhah', p. 156.

25. Bernstein, 'Midrash Halakhah', pp. 153, 156.

26. According to *b. Sanh.* 71, the law of Deut. 21.18-21 was only to be studied and had no practical application.

PART III

EXEGESIS AND LITERARY AFFINITIES

THE QUMRAN CULT: ITS EXEGETICAL PRINCIPLES

Jacob Milgrom

University of California at Berkeley

Like the other contributions to this volume, my paper is dedicated to the memory of Yigael Yadin. There is no facet of research on the Temple Scroll—be it textual, archaeological, philosophical, historical— that does not bear the lasting imprint of his *editio princeps*.[1] Our indebtedness to Yadin also holds true for his meticulous research in the biblical foundations of the cultic laws of the scroll. Here, however, his work not only needs to be advanced but also corrected. The reason is that in Yadin's exhaustive chapter on the impurity regulations of the Temple Scroll, where he develops its exegetical principles, he relies exclusively on the dictum laid down by Gedalyahu Alon.

Alon posits axiomatically that

> in the period of the Second Temple two conflicting trends established themselves: one insisted on restrictions, and limited the laws of purity to the sphere of the Temple and the priests, while the other aimed at enlargements and taught that laws of uncleanness applied to all Israel. . . this dispute has its origin in a certain duality that is found in the Torah itself. . . For there are Biblical passages that speak of uncleanness only in connection with the priests, the Temple, and holy things, whereas others are unqualified and are addressed to all Israel and to the prohibition of uncleanness in all circumstances, and not necessarily to sacred objects.[2]

This dictum is true but Alon, I submit, has misidentified it both in the Bible and in rabbinic writings.

For the minimalist view in Scripture—impurity limited to the realm of the sacred—Alon cites the following verses: Lev. 7.20-21; 12.4; 22.3-8; Num. 19.20 (p. 232 n. 108). To be sure, all four citations deal exclusively with the pollution of sancta. However, it should be observed that Lev. 12.4, 'She (the parturient) shall not touch any sancta nor shall she enter the sacred precinct', is preceded by the statement that during the first week or two weeks of her impurity (vv. 2, 5) she has the status of a menstruant. Thus, she is impure to the common as well as the sacred (cf. Lev. 15.19-24). Num. 19.20 indeed states the corpse-contaminated person defiles the sanctuary, but it should be borne in mind that he need not enter the sanctuary to defile it. Unless he purifies himself in accordance with the prescribed rites, he defiles the sanctuary from any point in the community.[3] Finally, Lev. 7.20-21 and 22.3-8 describe the penalties incurred by impure lay persons and priests who knowingly handle sancta. However, it should be noted that the prohibition for both is the same, the penalty for both (כרת) is the same, and the purification for both is the same. To be sure, the priestly rules were originally severer. This can be deduced from the purification of Ezekiel's corpse-contaminated priest (Ezek. 44.26-27) and P's corpse-contaminated Nazirite (Num. 6.6-12) both of which terminate with a purification offering. Nonetheless, as presently preserved in Scripture, there is no difference between priest and layman regarding the effects of contacting sancta in a state of impurity.

For the alleged maximalist view in Scripture—'addressed to all Israel and to the prohibition of uncleanness in all circumstances, and not necessarily to sacred objects'—Alon cites Leviticus 11 and 15 (p. 232 n. 109). Here, however, he is totally contradicted by the conclusion to Leviticus 15: 'You shall put the Israelites on guard against their impurity, lest they die through their impurity by defiling My Tabernacle which is among them' (v. 31). Thus, impurity incurred by genital discharges anywhere in the camp is liable to defile Israel's sanctuary - precisely the same fear, noted above, recorded for corpse-contamination (Num. 19.20) in the so-called minimalist view. Leviticus 11, it must be admitted, indeed omits any mention of the sanctuary or its sancta. This chapter, however, deals with carcasses which can transmit no more than a one-day impurity. But one-day impurities are no threat to the sacred unless their purification is neglected and their impurity is prolonged. If purification is willfully neglected, divine retribution will follow (Lev. 17.15-16); if accidental, a חטאת is required (Lev. 5.2-3, 5).[4] However, a minor impurity, such that lasts one day, is too weak to pollute the sacred from afar except in direct contact with it. No wonder, then, that Leviticus 11 omits any mention of the sacred; carcasses may be touched with impunity as long as the prescribed purification procedures follow.

Thus it can be seen that the Priestly source of the Bible predicates a uniform system of impurity. It registers neither a maximalist nor a minimalist stance. P posits a contiguous community with a sanctuary at its center. Any impurity, incurred anywhere in the community, if severe enough or if it is prolonged, if caused by priest or layperson, will pollute the sanctuary.

Yet, if the truth be told, there is a maximalist and minimalist mode of impurity embedded in the priestly writings—but it has not been identified by Alon and Yadin. For the question needs be asked: what if impurity occurs in the wilderness, outside the Tabernacle-camp or in Canaan, outside the Temple-city? On this matter P is silent. But another priestly work takes up this question—H, the Holiness source. H posits the holiness of the land. The Lord resides not just in His sanctuary but in His land. Hence, all who inhabit the land must be scrupulous to avoid impurity and to purify themselves if they become impure lest the land become polluted and vomit them out (cf. Lev. 18.25-28; 20.22). Therefore, all of Israel is commanded קדשים תהיו, 'Be you holy' (Lev. 19.2). A life of holiness is mandated for all inhabitants of the land, priests and laity alike. Even the גר, the resident alien, is held liable for the land's pollution and must bring a חטאת, a purification offering, for violating the prohibitive commandments.[5]

Thus, there are maximalist and minimalist views in Scripture regarding impurity, but they are not represented by priests and lay persons, nor by the sanctuary and the rest of the community, but by two different priestly sources: one (P) holds that the sacred sphere is limited to the Tabernacle and that its influence extends to the surrounding encampment whereas the other (H) holds that the sacred sphere is coextensive with the land and that all who inhabit it—aliens as well as Israelites—are responsible for maintaining its sanctity.

These two differing biblical traditions have left their imprint on later generations and are attested in rabbinic literature. To be sure, rabbinic laws clearly reflect the minimalist position; it is neatly encapsulated in Maimonides' Code and cited by Alon (p. 190 n. 2):

> Whatever is written in the Torah and traditional teaching about the laws relating to things impure and pure is relevant only to the Temple and its hallowed things and to *terumah* and second tithe, for it warns those impure against entering the Temple or eating anything hallowed, or *terumah*, or tithe. However, no such prohibition applies to common food and it is permitted to eat common food that is impure and to drink impure liquids. . . Similarly, it is permissible to touch things that are impure and to incur impurity from them, for Scripture warns none but the sons of Aaron and the Nazirite against incurring impurity from a corpse, thereby implying that for all others it is permissible, and that even for priests and Nazirites it is permissible to incur impurity from other impure things, but not from a corpse.[6]

First, Maimonides is in need of a slight correction. It is the high priest who is forbidden to incur impurity from a corpse (Lev. 21.11) but the ordinary priest is permitted to do so for his immediate blood relations (Lev. 21.1-3). Furthermore, this minimalist position among the rabbis is identical with its counterpart in the Bible, as ensconced in the laws of P (but not H). Ostensibly, there is a difference between these two minimalist positions: Scripture, but not the rabbis, mandates purification lest the sanctuary be polluted. However, it should be borne in mind that in rabbinic times the Temple was destroyed. Hence, the rabbinic view, as summarized by Maimonides, is correct: there was no need to be apprehensive of impurity impinging on a sacred sphere which had ceased to exist. Yet the question remains: what of those who lived in the land of Israel which, according to H, is holy even if it is bereft of the Temple? It should, therefore, come as no surprise that talmudic and gaonic sources report that, in contrast to Babylonia, there were those in the land of Israel who continued to follow the biblical law to bathe following nocturnal emissions and sexual intercourse (Lev. 15.16-18; cf. Alon p. 223 n. 89). Clearly, then, for this group, the maximalist position persisted: the land's holiness was independent of the Temple and those resident in it were bound by the laws of purification.

The maximalist view found among the rabbis also rooted itself in Scripture. The חברים who engaged in ritual immersion before prayer and Torah study were clearly interpreting their activities as extensions of Temple worship. Note the similar terminology: עבודה, 'Temple worship'; עבודה שבלב, 'worship of the heart', that is, prayer. Those who immersed themselves before Sabbaths and festivals also could have based their practice on biblical precedent. The Holiness source holds that not only had God sanctified a certain space, i.e. the land of Israel, He also sanctified certain times, i.e. the Sabbaths and festivals (Lev. 23). Therefore, in entering these sacred periods, one had to be ritually pure just as in entering the Temple precincts. Indeed, such purification rites before the Sabbath are actually attested as early as the Maccabees (2 Macc. 12.38). Moreover, the חברים who treated common food as sacrifice and, hence, purified themselves before mealtime could also claim biblical support. One such attempt merits quotation in full:

> With regard to Israelites, where does Scripture command washing the hands? In the verse 'Sanctify yourselves and be holy' (Lev. 11.44). On the basis of this verse, Rabban Gamliel [the elder] observed Levitical precautions of self-purification when he ate common food. He was wont to say that obedience to the precept of washing the hands for the sake of holiness was required not only of priests, but of priests, Levites, and Israelites—required of every one of them, as Scripture tells us: 'Speak to the *entire* (italics mine) congregation of the Israelites and say to them: You shall be holy' (Lev. 19.1-2).[7]

The biblical exegesis in this passage is noteworthy. The verbal form of the root קדש in the cited verse, Lev. 11.44, is in the *Hithpaʿel*, but it is interpreted as connoting 'sanctify oneself by ablutions' which, however, is a usage never found in the priestly writings but only in non-priestly sources (e.g. Exod. 19.22; 2 Sam. 11.4). Furthermore, since this very verse follows the series of prohibitions against eating forbidden food, it can be made to imply that one washes before eating. Finally, since the command to be holy (Lev. 19.2), i.e. to wash before meals, is enjoined upon all of Israel, the ritual of washing hands is no longer limited to the priesthood but is incumbent on every Israelite. This rabbinic exegesis is worthy of Qumran. If it showed up in a new fragment of the Temple Scroll, it would occasion no surprise. Thus, it can be concluded, that this maximalist position of some rabbinic circles is also the direct heir of Scripture—but of Source H, which posits that the holiness of the land mandates the holiness of its inhabitants.

That the maximalists and minimalists among the rabbis could equally claim that their views were anchored in Scripture helps immeasurably in gaining perspective on the authors of the Dead Sea documents, especially the Temple Scroll, *vis-à-vis* their Pharisaic contemporaries. As is well known, Qumran traced all its teachings to Scripture. And as maximalists, they had no difficulty in finding their warrant in Scripture's maximalist tradition (H). However, they also could not ignore Scripture's minimalist tradition (P). Thus both tendencies are reflected in the Temple Scroll, ideological vectors pulling in opposite directions and in unresolved tension. As a maximalist work, the Temple Scroll leans on the deuteronomic doctrine that Israel is a holy people (11QT 48.7, citing Deut. 14.2) but then qualifies it by adopting the minimalist stance: the attribute of holiness no longer applies to all of Israel but only to the 'true' Israel—the members of the sect (cf. 1QS 1.12-13; 2.9, 16; 5.13, 18; 8.17, 21, 24; CD 4.6; 8.28; 1QM 12.1). Furthermore, the Temple Scroll adopts the minimalists' restriction of holiness to the sanctuary (P) and never mentions the conflicting doctrine of the holiness of the land (H). As a consequence, whereas bearers of even minor impurities are banished from the Temple-city (11QT 45.7-12), bearers of major impurities such as gonorrheics, parturients, and menstruants are quarantined *within* ordinary cities (11QT 48.15-17). Yet inside the Temple-city a maximalist stance is taken. Its residents must live priestly, indeed celibate, lives and, going far beyond the plain meaning of the biblical text, the bodily imperfections that disqualify the priest from officiating in the Temple (Lev. 21.16-24) also disqualify any Israelite from residing in the Temple-city (11QT 45.12-15). In effect, the Temple Scroll has imposed maximalist demands upon a minimalist space and community.

Thus, the coexistence of minimalist (P) and maximalist (H) trends in Scripture has enabled the authors of the Temple Scroll and the rest of the Qumran literature to exploit both traditions in the service of their ideology: the imposition of maximalist conditions, i.e. holiness demands, upon a minimalist Israel, i.e., the sectaries of Qumran, within a minimalist space, the temple-city of Jerusalem.[8]

How does the Temple Scroll handle the conflicting laws of Scripture? Does it employ a basic exegetical principle? Yadin suggests that harmonization is one of the main organizing features of the Scroll (I, pp. 74-77 [Heb.: I, pp. 63-65]). However, most of the examples he cites should really be described as a unification process: the fusion of the various laws on a single subject into one law, such as vows, 53.9-54.5 (Num. 30.3-16); judicial decisions, 51.11-18 (Exod. 23.6; Deut. 1.16-17; 16.18-19); mourning rites, 48.7-10 (Lev. 19.28; Deut. 14.1-2), and contamination of foodstuffs and vessels, 49.7-10 (Lev. 11.33-34; Num. 19.15; for other examples, see items 1, 4, 7, 11, 12, 13, 14, 19, 20, 21, 33, 35, 36, 38, 39, 47, 71 in the section 'The Themes of the Scroll', I, pp. 45-70 [Heb.: I, pp. 38-60]). These unitary law blocks have this in common: the laws they have assembled are either the same or supplementary but they do not contradict each other. Nonetheless, there are a few combinations, three in my count, where the individual laws do conflict, necessitating true harmonization. These are: covering the blood, 52.11-12 (Lev. 17.13; Deut. 12.23-24); war spoils, 58.13-14 (Num. 31.27-28; 1 Sam. 30.24-25; cf. I, pp. 360-62 [Heb.: I, pp. 276-77]); and the 'ravaged virgin', 66.8-11 (Exod. 22.15-16; Deut. 22.28-29; cf. I, pp. 368-71 [Heb.: I, pp. 281-84]).

There is yet another exegetical principle, not dealt with by Yadin, that goes beyond harmonization and which I would call equalization or homogenization. By this I mean that a law which applies to specific objects, animals, or persons is extended to other members of the same species. I shall cite one example of each: (1) *Objects*. Everything within the house where death has occurred is impure (49.13-16; versus *m. Kel.* 10.1; *Sipre Num.* 126). (2) *Animals*. The prohibition of Lev. 22.28 falls on the father as well as the mother of the slaughtered animal (52.6; versus the majority view in *Ḥul.* 78b). (3) *Persons*. Blemishes which disqualify priests from officiating in the Temple (Lev. 21.17-23) disqualify all Israelites from entering the Temple-city (45.12-14).

The Temple Scroll's ruling on ablutions also falls into this homogenizing category: laundering is required in ɛddition to ablutions wherever Scripture only prescribes (or assumes) ablutions. For example, one who touches a carcass has to launder as well as bathe (51.1-2), though there is no warrant for it in Scripture. Of course, for the scroll, Scripture has to provide some warrant for this exegetical manoeuvre. And it does. The non-specific phrase יטמא עד הערב, 'He will be impure until evening', lends itself to the maximal ruling that laundering as well as bathing is required.

The homogenization is even more telling in the matter of corpse contamination. The scroll mandates both laundering and ablutions on the third day of purification from corpse contamination (49.18-19; 50.14) but, again, without any explicit biblical basis. The exegetical process, I surmise, is as follows: Since the seventh day of purification from corpse contamination explicitly prescribes aspersion, laundering and bathing (Num. 19.19), the scroll deduces that aspersion expressly required on the third day (Num. 19.12, 19) must also be supplemented with laundering and bathing. The homogenization occurring here is further enhanced by the scroll's other innovation that laundering and bathing are also required for the first day. After all, how could they be omitted for the third day on which aspersion is mandated but prescribed for the first day when there is no aspersion? Indeed, this major purificatory innovation is in itself a product of homogenizing exegesis. The case of the leper must have served as the model. Scripture requires the leper to launder and bathe on the first day of his week-long purificatory period (Lev. 14.8). The ablution entitles him to reenter the camp (*ibid.*) Similarly, by requiring the corpse-contaminated person to launder and bathe on the first day of his week-long purification, he need not be banished from his community (Num. 5.2-4).

The first-day ablution, I submit, is also required of the parturient, gonorrheic, and indeed of all other major impurity bearers even though there is no explicit statement to this effect in the Temple Scroll—again by the principle of homogenization. The power of this hermeneutic can be gauged by the fact that it has no clear biblical foundation and that it also violates the priestly system of impurities.[9]

The exegetical technique of homogenization is responsible for cultic laws of even greater import. Four such instances will now be cited.

(1) The fifty-day interval that Scripture mandates between the New Barley and New Wheat festivals (Lev. 23.15-16) is extended by the Temple Scroll to the New Wine, New Oil, and Wood Offering festivals (cols. 19-25). Homogenization has taken place. The need for it clearly stems from the biblical demand that the first-fruits of the wine and oil be brought to the sanctuary: 'I have assigned to you (priests) all the best of the new oil and of the new wine and grain that they (the Israelites) give to the Lord as their first-processed[10] fruits' (Num. 18.12). Moreover, since this verse brackets the new wine and oil together with the grain, it is reasonable to conclude with the

Temple Scroll that just as the two species of grain, the new barley and wheat, are brought to the sanctuary fifty days apart so must the dates for the new wine and oil be separated by a similar interval. This same triad is found again in connection with the biblical tithe: 'You shall consume the tithes of your new grain and wine and oil... in the presence of the Lord your God, in the place where He will choose to establish His name' (Deut. 14.23; cf. Neh. 13.5, 12). It is thus hardly any wonder that the scroll prescribes that the tithe be brought at the same time as the first-fruits (43.3-4) since, by the process of homogenization, whatever holds true for the new grain must hold as well for the new wine and new oil. Finally, Nehemiah's bracketing of the wood offering with the first-fruits: 'And I provided for the wood offering... and for the first-fruits' (Neh. 13.30) and, as Yadin has noted (I, p. 128 [Heb.: I, p. 103]), Nehemiah's specification that the wood offering take place at עתים מזמנות, 'appointed times' (*ibid.*), made it obvious to the author(s) of the scroll, again by homogenizing exegesis, that the wood offering must be likened to all the first-fruits regarding the time of its observance—after an interim of fifty days.

(2) The repeated (hence, polemical) insistence that the חטאת sacrifice must be accompanied by a libation and cereal offering (17.13-15; 18.4-6; 23.4-5, 11-17; 25.12-15; 28.6-9; etc.) is based on such a requirement (implied), for the חטאת of the leper (Lev. 14.10; cf. *m. Menaḥ* 9.16). Thus the scroll perceives the case of the leper as a generalization covering all other cases of the חטאת. Homogenization is at work.

(3) The term 'Levites' is inserted into the scroll's version of Deut. 19.16-17. Thus, 'If a malicious witness rises against any man to accuse him wrongly, then both parties to [the dispute] shall appear before me and before the priests and the Levites and before the judges who are in office in those days' (61.7-9). Whence this textual addition? The testimony of the Versions is negative. However, the possibility must be considered that the scroll's author(s) deduced from another deuteronomic verse, Deut. 17.9 (and reading הכהנים [ו]הלוים, 'the priests [or] the Levites', cf. Pesh.) that the Levites must be included in the highest tribunal stationed at the central sanctuary. This possibility turns to probability as soon as we realize that the identical reading is attested in another Qumran scroll (CD 3.21) in its version of Ezek. 44.15.[11] Surprisingly, this altered reading is actually recorded in a rabbinic source commenting on Deut. 18.1:

לא יהיה לכהנים הלוים. The verse speaks of priests *and* Levites. You say, the verse speaks of priests and Levites: perhaps it only speaks of Levitical priests? Hence it is written כל שבט לוי, 'the whole tribe of Levi' (*Midrash Tanaaim* to Deut. 18.1).

This astounding rabbinic comment echoes Qumranic exegesis. Since the verse expressly states that sacrificial gifts from the land and the altar are to be distributed to the entire tribe of Levi,[12] then the accompanying expression הכהנים הלוים, wherever it occurs, must always be rendered 'the priests and/or the Levites'. What applies to sacrificial gifts must then apply to the judiciary; the Levites are to join the priests on the judicial bench. Again, homogenization is at work.

(4) Homogenization is also responsible for one of the most far-reaching innovations of the Temple Scroll: the extension of the regulations of the Sinai encampment to the Temple-city. As mentioned earlier, blemishes disqualifying priests from officiating disqualify Israelites from residing in the Temple-city. How did the scroll derive this equation from the regulations at Sinai? I submit that the same exegesis utilized by Rabban Gamliel to demand of all Israel holiness by means of ablutions was employed earlier by the Temple Scroll to require holiness of all the residents of the Temple-city. Rabban Gamliel interpreted the *Hithpa'el* והתקדשתם of Lev. 11.44 to mean 'sanctify yourselves (through ablutions)'. The scroll interprets the *Hithpa'el* יתקדשו of Exod. 19.22 similarly, undoubtedly in keeping with the *Pi'el* usage of this root in the same chapter ויקדש את העם, 'and he (Moses) sanctified the people (by ablutions) (Exod. 19.14). All of Israel therefore attained holiness at Sinai and since the Temple-city is of equivalent holiness, the Sinaitic regulations must prevail there as well. Thus, the same impurities and imperfections which bar the priests from the Temple *ipso facto* must form the criteria in determining residence in the Temple-city. In the same way, the homogenization of the Temple-city with the Sinaitic encampment is responsible for the three-day minimum for purification (cf. Exod. 19.15a) and for the absolute prohibition against sexual relations in the Temple-city (45.11-12; cf. Exod. 19.15b) and, for that matter, against permitting any impurity bearer, even in the slightest degree, to enter or remain in the Temple-city (48.7-10).[13]

The exegetical technique of homogenization most closely resembles the later rabbinic hermeneutical rule of *binyan 'āb*, lit. 'a structure (emerging out) of the father'. In other words, it is the term for a general comprehensive principle. The similarity and virtual equivalence of homogenization and *binyan 'āb* is best clarified by examining some rabbinic examples. (1) The single occurrence of the phrase עז בת־בנתה, 'a she-goat in its first year' (Num. 15.27) constitutes a *binyan 'āb*, a general principle, that every other mention of a sacrificial she-goat implies a yearling (*Sipre* Num. 112). (2) From the verse אשר יאכל לכל נפש הוא לבדו יעשה לכם, 'Only what every person is to eat, that alone may be prepared for you' (Exod. 12.16), the rabbis deduce that it forms a general principle (*binyan 'āb*) for all the festivals (particularly) since it is the first [festival] (Pesach) to be mentioned'.[14] (3) The one verse which conjoins the punishment of stoning with the expression דמיהם בם, 'their bloodguilt shall be upon them' (Lev. 20.27) constitutes a *binyan 'āb*, a general principle, so that every crime containing the words 'his/their bloodguilt shall be upon him/them' (e.g. Lev. 20.9, 11) is also punishable by stoning (*b. Sanh.* 54a).[15]

These examples, so manifestly in the homogenization mode, demonstrate that the Temple Scroll's technique of homogenization is the forerunner of rabbinic *binyan 'āb*. Indeed, I am even willing to suggest that the Temple Scroll is the earliest known source for the *binyan 'āb*. We now know that other rabbinic rules of exegesis (*middôt*) are traceable to Greek sources.[16] To my knowledge, however, there is not a single instance of *binyan,'āb* in the apocrypha, the pseudepigrapha, the New Testament, Philo, or any other Hellenistic source. Furthermore, though some of the rabbinic *middôt* are attested in the Qumran documents,[17] homogenization, the forerunner of *binyan 'āb*, is amply and exclusively represented in the Temple Scroll. At this stage, it would be hazardous, if not presumptuous, to suggest that the author(s) of the Temple Scroll invented this principle, but its discovery does add strong support to the view, most recently articulated by George Brooke,[18] that the traditions of biblical interpretation, later systematized in the rabbinic *middôt*, have their origin in Second Temple times.

Finally, I wish to address the question concerning the *Sitz im Leben* of the homogenization technique. What motivated its use? Was its purpose to create new laws or to justify existing ones? Specifically, were enactments such as the pentacontad calendar, the Sinaitic sanctity of the temple-city, the three-day purification, the first-day ablution, etc., the product of Qumranic exegesis, or were they the legal codifications of prior tradition and practice? If the latter, if the Temple Scroll is the heir of its rules and not their creator and its purpose was simply to anchor them in Scripture, then homogenization was its technique to transform exegesis into eisegesis and text into pretext. To be sure, a number of the Temple Scroll enactments strongly support such a view. For example, the prohibition against importing skins of unsacrificed animals into the Temple-city (47.13-18) is congruent with the historically verifiable status of Jerusalem at the end of the third century. A proclamation of Antiochus III, reported in Josephus[19] and universally accepted by historians as authentic,[20] expressly confirms the special sanctity of Jerusalem. Thus, in this instance, the scroll perpetuates earlier law and custom. That is, the sacred status for the Temple-city not only reflects some previous legal theory but it verifies and reaffirms pre-existing historical reality. To be sure, this enactment is not a product of homogenization. Let us then consider one that is—the pentacontad calendar. There is evidence which suggests that the establishment of the New Wine and Oil festivals at fifty-day intervals was not the invention of the Temple Scroll.[21] If that is indeed the case, then the scroll merely provided these festivals with a biblical foundation. The possibility also exists that even this biblical underpinning was not original with the scroll but is a legacy of the past, in which case the homogenization technique may also stem from an earlier period.

Ten years ago, reacting to the lofty status of the Levites in the Temple Scroll, I wrote as follows:

> The quantity and thrust of these innovations are not the product of abstract speculation but are a polemic whose historical background can readily be discerned. It is a protest against the Wicked Priest (Jonathan Maccabeus?) who usurped the high priesthood and displaced the true Zadokite line... Thus the scroll gives new grounds for investigating the tensions and struggles amongst priestly families and between priests and Levites at the end of the Second Temple period.[22]

I would not write that today. Let us reconsider the basis for my premature conclusion—the Levites. The Temple Scroll restores their tithes (60.6-9), grants them parity with the priests on the king's advisory council (52.12-15), awards them the shoulder from every well-being offering (21.04), twice the portion of the other tribes from the prescribed well-being offerings for the New Wine and New Oil festivals (21.[1]; 22.12), and the right to pronounce the priestly blessing (60.11). What historic reality could possibly lie behind these unprecedented privileges? After all, the Qumranites are a priestly sect: their founder is a priest, final authority rests with a priest, each quorum of ten is headed by a priest, etc. What then could be responsible for this extraordinary Levitic windfall, gained at the expense of the priests, except the inexorable result of the Temple Scroll's biblical exegesis? To be sure, there exists historical precedent for the scroll's campaign to elevate the Levites. One need but recall that the books of Chronicles attempt to achieve greater parity between the priests and Levites. Together they convey the Ark and minister before it (1 Chron. 15.2; 16.4; 2 Chron. 5.5); together they serve on Jehoshaphat's high court (2 Chron. 19.8-11); and together they carry out the religious reforms of Hezekiah and Josiah (2 Chron. 29.5-36; 34.8-14).[23] Indeed, in the account of Hezekiah's reform the Chronicler accords the Levites greater merit than the priests: 'For the Levites were more upright in heart than the priests in sanctifying themselves' (2 Chron. 29.34b). However, as soon as we realize that the Chronicler himself based his Levitic bias on an earlier biblical precedent, i.e. Deuteronomy's insistence that the Levites be granted complete parity with the priests, then we have effectively removed the final historical prop that might have explained the post-exilic campaign on behalf of the Levites. Finally, when we add to the ahistorical status of the Levites other utopian and fantastic elements of the scroll, such as the gargantuan dimensions and lavishness of the Temple precinct and its installations, then it is absurd to seek a historical basis to all of its prescriptions.

However, the main reason for favouring the likelihood that the Temple Scroll is purely a product of its exegesis is that its authors are members of a fundamentalist sect. The basic axiom of fundamentalism has never changed through the ages: the prohibitions of Scripture are inflexible—even at the cost of one's life. In the face of death, a Jehovah's Witness will reject a blood transfusion. A right-to-lifer will refuse an abortion if the fetus is the product of rape, or if amniocentesis detects Down's symdrome or Tay-Sachs disease, if the mother's life is in danger, or even if all three factors are present. The common denominator among all fundamentalists—reaching as far back as Qumran—is that all problems are resolved by Scripture and its laws must be followed to the letter.

How did the Qumranites differ from their fellow Jews? In principle, not at all.[24] Their contemporaries, as indicated by their successors, the Pharisees and the rabbis, also believed in revealed Scripture, also devised exegetical techniques to interpret Scripture, also adhered to their interpretations scrupulously, and in the case of some of them, even at the cost of life.[25] There was only one difference, and it made all the difference. It is exemplified by their respective use of the exegetical technique of homogenization/*binyan 'āb*. In the Temple Scroll it produced Scripture. For the rabbis, it produced oral law. In the Temple Scroll, God Himself, so to speak, employs homogenization. The result is objective, definitive, and unalterable. In rabbinic writings, however, homogenization is employed by man. The result is subjective, tentative, and contestable. For Qumran, divergent opinions are intolerable; for the rabbis, they can be declared 'the words of the living God' (*b. 'Erub.* 13b).

NOTES

1. Y. Yadin, *Megillat ham-Miqdaš* (3 Vols.; Jerusalem: The Israel Exploration Society and the Shrine of the Book, 1977); English trans. *The Temple Scroll* (3 Vols.; Jerusalem: The Israel Exploration Society and the Shrine of the Book, 1983).

2. G. Alon, *Jews and Judaism and the Classical World* (trans. by I. Abrahams; Jerusalem: Magnes, 1977), p. 232; cf. Yadin, *The Temple Scroll*, I, p. 277 (Heb. I, p. 215).

3. Cf. J. Milgrom, 'Israel's Sanctuary: the Priestly "Picture of Dorian Gray"', *RB* 83 (1976), pp. 390-99 (reprinted in *Studies in Cultic Theology and Terminology* [Leiden: Brill, 1983], pp. 75-84).

4. Cf. J. Milgrom, 'The Gradual Purification Offering (Leviticus 5.1-3)', *JAOS* 103 (1983), pp. 249-54.

5. Cf. J. Milgrom, 'Religious Conversion and the Revolt Model for the Formation of Israel', *JBL* 101 (1982), pp. 169-76.

6. M. Maimonides, 'The Uncleanness of Foodstuffs', *The Book of Cleanness* (Vol. XVI of *The Code*; trans. by H. Danby; Yale Judaica Series; New Haven: Yale University Press, 1954), pp. 392-93.

7. *Tanna děbe Eliyyahu* (trans. by W.G. Braude and I.J. Kapstein; Philadelphia: Jewish Publication Society, 1981), pp. 202-203.

8. This argument is explained in J. Milgrom's 'The Biblical Foundations and Deviations of the Laws of Purity in the Temple Scroll', *Archaeology and History in the Dead Sea Scrolls. The New York University Conference in*

Memory of Yigael Yadin (ed. L.H. Schiffman; Baltimore: ASOR and Johns Hopkins University, in press).

9. Cf. J. Milgrom, 'The Priestly Impurity System', *Proceedings of the Ninth World Congress of Jewish Studies*, Vol. I, *Bible Studies* (Jerusalem: World Union of Jewish Studies, 1986), pp. 121-27.

10. For the significance of this rendering of ראשית, see provisionally J. Milgrom, 'First Fruits, OT', *IDBSup*, pp. 336-37.

11. Suggested to me orally by Yadin.

12. Cf. J. Milgrom, 'The Shoulder for the Levites' in Y. Yadin, *The Temple Scroll*, I, pp. 169-76 (Heb. I, pp. 131-36).

13. The Sinaitic model compels me to take issue with the thesis of L.H. Schiffman ('Exclusion from the Sanctuary in the Temple Scroll', *HAR* 9 [1985], pp. 301-20) that the perimeter of the עיר המקרש, 'the Temple-city', is congruent with that of the Temple's outer court. Israel's encampment at Mount Sinai, to be sure, is the equivalent of the Temple-city. However, since the people have to be brought from their encampment to the foot of Mount Sinai (Exod. 19.2), it is the latter and not the former which is equivalent to the Temple's outer court. Hence, if Israel's encampment is subject to the Sinaitic rules of holiness, then so is the residential quarter of Jerusalem. Besides, the Temple of the Temple Scroll is only equal to the dimensions of the old city but not congruent with it. Of necessity and fantastically, it would extend over the Kidron Valley and about the Mount of Olives; cf. M. Broshi, 'The Gigantic Dimensions of the Visionary Temple in the Temple Scroll', *BAR* 13/6 (1987), pp. 36-37. That only the mountain of Sinai is the prototype of the *temenos* of the Jerusalem Temple, but not Israel's encampment, see J. Milgrom, *Studies in Levitical Terminology* (Berkeley: University of California Press, 1970), pp. 44-45.

14. This *binyan 'āb* is not found in any known rabbinic source, but it is cited by Rashi in his commentary on the *Baraita* of R. Ishmael (the preface of *Sipra*). For other references see the *Encyclopaedia Talmudit*, Vol. IV, see under '*Binyan 'āb*' (Jerusalem: Talmudic Encyclopedia, 1952), p. 2 n. 16.

15. The *Baraita* of R. Ishmael distinguishes between the *binyan 'āb* based on one verse and on two verses (*Sipra*, nos. 5 & 6). The examples thus far cited illustrate the former. The latter is also exemplified in the Temple Scroll: the requirement of two purification animals for the priestly consecration, one for the priests and the other for the people (15.17-18; 16.14-18) is based on two biblical precedents, the inauguration of the cult (Lev. 9.2-3) and the Yom Kippur rite (Lev. 16.3, 5).

16. Cf. S. Lieberman, *Hellenism in Jewish Palestine* (New York: Jewish Theological Seminary of America, 1962[2]), pp. 68-82; D. Daube, 'Alexandrian Methods of Interpretation and the Rabbis', *Festschrift Hans Lewald* (Basel: Helbing & Lichtenhahn, 1953), pp. 27-44 (reprinted in *Essays in Greco-*

Roman and Related Talmudic Literature [selected with a prolegomenon by H.A. Fischel; New York: Ktav, 1977], pp. 165-82.

17. E.g. *gᵉzērâ šāwâ, zēker lᵉdābār, 'asmaktâ'* of E. Slomovic, 'Toward an Understanding of the Exegesis in the Dead Sea Scrolls', *RevQ* 7 (1969-71), pp. 3-15. For a possible *gᵉzērâ šāwâ* in Scripture itself, see M. Fishbane, *Biblical Interpretation in Ancient Israel* (Oxford: Clarendon, 1985), p. 157 n. 36.

18. G.J. Brooke, *Exegesis at Qumran: 4Q Florilegium in its Jewish Context* (JSOTS, 29; Sheffield: JSOT, 1985), pp. 1-79.

19. *Ant.* 12.146. The proclamation prohibits the entry of skins of impure animals, whereas the Temple Scroll also excludes the skins of pure but unsacrificed animals.

20. See especially E. Bikerman, 'Une proclamation sélucide relative au temple de Jérusalem', *Syria* 25 (1947), pp. 69-85, and my comments in 'Further Studies in the Temple Scroll', *JQR* 71 (1980), p. 98.

21. See the discussion in Yadin, *The Temple Scroll*, I, pp. 119-22 (Heb.: I, pp. 95-99).

22. J. Milgrom, 'Studies in the Temple Scroll', *JBL* 97 (1978), pp. 503-504.

23. The Chronicler may even have allowed the Levites to share the priestly prerogative of blessing the people (2 Chron. 30.27; cf. Deut. 10.8). True, the text reads הכהנים הלוים, 'the Levitical priests'. However, Chronicles assiduously avoids the deuteronomic terms. In its only other attestation in Chronicles (2 Chron. 5.5), it refers to the carrying of the Ark, a task which the Chronicler expressly assigns to the Levites (1 Chron. 15.2). In fact the latter's context makes it clear that the task of conveying the Ark to the Temple was divided between the priests and the Levites, the Levites carrying the Ark to Jerusalem (2 Chron. 5.4), and the priests installing it inside the adytum (2 Chron. 5.7). Thus the original reading most likely is הכהנים והלוים, 'the priests and the Levites' (2 Chron. 5.5), particularly since such is the corresponding text in Kings (1 Kgs 8.4) as well as the reading of many MSS and the Versions. Thus, the ostensibly remaining attestation of the deuteronomic term in 2 Chron. 30.27 must also be read הכהנים והלוים (with LXXᴬ, Tg., and Pesh.); it was the priests *and* the Levites who blessed the people.

24. And in practice, hardly at all, as seen in the picayune halakhic differences between them and the Pharisaic (!) high priesthood reflected in 4Q *394-99*; cf. tentatively, 'An Unpublished Halakhic Letter from Qumran', *Biblical Archaeology Today* (ed. J. Amitai; Jerusalem: Israel Exploration society, 1985), pp. 400-407.

25. E.g., 'If a man is commanded, "Transgress and suffer not death", he may transgress and not suffer death, except for idolatry, incest, and murder' (*b. Sanh.* 74a; cf. also *b. Yoma* 82a [*bar.*]).

THE TEMPLE SCROLL AND THE NEW TESTAMENT

George J. Brooke

University of Manchester

This paper is not an attempt to provide a comprehensive guide to the parallels between the Temple Scroll and the New Testament. For the most part discussion of their similarities has focussed on the topics of crucifixion and Jesus' teaching on divorce. There are, however, some intriguing similarities in exegetical traditions, similarities sufficiently close to warrant the speculation that some parts of the New Testament documents, at least at some stage in their history, were written with the group of people in mind who may have been responsible for the 'republication' of the Temple Scroll at the turn of the era.

Before the *editio princeps* of the Temple Scroll was ever published Yigael Yadin had already let it be known that in his opinion the reference to Deut. 21.22 in 11QT 64.6-9 meant that the author of the scroll and the group to which he belonged approved of hanging on the tree, almost certainly crucifixion, as the most dishonourable punishment reserved for political traitors.[1] Since Yadin associated the Scroll with mainline Qumran opinion, he suggested that the lacunae in 4QpNahum should be adjusted to allow for its author to be expressing approval for Alexander Jannaeus's mass crucifixion of Pharisees.[2]

Several studies have been written on what the approval of death by hanging on a tree might imply for our understanding of the scriptural interpretations applied to the death of Jesus.[3] There is no need to rehearse all the scholarly insight that has resulted from the publication of 11QT, but two comments deserve underlining here. Firstly, the dating of the manuscript of 11QT to Herodian times means that unless it was copied for purely antiquarian interest,[4] there were some Jews at a time close to that of Jesus' death who could have approved of crucifixion; undoubtedly it was because of Roman practice that the crucifixion actually took place, but perhaps the reading of Deut. 21.22 in the tradition of the Temple Scroll meant that those concerned to rid themselves of Jesus may have realized that it should be on a political charge that a death sentence of the sort that the Romans would carry out would be particularly appropriate.

Secondly, as Wilcox and Fitzmyer argue,[5] it is clear that our understanding of the allusions to Deut. 21.22 in early Christian apologetic should acknowledge the possibility that such apologetic was based on a similar text of Deuteronomy. In Acts 5.30 Peter declares, 'The God of our fathers raised Jesus whom you killed by hanging on a tree'; this is echoed in another speech of Peter's (Acts 10.39): 'And we are witnesses to all that he did both in the country of the Jews and in Jerusalem. They put him to death by hanging him on a tree'. In Gal. 3.13 the text is actually cited in the argument that asserts that because Jesus has taken upon himself the curse of the law, so the blessing of Abraham is to be available to all who believe in him. There is nothing in any of these texts that supposes that Deut. 21.22 could not apply to Jesus because he was not killed before he was hung on the tree. The reading of a text-type like that of the Temple Scroll is probable, indeed likely, given that none of these texts is exactly a representation of the LXX,[6] which for the order of the verbs agrees with the MT. The overall point is that here we are on the very borderline between what represents different text-types and what represents different interpretations of texts considered more, rather than less, fixed. In so many places the Temple Scroll forces us to reconsider not just the interpretation of law in the late Second Temple period, but the polemic of textual recensions.

The other matter in the New Testament which the Temple Scroll has illuminated and concerning which several scholars have expressed opinions[7] is Jesus' teaching on divorce. 11QT 57.17-18 prohibits polygamy and by saying that the queen shall be with the king all the days of her life implies that divorce is not allowed, at least for the king; a second wife may be taken, if the first dies. In CD 5.2 this law for the king, after Deut. 17.17, is democratized and an excuse is offered for David's polygamous behaviour, namely his ignorance of the law-book that some have supposed to be the Temple Scroll itself. Yadin has commented that the Temple Scroll and CD together provide pre-Christian evidence that some Jews would support the view of Jesus on divorce as expessed in Mark's version of his teaching (10.1-12), whereas Matthew's version with the exception clause (19.1-12) is closer to the Shammaite ruling.[8] What needs to be underlined here is that it is the Marcan tradition that is closer to what 11QT proposes; furthermore, in the juxtaposition of CD and 11QT, the law for the king, at least with respect to polygamy with excuses made for David, is applied to everybody.

The pre-eminence of the Marcan tradition and the reference to the figure of David in discussing the application of the law are both significant factors in a set of motifs that have yet to be thoroughly examined. Yadin has proposed that the Herodians in the New Testament (Mt. 22.16; Mk 3.6; 8.15) are to be identified with the Essenes.[9] Yadin's argument rests on reading the seven baskets of bread of Mk 8.8 and 20 in the light of 11QT 15.3-5, a text requiring much restoration but which seems to imply that at the feast of consecration or ordination there were to be seven baskets of bread, one for each daily offering of a ram. Yadin's identification also assumes that the Essenes were responsible in some way for the Temple Scroll; even if we are tempted to be sympathetic to Yadin's use of 11QT for identifying the Herodians, they would only be those responsible for the scroll, not necessarily Essenes proper. In relation to the actual text of Mark the logic of Yadin's argument for identifying the Herodians requires that an identification be made in a similar way for the five loaves and twelve baskets of crumbs mentioned in Mk 8.19. If the identification of the Herodians by the seven loaves and seven baskets of crumbs is correct, then, because of Jesus' warning in Mk 8.15 ('Beware of the leaven of the Pharisees and the leaven of Herod'),[10] we should expect the combination of five and twelve to be the hallmark of the Pharisees. Now this combination of five and twelve may be found by implication in one other place in the Gospel, in Mk 2.25-26, in the context of a debate with the Pharisees. Whether addressed by Jesus in his lifetime to Pharisees or by someone in the Marcan tradition to Pharisees or Pharisaic Jewish Christians, it is assumed that the Pharisees or Mark's readership at least will grant the line of argument involving the story of David and the shewbread. According to 1 Sam. 21.3 (MT) David asks for five loaves from Ahimelech and is given the shewbread (12 loaves).

A closer look at Mk 2.23-28 suggests some other parallels with the traditions represented in the Temple Scroll. Four preliminary points might be noteworthy. Firstly, this is a sabbath controversy; there need be nothing unusual about that except that observance of the Sabbath is stressed quite explicitly in *Jubilees*, especially ch. 50, and in the Damascus Document (12.4-6). Those responsible for those two works had much in common at some stage with those responsible for the Temple Scroll.[11] Their attitude to the law was stricter than many of their contemporaries, just as Mark's version of Jesus' saying on divorce is stricter than Matthew's version. Secondly, Mk 2.26 mentions that a certain Abiathar was high priest when David entered the house of God and ate the bread of the presence. Matthew and Luke omit this identification presumably thinking it was an embarrassing error. According to the Samuel narrative Abiathar, son of Ahimelech,[12] was joint high priest with Zadok during David's reign until he backed the wrong horse in the succession; but in the tradition in 1 Chronicles (18.16; 24.6), Ahimelech is son of Abiathar. Furthermore, with Zadok (in 1 Chron. 15.11), Abiathar and some Levites are addressed by David as 'The heads of the father's houses of the Levites'; the connection with levitical interests and the allegiance to the tradition of Chronicles are both features of 11QT and it looks certain here that the Marcan tradition is working with information from the Chronicler and not directly with 1 Samuel as represented by either the MT or the LXX.[13] Thirdly, Matthew inserts a tradition about those priests in the Temple who profane the Sabbath and, citing Hos. 6.6, underlines that God desires mercy, not sacrifice, an attitude which is echoed in 1QS 9.3-6. In this way Matthew makes the tradition reflect a more straightforward Qumran Essene attitude than does the Marcan pericope. Fourthly, and of least significance, I have argued elsewhere that the preceding pericope (Mk 2.18-22) may reflect knowledge of the feast of new wine (11QT 19.11-21.10); while John's disciples and the Pharisees fast Jesus suggests a feast: 'And no one puts new wine into old wineskins' (Mk 2.22).[14]

These little points add up to little, but for our purposes there is a more important aspect to the argument that Jesus uses in Mk 2.23-26. This is the very use of David's actions for interpreting the law.

Yadin has rightly observed that David features in the Temple Scroll, implicitly of course, as an authoritative interpreter of law; not only could 1 Chron. 28.11-19 be construed as evidence that there was a plan for the building of the temple such as the Temple Scroll might be, a plan which supplements and completes the law and which is entrusted to David,[15] but also in particular matters of legal interpretation what David does is taken as normative in some way. So, for example, the law concerning spoils of battle in 11QT 43.11-15 (interpreting Num. 31.27-30) uses 1 Sam. 30.24-25 to produce an interpretation which takes account of how David made provision for exactly equal shares for warriors and those who stay at home by securing the levy for the priests and Levites *before* the division takes place, not *after* as Numbers suggests; yet priests and Levites get exactly the same amount whichever way the sums are done—'Ingenious indeed', comments Yadin.[16] Other examples could be cited, though it is important also to add that David is not used in any way in the formulation of the law concerning the number of wives the king might have: one only says the scroll firmly! Thus David is not the sole authority in legal interpretation, but to some extent his actions are taken as normative.[17]

The significance of this for Mk 2.25-26 is that it is important for scholars to note that in some measure *torah* and *haggadah* can be interwoven in the very formulation of law or precedent. For example, D. Cohn-Sherbok has recently argued that Jesus' argument in Mark 2 cannot be valid from a rabbinic point of view, firstly because David's action did not take place on the Sabbath, so the analogy was not apt, and secondly because *haggadah* cannot be used to formulate precept, only to illustrate it.[18] That may be correct from a rabbinic point of view, but the use of Davidic *haggadah* in the formulation of the rules in the Temple Scroll suggests that the argument in this Gospel tradition may be valid from a different point of view. I would suggest that taken with all the minor signals mentioned above this Gospel pericope may contain an argument that would not have been out of line with those whose sympathies might lie somewhere on the levitical edges of Essenism and Pharisaism, close to those responsible for the republication of the Temple Scroll. Furthermore, all these connections with the traditions of the Temple Scroll lead me to suspect that Yadin's use of the ordination material in 11QT to identify the Herodians is not altogether inappropriate.

Together with these several similarities in Mark to exegetical traditions in the Temple Scroll, traditions that belong to the main literary components in the text of 11QT,[19] there are also some similarities between 11QT and the Fourth Gospel. These similarities belong to the more self-evidently redactional parts of the scroll, 11QT 1-3; 29.8-10. When taken together these redactional parts of the Temple Scroll can be seen deliberately to juxtapose exegetical traditions based on Exodus 34 with exegetical materials based on the Jacob cycle. Unfortunately at least the first column of the scroll is missing, but the part of the Introduction which survives uses the language of Exodus 34 and Deuteronomy 7 (the parallel passage) as its base. The whole of the scroll is thus to be viewed as the contents of a speech to Moses, as divine revelation, as the supplementary Law actually received but described neither fully nor accurately in the proto-Masoretic Pentateuch. In column 29 on the other hand it is the covenant with Jacob at Bethel that is mentioned, not that with Moses at Sinai. What might be the relationship of these two covenants?

The fourth Gospel has two introductions. There are allusions to various scriptural passages in each. In the Prologue proper, Jn. 1.1-18, Exod. 34.6 (in a version other than the LXX) lies behind the 'grace and truth' of 1.14 and 17.[20] Furthermore the emphasis in the Greek version of Exodus 33 and 34 on the 'glory' that is to be revealed to Moses may have influenced the Prologue's author's stress that 'grace and truth' define the type of glory to be seen in the word made flesh. Other prominent scriptural passages in Jn 1.1-18 are the allusions to Genesis 1 and the figure of Wisdom in Prov. 8.27-30 in Jn 1.1-5; both these texts and the pillar of cloud in Exod. 33.9-10 are taken up in the hymn of Sirach 24. Part of that hymn may well be echoed in Jn. 1.14; Sir. 24.8 reads: 'Then the creator of all things gave me a commandment, and the one who created me assigned a place for my tent. And he said, "Make your dwelling in Jacob, and in Israel receive your inheritance".' It is possible to construe Sirach 24 so that Wisdom's song in praise of herself ends at v. 22 to be followed immediately by the comment: 'All this is the book of the covenant of the Most High God, the law which Moses commanded us as an inheritance for the congregations of Jacob'.[21]

The allusions to these creation and wisdom texts in association with Exodus 33-34 are not just coincidental. To begin with it must be noted that *Jubilees* opens with a restatement of Exodus 34 linked with Genesis 1. The association of Exodus 34 with the presentation of a supplemented or rewritten law in both *Jubilees* and the Temple Scroll suggests that allusion to Exodus 34 may serve a similar function in the Johannine prologue. When the references to the Wisdom texts are also taken into account, then the association of the figure of Wisdom with the law in some form[22] confirms the suspicion that the Prologue is out to suggest that the incarnate Logos is the very content of the Law as it was revealed to Moses the second time he went up Mount Sinai. In this light Jn 1.18 reapplies the experience of Moses to what is now available for anyone through Jesus: 'No one has ever seen God'—not even Moses, as is made quite clear in Exod. 33.20; perhaps only Jacob at Peniel (Gen. 32.30)—'the only God who is in the bosom of the Father, he has made him known' (Jn 1.18). For the author of the Fourth Gospel Jesus Christ is the means of making explicit the character of God which was the content of the Law revealed to Moses. Here again is support for those who would see nothing antithetical in Jn 1.17: what was given to Moses has come through Jesus Christ. Earlier Paul may also have used Exodus 34 to identify what Moses saw with Christ himself.[23]

For the Prologue Sirach 24 is a key text. Following the premise that allusions should more often than not be understood in their original contexts, it is worth recalling that twice in Sirach 24 there are explicit references to Jacob, once as the place of Wisdom's dwelling (Sir. 24.8), and once Jacob's congregations are the inheritors of the book of the covenant, the law which Moses commanded (Sir. 24.23). In 11QT the covenant with Jacob is mentioned after the detailed listing of the festivals and their offerings; chs. 5–10 in the Fourth Gospel are also about the right ordering of the cult through the healing on the sabbath and the interpretations of the feasts of Passover, Tabernacles, and Dedication.

But this parallel is enhanced when the use of the Jacob traditions are compared. In 11QT 29 God recalls the covenant he made with Jacob at Bethel (Gen. 28.13-15). That covenant reads as a renewal of the covenant made with Abraham (Gen. 12.2-3, 7); in the second account of God's appearance to Jacob (Gen. 35.10-12) this Abrahamic covenant is combined with language from the priestly blessing of Gen. 1.22.[24] In this way Genesis 1 and Jacob at Bethel can be associated indirectly. Furthermore, as mentioned already, in Jn 1.18 there is the insistence that no one has ever seen God; yet Jacob does claim to have seen God face to face. For the Johannine Prologue as a whole we have Genesis 1, traditions identifying wisdom with the law entrusted to Jacob, Exodus 34, and a veiled allusion to or play upon Jacob's vision; these texts also lie behind the redaction of the Temple Scroll.

The Gospel's second introduction strengthens the function of these combined scriptural allusions. As the Gospel stands at the moment Jn 1.19-51, the second introduction, together with the sign at the marriage at Cana may form a week that matches that of Genesis 1;[25] the point to notice is not only the possible allusion to Genesis 1, but the way in which the Cana sign is preceded by material with allusions to the Jacob cycle, an effect reproduced for the second Cana sign at the end of John 4.

In the first case, 1.19-51, the author of the Gospel has the priests and Levites[26] sent from Jerusalem to find out who John the Baptist is by way of a prelude to introducing Jesus. The climax of this introduction in 1.51 is Jesus as the Son of Man with the promised vision of the angels of God ascending and descending on him. For all that 1.51 may be an independent saying (cf. Mt. 26.64; 16.27-28), since the time of Augustine commentators have seen in this verse an allusion to Gen. 28.12, Jacob's dream: 'And he dreamed that there was a ladder set up on the earth, and the top of it reached to heaven; and behold, the angels of God were ascending and descending on it'.

There is some very considerable confusion amongst scholars as to how to interpret this allusion to Jacob's dream.[27] Firstly, some commentators have argued on the basis of *Gen. R.* 69.3 (on Gen. 28.13) that the angels were descending on Jacob, reading 'on him' for 'on it'; applied to the Fourth Gospel this makes Jesus as Son of Man the replacement of Israel. Secondly, there are those who have relied on *Gen. R.* 68.12 (on Gen. 28. 12) in which Jacob appears in heaven while his body is on earth to make Jn 1.51 mean that Jesus as Son of Man is really with the Father, yet he is on earth at the same time. Thirdly, there are some scholars who have been influenced by the targumic reading in which God's *shekinah* appears on the ladder; applied to the Fourth Gospel this tradition shows that Jesus is the localization of the *shekinah*, a theme already present in the Prologue.

In light of the Temple Scroll all three categories of interpretation need reconsideration. In the first place, although the Fourth Gospel is concerned to identify Jesus with Wisdom and the law, as the one who displays the character of God, that in itself need not preclude him from also being portrayed in 1.51 in some sense as the replacement for Jacob/Israel. After all in 4.12 the Samaritan woman asks plainly: 'Are you greater than our father Jacob?' In Jn 1.45-51 it is true that something of the traditions concerning Jacob lies behind the portrayal of Nathanael. It is Nathanael whom Jesus hails as 'an Israelite indeed in whom there is no guile!' (1.47), possibly an ironic reference to Jacob, the first to bear the name Israel but in whom there was certainly some guile (Gen. 27.35); furthermore, the ancient popular and playful etymology of Israel as 'the one who sees God' matches John the Baptist's description of his purpose as baptizing with water so that Jesus might be revealed to Israel and Jesus' promises to Nathanael that he will '*see* greater things than these' and that he will '*see* heaven opened' (1.50-51). Perhaps the relationship between Nathanael, Jesus and the figure of Jacob is that whilst Nathanael is the representative Israelite, Jesus as an individual supplants the position of honour accorded Jacob himself.

Secondly, *Gen. R.* 68.12 may be more significant than is commonly supposed nowadays. Although the actual form of the tradition presented in it cannot be dated convincingly earlier than the middle of the first millennium, it may well contain elements of traditions that are much older. For our purpose it seems significant that while nearly all the rabbinic sources simply transfer all the imagery associated with Bethel to Jerusalem, *Gen.R.* 68.12, together with representing something of the interpretation of the passage to be found in the *targums*, speaks of the ladder firstly as the stairway of the temple and secondly as Mount Sinai, the place of the giving of the law.

The combination of temple and Sinai in this kind of juxtaposition may be very ancient, but there could be more to the content of what was disclosed to the sleeping Jacob. To discover what that content might be we can turn to the third matter which the *targums* iluminate. C. Rowland has argued[28] that the *targumic* renderings of Gen. 28.12 are important for disclosing the content of the revelation: he suggests that *Tg. Ps. -J.* reflects the belief that the most secret things of God were hidden even from angels (*1 Enoch* 14.21; 1 Pet. 1.12); but by looking at the features of Jacob the angels can look at the features of one whose form is found on the throne of glory itself. For Jn 1.51 this exegetical tradition would then imply that, as Jacob, so Jesus is on the earth as the one whom the angels in heaven sought to look at, the one who embodies the mystery of God himself. It is in this way that Jesus supplants Jacob and so 1.51 at the climax of the second introduction matches 1.18 at the climax of the first: for the author of the Fourth Gospel Jesus is the one who discloses the very character of God, glory embodied in the Word made flesh—that glory is to be seen in the first sign at Cana. And this parallel between the endings of the two introductions is just the juxtaposition of Exodus 34 and the Jacob cycle which we see also in 11QT.

For the authors of *Jubilees* and the Temple Scroll it is the proper cultic ordering of the Temple and its regulations that need to be declared over against the impure Jerusalemite practice. For the author of the Fourth Gospel the law is the grace and truth that is embodied in and disclosed by Jesus; his use of the Jacob tradition, if close in his understanding also to that of the *targums* gives weighty support to his notion of incarnation: in the human Jesus can be seen the image of God himself. Not surprisingly, as for the authors of *Jubilees* and the Temple Scroll, the combination of traditions from Exodus and Genesis leads the author of the Fourth Gospel to portray the true significance of the temple, the sabbath, the festivals, the very nature of worship itself. So much for the two Introductions to the Fourth Gospel and the juxtaposition of Exodus 34 and Genesis 28 at the end of each.

The other prominent Jacob tradition in the Fourth Gospel is in the narrative of the woman at the well (Jn 4). In the first place the dialogue between Jesus and the Samaritan woman is set at the 'city of Samaria called Sychar near the field that Jacob gave to his son Joseph. Jacob's well was there' (Jn 4.5-6). The use of the figure of Jacob gives some measure of legitimation to the Samaritan woman; she is no descendant of the Schechemites who raped Dinah and who were murdered by Simeon and Levi (a point that is made much of in *Jubilees*), but a descendant of Jacob who bought some land from the Shechemites before the unhappy incident took place. Then the Samaritan woman asks straightforwardly: 'Are you greater than our father Jacob, who gave us the well, and drank from it himself, and his sons, and his cattle' (4.12)

As usual in the Fourth Gospel the meaning of the text does not only rest on the surface. Although there is no mention of Jacob purchasing or digging a well at Shechem, there are plenty of texts in which Jacob is associated with a well. The mention of the well may correspond with Jesus' phrases 'the gift of God' and 'living water' (4.10) both of which were used to describe the Torah.[29] In the Damascus Document (CD 6.4-11) the well of Num. 21.18 is identified explicitly with the law. CD goes on to identify this law with the covenant that the faithful will keep according to Deut. 7.9 (MS B); the proximity of CD to the Temple Scroll has already been noted, so it is not impossible, given the use of Deuteronomy 7 in 11QT 2.7-11, that the covenant to which it refers includes that made with Jacob at Bethel (11QT 29.7-10). In any case in ch. 4 the Fourth Gospel identifies the well with Jacob. Additionally for Jn 4.14 as R.E. Brown has shown,[30] the best parallel is Sir. 24.21 where Wisdom claims that 'those who drink me will thirst for more'. Sir. 24.23-29 goes on to describe how the law fills men with wisdom like rivers overflowing their banks. We have already noted how in this context there is explicit mention of the congregations of Jacob—as Brown says of these verses in ch. 4: 'In John Jesus is presented as divine wisdom and as the replacement of the Law'.[31] In light of the discussion of these motifs in the Prologue, Brown's statement might be altered to say rather that Jesus is the law, its meaning made explicit through being supplemented by his person; it is not so much a matter of Jesus replacing the law. We may suggest, then, that 11QT is also written to disclose the true meaning of the law.

After the Samaritan woman has perceived something of this inasmuch as she is able to identify Jesus as a prophet (like Moses; 4.19), the dialogue develops around the topic of worship. Since this is the principal purpose of the reworking of the Pentateuch in both *Jubilees* and the Temple Scroll, there need be no surprise that true worship is the most significant aspect of the law that the Samaritan woman should grasp. The first topic in the dialogue between the woman and Jesus in this section concerns the place of worship. Intriguingly Jesus says to the woman, 'The hour is coming when neither on this mountain nor in Jerusalem will you worship the Father'. 'Where then?', the reader might ask. Might some of those hearing this dialogue wish to respond by saying, 'At Bethel?' J.C. Vanderkam[32] has lent his detailed support to those who see in the Jacob cycle in the book of *Jubilees* allusions to the battles of the

Maccabees against the Seleucids. J. Schwartz has taken this further with regard to Bethel.[33] He argues that before Bethel's capture and reinforcement by Bacchides (1 Macc. 9.50; *Ant.* 13.12-17), Judas Maccabee was in retreat from Jerusalem in the mountains of the Gophna region (*War* 1.45) close to Bethel. Schwartz proposes that it is these circumstances in 162 BCE that provide the historical setting for the cult to be restored at Bethel which *Jub.* 31-32 seems to stress. There are several attractive aspects to Schwartz's theory; for our immediate purpose it is worth noting that in the late Second Temple period there were those who still harboured notions about the cultic importance of Bethel. If some of these people, especially Levites, eventually found their way into the Qumran community, it is clear from the archaeological evidence that no cultic centre was physically established at Bethel in the Maccabean period.[34]

The dialogue in the Fourth Gospel continues with Jesus saying 'We worship what we know for salvation is from the Jews'. Much has been written on this statement; Brown[35] favours those who see here something comparable with Ps. 76.1: 'In Judah God is known'. This comparison is significant both because Psalm 76 is an Asaph psalm and so may justifiably be associated with Bethel,[36] and because of the psalm's overall content with its reference to Salem, its description of God as 'more majestic than the everlasting mountains', and as 'God of Jacob'. The reference to God being greater than any mountain may be echoed in Jn 4.21, and the title of God as God of Jacob fits the context of John 4. Moreover, the occurrence of Salem may be relevant to how the place of John the Baptist's activity is to be understood ('At Aenon near Salim' [3.23]), since in *Jub.* 30.1 Jacob goes up to 'Salem which is east of Shechem';[37] this seems to be the name for the land which was rightfully his, before the rape of Dinah. In this way there are several tantalizing allusions within John 3 and 4 to the Jacob traditions as represented in Psalm 76 and *Jubilees* as well as in Genesis itself. Perhaps these would amount to nothing if it were not the case that in Jn 4.5-6 and 12 Jacob is named explicitly. In addition it is likely that 1QS 4.19-22 illuminates the meaning of Jn 4.23-24 on the nature of true worship.[38]

As Jesus is on the cross his thirst is assuaged with vinegar to fulfill the scripture (19.28-29); Psalm 69, which lies behind this incident, is also referred to in 2.17. In relation to Jesus' attack on those who were selling doves in the temple, 'His disciples remembered that it was written, "Zeal for thy house will consume me" (Ps. 69.9)'. There follows a reference to the forty-six years that it has taken for the Herodian rebuilding of the temple. Several minor points might add up to something. Firstly, in 11QT 60.9 there is a particular regulation to guarantee that the Levites secure their tithe from doves, which was twice the percentage that it was for booty, game, and wild animals. Secondly, Josephus records both that the Second Temple was constructed by Levites aged twenty and over (*Ant.* 11.79) and that in order not to offend religious scruples Herod had been careful to have the rebuilding of the temple undertaken only by priests, those qualified to be in the temple precincts (15.419-21). Jesus' attack on the sellers of doves at a time when the principal temple buildings were just considered complete might thus be seen as a double blow against Levites, given that some of these Levites might have considered Herod's work as near a fulfilment of their hopes as they might expect, leaving only the eschatological intervention of God himself. In addition Psalm 69 is commonly thought to reflect the views of the pietists who earnestly desired the rebuilding of the temple after the exile; the psalm implies their desire was misplaced and the Fourth Gospel underlines this for Herod's new building too. Lastly, it is worth noting that 11QT 14.9-18 suggests that the purifying of the sanctuary, usually associated with the Day of Atonement, should rather be associated with the celebrations for the spring New Year in Nisan, which is, according to *Jub.* 27.19, the time that Jacob arrived in Bethel; together with these other minor points, perhaps part of the reason for the cleansing of the temple being in the place it is in the Fourth Gospel is the result of some such calendric adjustment as well as the literary possibility that just as in the Temple Scroll the cleansing of the sanctuary follows the regulations for the construction of the altar, so the cleansing of the temple should precede the adjustment to the festivals that will follow later in the Gospel.

The possibility exists, therefore, that some of the members of the Johannine community were those whose fellows (perhaps Levites) may at one time have thought that their aspirations for Bethel had been realized in Jerusalem. These disciples came to recognize that their desire for the Temple was misplaced; the author of the Fourth Gospel tries to show them what the Johannine church considers to be the real content of the law given to Moses the second time he ascended the mountain. In so doing the cultic traditions associated with Jacob receive the same christological adjustment as the practice of the Sabbath and the festivals. This is not literary dependence so much as the deliberate taking over of ideas which belong together particularly in the background of one section of the community. The Pentateuch in the form that it is preserved in the Temple Scroll and *Jubilees* seems to make sense of several disparate ideas in the Fourth Gospel. It may also help account for the Fourth Gospel's stress on divine initiative; to begin in the Holy of Holies and to have a perspective of divine disclosure as at Sinai will result in the story starting with God and working out from the centre to include even the Greeks (Jn 12.20-26).

It is not possible to demonstrate that any of the authors of the New Testament books knew the Temple Scroll. It does seem, however, not only that there are common exegetical traditions, but also that some members of the early Christian communities came from a group whose views had earlier been expressed through such documents as the Temple Scroll. The hopes they may have once fostered for Bethel had proved impossible to fulfil; they had associated themselves with the Qumran community's disapproval of cultic practice in Jerusalem; perhaps they had had their hopes raised by Herod's rebuilding programme, only to have their priesthood and other characteristics of their understanding of the cult denied once again. If some of them had been retained to run the sale of offerings after the principal elements of Herod's temple were complete, they may have been put in their place by Jesus. Or, later, as some of them became associated probably with either the nascent Marcan or Johannine communities, they were shown through the adaptation and adjustment of their own exegetical traditions how Jesus fulfilled all their hopes and expectations. If at any stage they had been designated 'Herodians', they would have soon wanted to lose that name!

NOTES

1. 'Pesher Nahum (4QpNahum) Reconsidered', *IEJ* 21 (1971), pp. 1-12.

2. M. Hengel for one (*Crucifixion in the Ancient World and the Folly of the Message of the Cross* [London: SCM, 1977], pp. 84-85) approves of

Yadin's understanding and supposes that the tradition of the hanging of the sorceresses in Ashkelon, preserved in *m. Sanh.* 6.5, is so unusual that it may well reflect an actual event, perhaps the Pharisees getting their own back when they came into favour once again under Alexandra Salome.

3. J.M. Baumgarten, 'Does *TLH* in the Temple Scroll Refer to Crucifixion?', *JBL* 91 (1972), pp. 472-81; reprinted in *Studies in Qumran Law* (SJLA, 24; Leiden: Brill, 1977), pp. 172-82; J.M. Baumgarten, 'Hanging and Treason in Qumran and Roman Law', *Eretz-Israel* 16 (1982), pp. 7-16; A. Dupont-Sommer, 'Observations nouvelles sur l'expression "suspendu vivant sur le bois" dans le Commentaire de Nahum (4QpNah II 8) à la lumière du Rouleau du Temple (11Q Temple Scroll LXIV 6-13)', *CRAIBL* 1972, pp. 709-20; J.A. Fitzmyer, 'Crucifixion in Ancient Palestine, Qumran Literature, and the New Testament', *CBQ* 40 (1978), pp. 493-513; J.M. Ford, '"Crucify him, crucify him" and the Temple Scroll', *ExpTim* 87 (1975-76), pp. 275-78; D.J. Halperin, 'Crucifixion, the Nahum Pesher, and the Rabbinic Penalty of Strangulation', *JJS* 32 (1981), pp. 32-46; M. Hengel, *Crucifixion*, pp. 84-85; L. Merino Díez, 'La crucifixíon en la antigua literatura judía (Período Intertestamental)', *Estudios Ecclesiasticos* 51 (1976), pp. 5-27; L. Merino Díez, 'El suplicio de la cruz en la literatura judía intertestamental', *SBFLA* 26 (1976), pp. 31-120; L. Rosso, 'Deuteronomio 21, 22: Contributo del Rotolo del Tempio alla Valutazione di una Variante Medievale dei Settanta', *RevQ* 9 (1977-78), pp. 231-36; R. Vincent Saera, 'La halaká de Dt 21, 22-23 y su interpretación en Qumrán y en Jn 19, 31-42', *Salvación en la Palabra. Targum-Derash-Berith. Homenaje al prof. A. Diez Macho* (ed. D. Muñoz Léon; Madrid: Ediciones Cristiandad, 1986), pp. 699-709; M. Wilcox, '"Upon the Tree"—Deut. 21.22-23 in the New Testament', *JBL* 96 (1977), pp. 85-99.

4. As the contribution of H. Stegemann to this volume suggests.

5. J.A. Fitzmyer, 'Crucifixion in Ancient Palestine', pp. 509-10; M. Wilcox, '"Upon the Tree"—Deut. 21.22-23 in the NT', pp. 90-91, 99.

6. E. Haenchen (*The Acts of the Apostles: A Commentary* [ed. R.McL. Wilson; Oxford: Blackwell/Philadelphia: Westminster, 1971) says Acts 5.30 *alludes* to Deut. 21.22-23 in the LXX (p. 251) and that the same text in Acts 10.39 belongs to early Christian scriptural proof (p. 353); H. Conzelmann (*Die Apostelgeschichte* [HNT, 7; 2nd edn, Tübingen: Mohr, 1972]; Eng. trans. *Acts of the Apostles* [Hermeneia; Philadelphia: Fortress, 1987], p. 42) does not mention the LXX and more aptly asks whether Deut. 21.22-23 in Acts 5.30, 10.39, and Gal. 3.13 belongs to a traditional Christian apologetic tradition. Most recently, R. Pesch (*Die Apostelgeschichte* [EKK, 5/1; Neukirchen-Vluyn: Neukirchener Verlag, 1986], p. 217 n. 31) refers not to the LXX but to the interpretation of Deut. 21.22-23 in 11QT for understanding the text of Acts. Yadin himself drew attention to the significance of 11QT for the better understanding of Gal. 3.13 (*The Temple Scroll*, I, p. 379 [Heb.: I,

p. 290]). H.D. Betz (*Galatians* [Hermeneia; Philadelphia: Fortress, 1979], pp. 151-52 n. 133) allows that Paul's use of Deut. 21.22-23 may have been based on a *Vorlage* like that of 11QT. The version of Deut. 21.22-23 in the Temple Scroll eases the difficulties in all these NT passages. Of the four Passion Narratives it is those of Mark and John that came closest to representing something of Deut. 21.22-23 in their description, Mark in the stress on the need to take Jesus from the cross because evening had come (Mk 15.42-44), John by having the soldiers break the legs of those not dead so that the law might be kept (Jn 19.31-33).

7. A. Ammassari, 'Lo statuto matrimoniale del re di Israele (Deut. 17, 17) secondo l'esegesi del 'Rotolo del Tempio' (57, 15-19) e le risonanza neotestamentarie (Ef. 5, 23-33; Apoc. 21, 9-10)', *Euntes Docete* 34 (1981), pp. 123-27; P.R. Davies, *Behind the Essenes: History and Ideology in the Dead Sea Scrolls* (BJS, 94; Atlanta: Scholars, 1987), pp. 73-85; J.A. Fitzmyer, 'The Matthean Divorce Texts and Some New Palestinian Evidence', *TS* 37 (1976), pp. 197-226; J.A. Fitzmyer, 'Divorce among First-Century Palestinian Jews', *Eretz-Israel* 14 (1978), pp. 103-10; J.R. Mueller, 'The Temple Scroll and the Gospel Divorce Texts', *RevQ* 10 (1979-81), pp. 247-56; J. Murphy-O'Connor, 'Remarques sur l'exposé du Professeur Y. Yadin', *RB* 79 (1972), pp. 99-100; C. Schedl, 'Zur Ehebruchklausel der Bergpredigt im Lichte der neugefundenen Tempelrolle', *Theologisch-praktische Quartalschrift* 130 (1982), pp. 362-65; G. Vermes, 'Sectarian Matrimonial Halakhah in the Damascus Rule', *JJS* 25 (1974), pp. 197-202; reprinted in *Post-Biblical Jewish Studies* (SJLA, 8; Leiden: Brill, 1975), pp. 50-56; Y. Yadin, 'L'attitude essénienne envers la polygamie et le divorce', *RB* 79 (1972), pp. 98-100. See also the article on divorce by H.A. Mink in *Tekster og tolkninger—ti studieri Det gamle Testamente* (ed. K. Jeppesen & F.H. Cryer; Aarhus: Anis, 1986).

8. Y. Yadin, *The Temple Scroll: The Hidden Law of the Dead Sea Sect* (London: Weidenfeld & Nicolson, 1985), pp. 201-202; cf. *The Temple Scroll*, I, p. 357 (Heb.: I, pp. 272-73). Although when he discusses divorce, E.P. Sanders (*Jesus and Judaism* [London: SCM, 1985], pp. 256-60) makes no mention of 11QT, he does refer in detail to CD 4-5 and his conclusions are significant: he shows that Jesus in his teaching on divorce neither contradicts the law nor is entirely satisfied with it—this is exactly the position of 11QT in relation to the Pentateuch on many matters.

9. *The Temple Scroll*, I, pp. 138-39 (Heb.: I, pp. 111-12), *The Temple Scroll: The Hidden Law*, pp. 80-83. Yadin also mentions how Jn 6.4 explicty speaks of the Feeding of the 5,000 happening as Passover drew near; this corresponds with the timing of the 11QT feast of Ordination.

10. Instead of Ἡρῳδου, P[45], *W*, Θ, and others read τῶν ˙ Ἡρῳδιανῶν.

11. In commenting on Mk 2.23-28, J.D.G. Dunn ('Mark 2.1–3.6: Between Jesus and Paul', *NTS* 30 [1984], p. 402) draws attention to *Jub.* 2.29-30; 50.6-13 to illuminate the position concerning the Sabbath in contemporary

Judaism, but he does not draw out the significance of his remarks. For more on *Jubilees*, CD and 11QT see the contributions by J.C. VanderKam and P.R. Davies in this volume and the bibliographical notes there; see also P.R. Davies, *Behind the Essenes*, pp. 107-34.

12. D, W, *it sy*[s] and others omit the phrase referring to Abiathar, as do Matthew and Luke, sensing its difficulty. Several Scholars reflect the statement of V. Taylor (*The Gospel according to St. Mark* [2nd edn, London: Macmillan, 1966], p. 217): 'The statement about Abiathar is either a primitive error or a copyist's gloss occasioned by the fact that, in association with David, Abiathar was better known than his father'. C.E.B. Cranfield (*The Gospel according to St. Mark* [CGTC; Cambridge: Cambridge University Press, 1959], p. 116) helps Jesus out of the difficulty by suggesting that the phrase could mean 'in the days of Abiathar the High Priest' and so need not refer to his actual high priesthood; more helpfully he says: 'It may be that there is some confusion between Ahimelech and Abiathar in the O.T. itself—cf. I Sam. xxii. 20 with II Sam. viii. 17, I Chr. xviii. 16, xxiv. 6'.

13. In *Ant.* 6.243-44 Josephus fails to mention the giving of the shewbread to David; perhaps this illustrates that there was some debate about the suitability and significance of the action. J.D.G. Dunn ('Mark 2.1-3.6: Between Jesus and Paul') argues persuasively that the whole section in Mk reflects debates within Judaism and Jewish Christianity before the time of Paul. The Samuel passage concerned is not preserved amongst the Qumran fragments of Samuel: E.C. Ulrich, *The Qumran Text of Samuel and Josephus* (HSM, 19; Missoula: Scholars, 1978), p. 273.

14. 'The Feast of New Wine and the Question of Fasting', *ExpTim* 95 (1983-84), pp. 175-76.

15. On the supplementary nature of the Temple Scroll see the contribution of H. Stegemann to this volume; on the importance of 1 Chron. 28.11-19 for understanding the function of 11QT see Y. Yadin, *The Temple Scroll*, I, pp. 81-82, 182, 403 (Heb.: I, pp. 70, 141, 308); *The Temple Scroll: The Hidden Law*, pp. 115-17.

16. *The Temple Scroll: The Hidden Law*, p. 78; for the details see *The Temple Scroll*, I, pp. 76, 360-61 (Heb.: I, pp. 57, 276).

17. In a similar way, according to 11QPs[a] 27.2-11, David's psalmodic compositions are a demonstration of the correct calendric attitude; see W.H. Brownlee, 'The Significance of David's Compositions', *RevQ* 5 (1964-66), pp. 569-74.

18. 'An Analysis of Jesus' Arguments Concerning the Plucking of Grain on the Sabbath', *JSNT* 2 (1979), pp. 31-41, especially p. 36.

19. See the definition of the main sources and redactional sections of 11QT identified by A.M. Wilson and L. Wills, 'Literary Sources of the Temple Scroll', *HTR* 75 (1982), pp. 275-88. On 11QT 29.7-10 in particular see Yadin, *The Temple Scroll*, I, pp. 182-86 (Heb.: I, pp. 140-44); P. Callaway,

'Exegetische Erwägungen zur Tempelrolle XXIX, 7-10', *RevQ* 12 (1985-87), pp. 95-104.

20. Many scholars accept this identification: e.g. C.K. Barrett, *The Gospel According to St. John* (2nd edn, London: SPCK, 1978), pp. 167, 169; R.E. Brown, *The Gospel According to John I-XII* (AB, 29; Garden City, N.Y.: Doubleday, 1966), p. 14; R. Schnackenburg, *The Gospel according to St John* (New York: Herder & Herder; London: Burnes & Oates, 1968), Vol. I, p. 272.

21. To find Genesis 1 linked with Exodus 34 and the temple is to see another example in support of the view that the temple is to be understood as a microcosm; see e.g. M. Weinfeld, 'Sabbath, Temple, and the Enthronement of the Lord—The Problems of the Sitz im Leben of Genesis 1.1-2.3', *Mélanges bibliques et orientaux en l'honneur de M. Henri Cazelles* (AOAT, 212; ed. A. Caquot & M. Delcor; Neukirchen-Vluyn: Neukirchener Verlag, 1981), pp. 501-12.

22. As proposed, for example, by B. Lindars, *Behind the Fourth Gospel* (Studies in Creative Criticism, 3; London: SPCK, 1971), p. 48; R.E. Brown, *John I-XII*, pp. cxxii-cxxv.

23. See the detailed analyses of 2 Cor. 3.1-18 by A.T. Hanson, *Jesus Christ in the Old Testament* (London: SPCK, 1965), pp. 25-35; 'The Midrash in II Corinthians 3: A Reconsideration', *JSNT* 9 (1980), pp. 2-28. Cf. Rom. 11.7, 25.

24. Similarly, in 4Q158, frg. 1, Gen. 32.29-30 includes phraseology of Isaac's blessing of Jacob in Gen. 28.3.

25. R.E. Brown (*John I-XII*, pp. 105-106) cautiously agrees with other scholars who have proposed this.

26. Few commentators attempt any explanation of why Levites are mentioned in Jn 1.19; e.g. E. Haenchen (*John 1* [Hermeneia; Philadelphia: Fortress, 1984], p. 143) argues that they are present neither as temple police nor as the party interested in purity, but simply to stress the religious significance of the scene. The Levitical bias of 11QT suggests that they may have been mentioned in Jn 1.19 because they formed part of the author's readership; the bias towards the Levites in 11QT was first summed up by J. Milgrom, 'Studies in the Temple Scroll', *JBL* 97 (1978), pp. 501-506.

27. The comments in this paragraph are based on the summary of scholarly opinions by R.E. Brown (*John I-XII*, pp. 90-91).

28. 'John 1.51, Jewish Apocalyptic and Targumic Tradition', *NTS* 30 (1984), pp. 498-507. Jacob traditions are prominent in several items of intertestamental literature, especially PrJos which may well come from the same school as 11QT. PrJos, Frg. A, speaks of Jacob as the firstborn who tabernacles among men.

29. See R.E. Brown, *John I-XII*, pp. 176, 178.

30. *John I-XII*, p. 178; surprisingly, G. Reim (*Studien zum alttestamentlichen*

Hintergrund des Johannesevangeliums [SNTSMS, 22; Cambridge: Cambridge University Press, 1974], pp. 192-93) makes no mention of this parallel.

31. *John I-XII*, p. 179.

32. *Textual and Historical Studies in the Book of Jubilees* (HSM, 14; Missoula: Scholars, 1977), pp. 217-41.

33. 'Jubilees, Bethel and the Temple of Jacob', *HUCA* 56 (1985), pp. 63-85.

34. See J.L. Kelso, *The Excavation of Bethel (1934-1960)* (AASOR, 39; Cambridge: American Schools of Oriental Research, 1968), pp. 38-40.

35. *John I-XII*, p. 172.

36. See e.g. M.D. Goulder, *The Psalms of the Sons of Korah* (JSOTS, 20; Sheffield: JSOT, 1982), pp. 59-65.

37. This justifies reading MT Gen. 33.18 as Salem, although Sam. has שלום.

38. According to R. Schnackenburg, 'Die "Anbetung in Geist und Wahrheit" (Joh 4, 23) im Lichte von Qumran-Texten', *BZ* 3 (1959), pp. 88-94; O. Betz, '"To Worship God in Spirit and in Truth": Reflections on John 4, 20-26', *Standing Before God: Studies on Prayer in Scripture and Tradition in Honor of J.M. Oesterreicher* (ed. A. Finkel & L. Frizzell; New York: Ktav, 1981), pp. 53-72, esp. pp. 62-65.

THE TEMPLE SCROLL AND THE DAMASCUS DOCUMENT

Philip R. Davies

University of Sheffield

The question I address in this paper is whether 11QT, or anything like it, can be inferred from CD, and if so, what its status would have been within the community which produced CD. I am not concerned primarily with possible quotations or allusions or similarities in language, for these have already been satisfactorily discussed.[1]

The 'base-text' of this paper is CD 6.3b-11a, the so-called 'well-midrash'. It forms an intrinsic part of what I have called[2] a *Heilsgeschichte* which begins at 5.16 and culminates in the foundation of what I will very loosely call a 'community', following the 'epoch of the desolation of the land', i.e., the destruction and exile under Nebuchadnezzar. Four stages are portrayed in the process of forming this 'community', which are (1) God's 'remembering of the covenant of the former ones', (2) the raising of men of 'wisdom' and 'understanding' from Aaron and Israel, (3) divine communication ('causing them to hear/obey') and (4) the digging of a 'well' by the recipients of that communication. It is this last stage which introduces the 'well-text' (Num. 21.18): 'the well which princes dug, which nobles of the people excavated with a מחקק'. The midrash proceeds to identify the 'well', then the 'princes', then the מחוקק, then the 'nobles of the people'.

We are certainly dealing not merely with details conjured up out of an individual passage but with an independent tradition. This is obvious from a comparison of this passage with another *Heilsgeschichte* in CD 2.14ff. The pertinent section begins at 3.9b-4.6, from which the following similarities emerge:

(1) Each passage is a *Heilsgeschichte* culminating in a midrash which forms an intrinsic part of the whole and cannot be detached as an originally independent item (Num. 21.18; Ezek. 44.15).

(2) Each midrash also employs as a designation for the founders of the community the term שבי ישראל היוצאים מארץ יהודה. In both cases the term is not derived from the biblical text but applied to its interpretation.

(3) Each passage closes with the expression 'end of days'.

(4) Both midrashim cover not only the *foundation* but also the consummation of the community and *make a chronological differentiation between parallel terms in the biblical text*. Thus in the Ezekiel midrash the 'sons of Zadok, the levitical priests' of the biblical text are taken as three separate entities and interpreted in a chronological sequence, the 'priests' being the שבי ישראל היוצאים מארץ יהודה, the 'Levites' those who joined them, and the 'sons of Zadok' those who belong at the 'end of days'. In the Numbers midrash we have also the 'princes' who *dug* the well, using the מחוקק, while the 'nobles of the people' are הבאים 'those who *come to dig*', their 'digging' being to walk in accordance with the laws 'during the epoch of wickedness' until a יורה צדק will arise *at the end of days*.

(5) In both midrashim we have the equation well = law (תורה). This *torah* will be the primary object of attention in what follows.

Both passages cited, and both their midrashim, convey the same sequence of events using the same literary techniques. At the climax of each sequence lies the 'well', the law. We can learn from these passages—whether or not they are historically reliable, which is another issue—the basic elements in the community's expressed belief about its own foundation, constitution and destiny, all of which revolve around the possession of *torah*. This community understands itself to be in possession of a *torah*, acquired by divine revelation, possession of which is its *raison d'être*. This law governs the life of the present members of the community in the 'epoch of wickedness' (6.10), an epoch which will be ended, according to 6.11, by the arrival of one who will 'teach righteousness'. Elsewhere in CD the belief in a prescribed end to the duration of the present epoch is confined to the words 'end of days' (4.4) or 'completion of the end of these years/ number of years' (4.9, 10).

What, then, do we learn from CD about the nature of this law which constitutes the purpose of the community? First, it is called *torah* (4.8; 6.4). But it is obviously not exactly equivalent to the scriptural text of the law of Moses, for this has been received by all Israel. Yet it obviously does not replace or contradict what we now regard as the scriptural text. For CD 4.13bff., claiming that Israel has been led into error by Belial into taking wickedness for righteousness, argues on the basis of scriptural texts, which constitute what 'Moses said' (5.8). In CD 5.21, too, we find the pre-exilic generations accused of rebellion 'against the commandments of God by the hand of Moses' which implies recognition of a given *torah* before the revelation of *torah* to the community. Add to these points the numerous allusions to what we can recognize as the scriptural text in CD—for instance, the Numbers midrash itself—and we must conclude that this scriptural text as we now know it—or something approximate to it—is accepted in CD as Mosaic law. I say Mosaic law, not *the* Mosaic law. The difference is quite crucial. Moreover, it is crucially important to define the scriptural Mosaic law more carefully. It is the law given to Moses *and revealed to Israel*. The author of that sciptural text is Moses. But he is not the author of the law. The law is *what God revealed*. Now, clearly, this law has been revealed in two ways: first through what Moses wrote, and second through the community.

A critical issue surrounding the Temple Scroll in much recent discussion has been the question of its relationship to the Pentateuch. As far as understanding CD is concerned, the issue is represented as the relationship between the scriptural text of Mosaic law and the law which God revealed—and reveals—to the community. 3.14 refers to the new revelation (לנגלות) as 'hidden things (נסתרות) in which all Israel had gone astray', sabbaths, festivals, עידות צדקו ודרכי אמתו and חפצי רצונו. These God 'opened before them' (3.16). Is this process of revelation to be construed as a new Sinai, inscribed on a new *torah* code? All the evidence suggests not. Rather, the new revelation of *torah* to the community cannot be anything other than *exegesis of the already existing text of Mosaic torah we know as scriptural.*

The characterization of *torah* in CD accords with Baumgarten's view so far as 'revelation' is concerned. As far as 'exegesis' goes it agrees with Schiffman. The distinction between 'revealed' and 'exegetical' is one of a number of misleading issues which had dogged our understanding of 11QT.[3] Although I am broadly in agreement with Schiffman's analysis of legal terminology in the Scrolls, I disagree with him in his rejection of 'revelation' and in his inclusion of CD but exclusion of 11QT from 'Qumran law'—both ought to be in or out. I wish to go beyond what Schiffman has established. For Schiffman has somewhat confused the issue by not recognizing the difference between *torah* and laws governing community life. Were space permitted, I would develop the argument that in CD the community is governed by *torah*. But the rules in 1QS are not *torah*. They are not derived from scripture, but have been laid down by the founder of the community, whose authority is based on his claim to be the 'teacher of righteousness' of CD 6.11 and thus one who will mark the end of the period in which the law will be in operation (see below). In support of this argument can be cited both the analysis of 1QS by J. Murphy-O'Connor, which identifies the core of Qumran community legislation as a 'Manifesto' of the 'Teacher of Righteousness', and also the recent criticisms of Schiffman by Weinfeld, who demonstrates the coherence of Qumran rules of organization (yet he too fails to see the distinction between 1QS and CD) with other guilds and religious associations of the Hellenistic-Roman period.[4]

The exegetical nature of the revealed *torah* possessed by the CD community becomes evident from a number of considerations. The simplest and most obvious of these is in the Numbers midrash, where the מחוקק of the scriptural text is called the דורש התורה, '*interpreter* of the law', not 'teacher' or 'giver' of the law. Another consideration is the use of a set of terms to qualify the word *torah* when it is used of the law in the community. The most common is פרוש. We have in CD 6.14ff. (item 4) a selection from the פרוש התורו 'for the epoch of wickedness' (cf. the same phrase in 6.10). These 'instructions', as I have called them,[5] seem to be based on scriptural formulations, and to be arrived at much in the manner outlined by Phillip Callaway in his examination of 11QT laws (in the present volume), by a mixture of scriptural allusion, straight scriptural quotation and less direct but quite obvious derivation from scriptural formulations. In other words, here is an example of how the community's law actually was 'revealed'—through exegesis. The results of this exegesis are denoted by either כמצוה, פרוש (ה), or כמשפט. As Schiffman has shown, פרוש is 'another term for the law derived from Scripture by interpretation';[6] and if differences of nuance lie in the other two terms, I cannot find them. In the *Laws* (CD 9–16) we can also find פרוש and משפט.

A further consideration discloses the ongoing process of interpreting law within the community. Again, it starts with the Numbers midrash. The 'well' is dug by a דורש, but the community is initially composed of 'wise' men having 'understanding'; wisdom and understanding are also the qualities sought in CD of contemporary members of the community, for those raised by God are called נבונים ('men of understanding') and חכמים ('wise'). The language of insight and wisdom in fact pervades the *Admonition* and emphasizes the *interpretative* qualities sought of the covenant members. Thus, in the three opening discourses we find 'hear/cause to hear' (1.1; 2.2, 12; cf. 6.3), 'uncover (אגלה) the ear' (2.2), or 'uncover the eyes' (2.14), 'consider' (להבין) (2.14). The essential requirement of members of the covenant is not obedience but *insight, understanding* or *knowledge*.

The picture presented by the Numbers midrash is of the law as a continuously creative process within the community. The act of digging does not, as it turns out, denote a once-for-all procedure of establishing the law, but the initiation of a *continuous process*. In 6.8-9, the 'nobles' are 'those who come (or have come) to dig the well'. Digging the well goes on still.

Let us note, however, that this *torah* will not last for ever, but, according to 6.11, only until one comes who will 'teach righteousness at the end of days'. (Perhaps the translation 'judge properly. . . ' is better, because with a righteous judge a body of laws is evidently not needed?) From the *Laws* it seems that this person is identified as the 'messiah of Aaron and Israel' (12.23; 14.9[?]).[7] The Qumran community would appear to have been founded by one claiming this role. That is why the laws of the CD community were probably superseded at Qumran by a new regime. The 'Teacher of Righteousness' is evidently not the person referred to by the term 'Interpreter of the Law' in 6.7; I find myself wondering whether such an individual as the 'Interpreter' ever existed, or whether he is an halakhic fiction (he is absent from both 1.1ff. and 3.13ff.). I am reminded in both midrashim of the opening of *m. 'Abot*, משה קבל תורה מסיני ומסרה ליהושע , a wonderful fiction to describe the origin of a patently rabbinic and thus both recent and contemporary activity. Is CD a precursor of this hermeneutic, whereby every new community exegesis is ascribed to the 'new Moses' who 'interpreted the law' when the community was founded? I think the analogy is admissible, but with the important difference that the law derived by exegesis is not Mosaic, but divine.[8] The difference between this and the mishnaic theory of the 'oral law' is not in the end more than a matter of metaphor. But it might explain why the Temple Scroll, while derived from *Mosaic* law (the code Moses wrote), is ascribed to God.

We have now reached the point of asking what kind of sense, if any, such a document as 11QT might have within the community described in CD. The scriptural text, as we have seen, is the *torah* as written by Moses, and any law properly derived from it by exegesis will also be *torah*. The entirety of *torah* cannot be contained either in a scriptural (or any other) text, nor can it be held to have been entirely 'revealed' until the process of exegesis is exhausted, which remains a theoretical terminus only. Yet it is necessary from time to time for the results of exegesis—providing a more exact definition of *torah*—to be codified. Such a code, of course, will not contradict or supplement the law that Moses wrote, but define it more exactly— that is to say, spell out more precisely what the law *was* (or *is*) that God revealed to Moses.

Another issue surrounding 11QT which has failed to identify the real nature of the problem is the distinction between 'oral' and 'written' law. For even the rabbinic 'oral law' became written. Schiffman's distinction between *esoteric* and *public torah*, on the other hand, is appropriate, and he correctly suggests that the law of the community would be the former, since it claimed to be in sole possession of that law which God had revealed to it. One also finds it argued, however seriously, in the rabbinic literature that the written law, revealed at Sinai, was available to all the world, but the oral law was not written because it was for Israel only. But how private *was* the *Mishnah*, once written? Perhaps its language preserved it from non-Jews, but was this by intention or by consequence? There is no point in denying that the community in CD consigned to writing the results of its exegesis, whilst regarding these results as comprising a divine revelation to itself. The notion of writing down secret things is not confined to apocalyptic books.

The existence of such written law is in any case implied in CD. We have already noted the 'injunctions' in CD 6.14ff., which may have existed as a separate literary source. We find another such lawbook referred to as the 'book of the הגו' in CD 13.2ff. A priest 'instructed in the book of the הגו' makes rulings. In cases of a נגע לתורת, the משפט, the ruling must be made after the מבקר has instructed him in the

פרוש התורה. In 14.6-7 the priest appointed at the 'head of the רבים must be instructed in the book [of the הגו?] and in all the משפטי התורה'. Alongside the book of the הגו we also encounter the 'יסורי (emended from יסורי) of the covenant' (10.6). Then there are the *Laws* themselves of CD 9–16. The system by which the community created its law is not entirely clear, but it was encoded, it seems, in more than one written source. None of these sources, it seems, was intended to represent a complete restatement of Mosaic law, but simply a convenient literary resource for purposes of regulating life under the law within the community. For, of course, the law was refined exegetically in order to be obeyed.

The 'Temple' or 'Torah' scroll may well be one of several literary forms in which Mosaic law according to the community was encoded, and if this is the case, we can understand that it was neither a replacement for the scriptural law, nor a complete *Torah*, nor a supplementary *Torah*—all of which have been suggested. It is a פרוש התורה, a more precise, more defined *torah*, which expands, abbreviates and rearranges in ways familiar from the *Mishnah*, although, unlike the *Mishnah*, it adheres largely to the biblical sequence.

I do not propose to review again the more exact parallels between CD and 11QT which complement the approach taken here. I do not believe that those who have noted differences between them have been able to give a satisfactory account of the *similarities*—and any explanation must do justice to both. It seems to be that 11QT constitutes one of the many and varied forms of written *torah* according to the community (expanded Pentateuch texts being another, a possibility we can only explore when they are published). The community was apparently defined by and obsessed with law, not wicked priests or Hellenism, and we may expect, as we find in the *Mishnah*, differing schools of thought. Discrepancies between Hillel and Shammai do not vitiate the integrity of the 'oral law'. Why do halakhic variations between 11QT and CD worry us? One can find evidence of a long and complicated process of compilation in the *Mishnah*. So too in 11QT. I have now referred several times to the *Mishnah* in this essay; however, I am not proposing that we draw *exact* parallels between the processes of the CD community and of the rabbis, but it is always important to use analogies of this kind to protect ourselves from inconsistent thinking in applying different sets of expectations to different phenomena. I see no reason to require of the CD community a rigorously consistent body of law, which neither the Bible nor the rabbis were able to manage. What some scholars find problematic in Qumran law others do not find problematic in rabbinics, nor others in the Bible.

By way of taking up just one particular case where CD and 11QT are muturally enlightening, let me comment on the 'city of the sanctuary' (עיר המקדש); CD forbids any sexual intercourse within its bounds (12.1f.). The implication usually drawn is that Jerusalem was regarded here as especially holy by virtue of being close to the Temple. Nevertheless it is strange that this law, which implies (married) members of the community living in Jerusalem, should deny them a basic privilege of marital status. The reason for this law can be explained from the extent of the Temple in 11QT, according to which, as Maier has shown (see his article above), the outer court of the Temple includes the major part of the city. Most of those living in Jerusalem were therefore living in the Temple precincts, even if these precincts were not as yet architecturally realized. In a literal sense, the city—or most of it—*was* the city of the sanctuary!

I wish to conclude with a few brief comments on the interesting theses of Hartmut Stegemann. The fact that at Qumran 11QT is not influential, as he rightly states (though he is probably not entirely right, given 1QM 2), makes perfect sense on the supposition that the Qumran community regarded such laws in much the same way that Christians regarded their 'Old Testament'—inspired but to be viewed under a new dispensation. Under this new dispensation (in both instances) a radically new attitude to the Temple prevailed.

The date of the origin of 11QT—or, more correctly, of the body of *torah* which this manuscript contains—remains uncertain but not very important, since it probably represents a long tradition. Again, I am inclined to pursue the line taken by Stegemann and implied by Maier. However, perhaps we ought not to speculate about what Ezra did or did not accomplish since no two scholars seem to agree on this, and the idea of a priestly '*Tosefta*' or sixth Mosaic book is really no more than speculation. I suspect that the origin of 11QT, or at least its tradition, is connected not with Ezra's law-book and its effect upon earlier priestly codes, but with the origins of the CD community. (I stress that I am speaking of *origins*, and do not preclude the possibility that the manuscript was copied, edited, or re-issued in the Herodian period for some particular purpose.)

Despite such reservations, we certainly ought not to rule out a possible connection between the events related in Ezra and Nehemiah, the beginning of the formation of 11QT and the origin of the community represented in CD. The relationships between *Jubilees*, 11QT, CD and possibly *1 Enoch*, which exist on several levels— historical summaries,[9] eschatology, calendar—must also be positively appraised in any such investigation. Connections between the ideology of CD and biblical literature relating to the Judaean community in the fifth century have already been made. Reference to a group called שבי ישראל who went out of the land of Judah have been taken by Murphy-O'Connor to refer to the Babylonian exile, while the phrase השבי in Neh. 1.3; 7.6; 8.17 (the last השבי מן השבים) has also been remarked. Parallels have also been drawn by Morton Smith,[10] who drew attention to the covenant decribed in Nehemiah 9. The prayer of Nehemiah 10 is markedly similar to 4QDibHam,[11] very probably another pre-Qumran text. One may still take seriously the possibility of the claim of CD to trace the origin of the community to the aftermath of the Babylonian exile. Of those who returned to Jerusalem in the century after the degree of Cyrus we know four things: they came in small groups and not as a single migration; they contained a large priestly element; they kept lists of their names and ancestry (cf. CD 4.5); and they regarded themselves as the true heirs of the covenant.

If the origins of 11QT are as old as Stegemann suggests, why not the origin of the community of CD also? At all events, there is simply too much evidence to permit us the option of denying a relationship between 11QT, CD, Qumran, and *Jubilees*. The fact that we cannot easily define or explain that relationship does not permit us to turn our back on the problem and sever any connection between them.

NOTES

1. Detailed consideration was given by Y. Yadin, *Megillat ham-Miqdaš* (3 Vols.; Jerusalem: The Israel Exploration Society and the Shrine of the Book, 1977); English trans. *The Temple Scroll* (3 Vols.; Jerusalem: The Israel Exploration Society and the Shrine of the Book, 1983); Yadin concluded, however, that both CD and 11QT were from the Qumran sect. See also B. Levine, 'The Temple Scroll: Aspects of its Historical Provenance and Literary Character'. *BASOR* 232 (1978), pp. 5-23; E. Schürer, *A History of*

the Jewish People in the Age of Jesus Christ (ed. G. Vermes, F. Millar, & M. Goodman; Edinburgh: T. & T. Clark, 1987), III, pp. 412-13.

2. *The Damascus Covenant* (JSOTS, 25; Sheffield: JSOT, 1983), p. 106; *Behind the Essenes* (BJS, 94; Atlanta: Scholars Press, 1987), p. 107.

3. See J. Baumgarten, 'The Unwritten Law in the Pre-Rabbinic Period', *JSJ* 3 (1972), pp. 7-29; L.H. Schiffman, *The Halakhah at Qumran* (SJLA, 16; Leiden: Brill, 1975), pp. 76, 134; L.H. Schiffman, *Sectarian Law in the Dead Sea Scrolls: Courts, Testimony and Penal Codes* (BJS, 33; Chico: Scholars Press, 1983), pp. 1-19, 211-17.

4. J. Murphy-O'Connor, 'La genèse littéraire de la Règle de la Communauté', *RB* 76 (1969), pp. 528-49; M. Weinfeld, *The Organizational Pattern and the Penal Code of the Qumran Sect* (NTOA, 2; Göttingen: Vandenhoeck & Ruprecht/Fribourg: Editions Universitaires, 1986), esp. pp. 71-77.

5. *The Damascus Covenant*, pp. 125-42.

6. *The Halakhah at Qumran*, p. 36.

7. For the arguments, see my 'The "Teacher of Righteousness" and the "End of Days"', *Mémorial Jean Carmignac, RevQ* 13 (1988), pp. 313-17.

8. Much of this understanding of the relationship between 11QT and the scriptural law of Moses I owe to a conversation with M. Bernstein, and it invites a comparison with the distinction between what God says and what Habakkuk says in 1QpHab—i.e., God told Habakkuk, Habakkuk did not understand, implicitly neither did his readers until God gave the Qumran community to understand. The origin of the book of Habakkuk, on the Qumran reading, is the prophet; the origin of the *pesher*, strictly, is God—via the 'Teacher of Righteousness'.

9. For an examination of these, see *Behind the Essenes*, pp. 107-34.

10. Morton Smith, 'The Dead Sea Sect in Relation to Early Judaism', *NTS* 7 (1961), pp. 347-60.

11. For a full discussion of the history of this prayer, see A. Lacocque, 'The Liturgical Prayer in Daniel 9', *HUCA* 47 (1976), pp. 119-42. Despite Lacocque's conclusion, the evidence points to a prayer of Diaspora origin.

THE TEMPLE SCROLL AND THE BOOK OF JUBILEES

James C. VanderKam

North Carolina State University

During the very brief history of research on the Temple Scroll, scholars have expressed rather different theories about the relationship between it and the book of *Jubilees*. No one doubts that in some sense the two are related; disagreement has arisen in trying to define the precise nature of that kinship. The two are, of course, very different kinds of compositions. The Temple Scroll is a legal work with no preserved narrative framework, while *Jubilees* is a narrative book with some legal sections. Hence, in treating the relationship between them, one is dealing almost exclusively with the legal parts of *Jubilees*. And, since the detailed prescriptions regarding the temple structure in the scroll find no parallel in *Jubilees*, the overlapping material in the two books is limited primarily to matters connected with the sacred calendar, festivals, and their sacrifices. The laws regarding these topics are scattered throughout *Jubilees* but with few exceptions are concentrated in 11QT 13.9–30.2

Because this essay focuses on the relationship between two literary works, it is important to define the term *relationship*. By it one could mean at least two forms of connection. Obviously, it would include the provision that the two share some part(s) of their content, but the term may be used in both stricter and looser senses. The stricter notion of relationship would entail that the author of one work derived material directly from the other composition, while the looser form would mean that the two merely express a similar viewpoint about the material that they share. Within the latter category there is room for several levels of relationship, ranging from close to remote. In this paper it will not be argued that the Temple Scroll and *Jubilees* are related in the stricter sense; the evidence suggests otherwise. Rather, it will be shown that they enjoy a kinship that is close but falls within the looser category.

The paper is divided into three sections. The first surveys the general positions which scholars have taken regarding the relationship of the scroll and *Jubilees*; the second explores the teachings of the two about calendrical issues; and the third examines their laws for festal sacrifices.

1. *Positions Regarding the Relationship between the Temple Scroll and Jubilees*

Y. Yadin offered no programmatic statement about the connections between the two compositions but in his introduction and notes to the scroll he referred to *Jubilees* far more frequently than to any other apocryphal or pseudepigraphic work. In fact, he mentions it with a frequency approaching that of some of the major texts from Qumran.[1] In a paragraph about 'The Scroll and the Qumran Sect', he remarked: 'Nor should we overlook the parallels—at times even *in ipsissima verba*—between the text of the scroll and the laws in the Book of Jubilees. . .'[2] Elsewhere, in a discussion of the columns which describe the scroll's series of firstfruits festivals, he wrote: 'The importance of these columns is also enhanced by the fact that their content establishes conclusively that the laws in the scroll are based on the calendar of the Book of Jubilees and of the Dead Sea Scrolls'.[3]

B.Z. Wacholder voiced a stronger, more specific theory about the issue of interrelations. In his *The Dawn of Qumran* he argued that the Temple Scroll, which he prefers to call 11Q Torah, was used by the author of *Jubilees* as 'a pillar of his own work'—a book from which he not only borrowed but which he also propagated as divine revelation from Sinai, as God's second *Torah*.[4] He based his claims on a fairly detailed comparison of the two texts on a variety of points, including some from the festal calendar.[5] When he wrote his book, Wacholder did not think, however, that the scroll presupposed the calendar which would later be described in *Jubilees* and some texts from Qumran.[6] More recently, he has changed his mind and proposed that *Jubilees* and the Temple Scroll, in that order, are two parts of a single composition.[7] He now finds that the new temple which figures in *Jub.* 1.27-29 prepares for the sanctuary which the scroll depicts in detail. The same, he thinks, may be said about the sacrificial data in *Jubilees*. Moreover, he holds that the end of *Jubilees* and the beginning of the Temple Scroll dovetail: '... the beginning of the legal section at [*Jub.*] 49.7 marks the proper beginning of 11Q Torah...'[8] Though he is not explicit about it, presumably he now believes that the two operate wth the same calendar.

Despite the detailed work of Yadin and Wacholder, it is fair to say that the only scholar who has published a systematic study of the relationship between the scroll and *Jubilees* is L. Schiffman. His work is distinctive in that he has made a full comparison of the two in a single area—their sacrificial laws.[9] In his essay he investigated their teachings about procedures and sacrifices for eleven cultic occasions and found that the two works disagree completely or partially for seven of them. On this basis he concluded that, though the two texts probably belonged to the world of thought from which the views of the Qumran sectaries emerged, each '... represents an independent view of the festal sacrificial cycle, based on exegesis of the Scriptural texts and a certain shared common heritage. There can be no possibility, however, of seeing the sacrificial codes of Jubilees as based on those of the *Temple Scroll*.'[10] Schiffman's essay will receive extended treatment in the third part of this paper.

These three experts have come to sharply diverging results concerning the relationship of the Temple Scroll and *Jubilees*. While Yadin and Wacholder, each in his own way, discovered the most intimate connections between them, Schiffman has separated them to an appreciable extent. In light of such disagreement, it should be useful to approach the question again. In the following pages the two compositions will be compared in the closely related areas of the calendar and sacrificial laws. It should be noted that by confining attention to these subjects one may be comparing the views of *Jubilees* with those of a source of the Temple Scroll and not, in the first instance, with those of the writer of the scroll. That is, A. Wilson and L. Wills have argued that the festal section (13.9–30.2) is distinguished from the remainder of the Temple Scroll not only by content but also by literary, linguistic, and stylistic traits.[11] Nevertheless, even if these columns were once an independent work, the fact that the author of the scroll incorporated them into his composition indicates that he accepted their teachings.

2. The Calendar

As noted above, Yadin concluded that the calendar underlying the festivals of the Temple Scroll was that of *Jubilees* and the Qumran texts. While the dating formulae for the first-fruits holidays constituted part of his evidence, it is important to remember, in light of the subsequent debate, that Yadin never claimed—either in the Hebrew or in the English edition of the scroll—that this conclusion was forced upon him by the evidence of the scroll alone. 'We might have failed to unravel the author's system had it not been for a tiny fragment fortunately discovered at Qumran, which lists the festivals by months and days. It reads: "on the twenty-second day of it (the sixth month) is the feast of oil (מועד השמן)."'[12] The only ancient Jewish calendrical system which could both accommodate the calendrical specifications of the scroll and locate the oil festival on 6/22 (= the sixth month, the twenty second day) is the 364-day arrangement of *Jubilees*.

Yadin's thesis received a forceful challenge from B. Levine.[13] He is not convinced, as Yadin had asserted, that the Temple Scroll is a sectarian document from Qumran, and in order to undermine Yadin's case he uses the issue of the calendar.[14] In his opinion, the dating specifications of the first-fruits holidays do not point to any particular calendrical system. They prescribe only that the festivals are to be observed on the day following the completion of a seven-week count from the previous one. As one is never told the day on which the count begins, one does not learn the day on which it ends.[15] He finds it significant that the author deleted the crucial yet notorious phrase ממחרת השבת when reproducing the words of Lev. 23.15. Surely the literal meaning of these words—Sunday—would have been important for the writer had he wished to emphasize that all of these holidays fell on Sunday.[16] Other ancient groups who later opposed the rabbinic calendar exploited this literal sense. 'The specific formulation of the Scroll's prescriptions for the "set times" is ambiguous and by no means compels us to conclude that the Scroll's author was operating on the Qumran-Jubilees calendar. All that is certain is that he is going further than the Torah in ordaining two additional *mô'ădîm*, each at the end of a 49-day cycle'.[17]

Though Wacholder initially echoed Levine's negative verdict,[18] it has not been generally accepted. J. Milgrom, in his rejoinder to Levine's review article,[19] noted that in 11QT 18.10-13 the word שבת

means literally 'sabbath' and שבתות תמימות refers to weeks which terminate on the sabbath day. Thus the 'morrow of the sabbath' would be Sunday. He also explains the omission of ממחרת השבת from this context by observing that once the words שבע שבתות תמימות were inserted into the citation of Lev. 23.15, an ambiguity regarding the meaning of שבת in the expression ממחרת השבת could have resulted, had the phrase been retained. That is, it might have implied that the sabbath under discussion was the one which followed the omer ceremony. 'To avoid this ambiguity, the term would have been deleted. Thus the omission of *mimmohŏrat haššabbāt* can be explained purely on stylistic grounds: it adds nothing but confusion.'[20]

Levine's essay, which does of course treat more topics than just calendrical ones, also elicited a lengthy response from Yadin himself.[21] He considered the issue worthy of debate because 'if the Scroll's calendar *is not* that of the Qumran sect, the Scroll *ipso facto* is not of this origin'.[22] Though his response to Levine's calendrical challenge covers several pages, the substance of his remarks can be condensed to a single point: he found much of Levine's argumentation irrelevant because he virtually ignored the key piece of evidence for Yadin's conclusion, viz. the Qumran fragment which dates the oil festival to 6/22.[23] That is, Yadin agreed that the scroll alone did not demand what he concluded; the fragment was decisive.

After summarizing the debate about the calendar presupposed in the Temple Scroll, a few clarifying comments are in order. The term *calendar* in discussions of this sort can be used in different senses. It can refer to a system which specifies the number and arrangement of days and months in a year, or it can signify a series of religious festivals which are dated to various points in a year.

If one limits the discusion to the problem of whether the scroll operates with the 364-day calendar best known from *Jubilees*—that is, the system in which each of the four parts of the year consists of three months of 30, 30 and 31 days respectively—then the solution is simple. The only logical answer is that the scroll does presuppose this system; no other arrangement accounts for all of the evidence. As Yadin reiterated, the calendrical fragment that Milik cited is the quintessential piece of the puzzle. Although this fragment does not belong to the Temple Scroll, it does constitute part of the calendrical writings from Qumran where copies of the scroll were found. And, as

Yadin has demonstrated at great length, there are many affinities
between the Temple Scroll and the major writings from Qumran. It
seems highly unlikely that the מועד השמן mentioned in the fragment
points to any other set time than the oil festival of the scroll. It is true
that the scroll does at times use the word יצהר in connection with this
holiday, but it also names the festival מועד יום הקרב שמן חדש (43.10)
and שמן is frequent in other references to it (יצהר: 22.16; 43.9; שמן:
21.14-16; 22 frg. 2.5, 6; 22.03, 05, 15). It is difficult to imagine what
other holiday the fragment could intend, since an oil festival is
attested neither in the Bible nor in rabbinic literature.

Once one accepts the inference that the oil festival of the Temple
Scroll was to be celebrated on 6/22, debate about the calendar that
underlies the document may cease because only in the 364-day
system of *Jubilees* and Qumran would one arrive at this date after
following all of the scroll's instructions about counting the intervals
between the omer ceremony and the harvest festivals of weeks (1/
26+50 = 3/15; 3/15+50 = 5/3; 5/3+50 = 6/22). If the scroll were
based upon the rabbinic calendar, which is attested only in later
sources, the oil festival would fall on approximately 6/17. One
implication of Yadin's solution is that in the Temple Scroll the phrase
ממוחרת השבת which is employed in connection with the festivals of
weeks, wine, and oil, has its literal sense—Sunday. Thus all of the
first-fruits festivals were to be celebrated on Sundays.[24]

Though there is virtually no room left for doubt that *Jubilees'*
yearly calendar underlies the Temple Scroll, the scroll and *Jubilees*
do differ significantly in the second sense of the word *calendar*, i.e., a
series of annual religious festivals. There are no discernible conflicts
for the dates of the holidays which are found in both texts, but the
festivals that are mentioned are hardly the same in both works:

Temple Scroll	Jubilees
1. first of the first month	1. first of the first month
2. days of ordination	2.
3. passover (1/14)	3. passover (1/14)
4. festival of unleavened bread (1/15-21)	4. festival of unleavened bread (1/15-21)
5. waving of the omer	5.
6. [second passover]	6.
7. festival of weeks	7. festival of weeks (3/15)
8.	8. first of the fourth month

9. festival of new wine	9.
10. festival of new oil	10.
11. days of the wood offering	11.
12. first of the seventh month	12. first of the seventh month
13. day of atonement (7/10)	13. day of atonement (7/10)
14. festival of tabernacles (7/15-22)	14. festival of tabernacles (7/15-22)
15.	15. first of the tenth month

Of the fifteen festivals which are named in the two works combined, the Temple Scroll mentions thirteen (if the second passover figured at the lost top of col. 18)[25] and *Jubilees* nine. The scroll includes the day of the omer waving and the first-fruits festivals of wine and oil as well as the days of ordination and of the wood offering. None of these occurs explicitly in *Jubilees*. It does, however, name four days of remembrance, only two of which are marked in the Temple Scroll. Such major deviations between the two texts have caused some scholars to raise the question of just how closely they can be related.

The differences are there and are undeniable, but it is more instructive to ask why they exist than simply to list them and conclude that two books so sharply divergent can hardly be closely related. A careful study of the lists of festivals in *Jubilees* and the Temple Scroll leads to the thesis that they differ, not because of some fundamental disagreement about cultic matters, but because of the simple fact that they are based upon different parts of the *Torah*. That is to say, *Jubilees* builds upon Genesis to mid-Exodus, while the Temple Scroll deals with the material from mid-Exodus through Deuteronomy. The particular parts of the pentateuch which underlie each book dictate which festivals are incorporated into them. *Jubilees* develops those holidays which are explicit or implicit in Genesis and the first part of Exodus; the Temple Scroll details those festivals which are explicit or implicit in the remainder of the *Torah*.

Before turning to the ample documentation for this thesis, it is worth noting that there are rather transparent indications in *Jubilees* that the absence of a festival from the book does not imply rejection of it or even disagreement about its importance. The omer holiday is a prime example. It is never mentioned in *Jubilees*, yet it would be absurd to claim that the author rejected it as a sacred occasion or that he was ignorant of it. After all, it is presented in Lev. 23.9-15 and Deut. 16.9, and the writer was thoroughly familiar with these two books of Scripture. Moreover, the dating of this holiday provided the unnamed starting point for calculating the proper time for his all-important festival of weeks. One should, therefore, search for an explanation that both accounts for the absence of the holiday from *Jubilees* and does not involve asserting that the author disagreed with the pentateuch and the Temple Scroll regarding it.

An obvious objection to the hypothesis that *Jubilees* elaborates festivals which are explicit or implicit in Genesis–mid-Exodus is that some of its holidays seem to have no biblical basis while others are introduced only later in the Bible in the legal parts of the pentateuch—that is, in chapters which appear after the narrative of *Jubilees* ends. In the following paragraphs it will be shown that, while the writer of *Jubilees* does introduce novelties into his biblical base, he does this only if the scriptural text supplies some stimulus for the new material.

A. *The Festivals in Jubilees*
1. *The Four Days of Remembrance* (1/1; 4/1; 7/1; 10/1)
The author ties these occasions to the story of the flood. Genesis itself mentions two of them (but not as holidays): 1/1 (Gen. 8.13) was the date on which the waters were dried from the earth and Noah looked out from the ark; and 10/1 (8.5) was the date on which the tops of the mountains became visible. *Jubilees* repeats and amplifies the biblical data. On 1/1 God told Noah to build an ark, and exactly one year later the land appeared (*Jub.* 6.25; 5.30); and on 10/1 the summits of the mountains became visible (5.30; 6.27). To these dates the writer adds 4/1 as the time when the openings of the depths closed (6.26; 5.29) and 7/1 as the occasion when these openings were unstopped so that the flood waters could flow down into them (6.26; 5.29).

The latter two dates seem to have resulted not only from considerations of symmetry but also from the results of calculation. The first of the fourth month was suggested by the facts that the flood began on 2/17 (Gen. 7.11; *Jub.* 5.23) and that the rains continued for 40 days and nights (Gen. 7.12, 17; *Jub.* 5.25). The rains would thus have ended on 3/27, just four days before the beginning of the second quarter of the year. The author arrived at the first of the seventh month also by reasoning from scriptural numbers. Gen. 7.24; 8.2-4 state that the 150-day period during which the waters prevailed upon the earth ended on 7/17 (cf. *Jub.* 5.27). By this date the water level had dropped far enough for the ark to settle atop a mountain. This implies that the process of abatement had begun before 7/17. Since 7/1 was the beginning of the third quarter of the year (and a holiday according to Lev. 23.23-25; Num. 29.1-6; Ezek. 45.18-19), it was the logical candidate for the time when the water began to recede. So, *Jub.* 6.26b reads: 'on the first of the seventh month all the openings of the earth's depths were opened, and the waters began to go down into them'.[26]

In this way the writer arrives at four symmetrical holidays for events during the year of the flood. Two were explicit in Genesis, and the other two could be derived from it by calculation. His calling them memorial days may have resulted from the name זכרון תרועה for the first of the seventh month in Lev. 23.24 (= 11QT 25.3; see *Jub.* 6.23-31). It is possible, moreover, that Gen. 8.22, which promises that 'while the earth remains, seedtime and harvest, cold and heat, summer and winter. . . shall not cease', contributed to the idea that these memorial days marked the beginnings of new seasons or parts of the year.[27]

2. *Jubilees' Festivals that are Found in the Legal Parts of the Torah*

Jubilees departs from the pentateuch by tracing to patriarchal times the festivals of weeks and tabernacles and the day of atonement. These, too, can be shown to be implicit in the text of Genesis.

a. *The Festival of Weeks*. This holiday, which is absent from Genesis but highly significant in *Jubilees*, was suggested to the author of the latter by several hints in the biblical text. One of the contexts in which he offers a precise date for the festival (3/15) is in the Abraham stories. *Jub.* 15.1 reads: '. . . in the third month, in the middle of the month—Abram celebrated the festival of the first-fruits of the wheat harvest'.[28] The book relates that Abraham and his household were circumcised (15.1-24) and also that Isaac was born (16.13) on that date. It would be simple to attribute these assertions to the author's familiar penchant for placing important events on key religious dates were it not for the fact that Genesis itself provides the apparent catalyst for his inference.

One reads in two places in Genesis that Sarah would give birth to a son one year in the future on the מועד (17.21; 18.14; 21.2 records that she did bear the child at that time). The word means something like 'specific time' in these passages,[29] but it is also a common term for special set times, i.e. festivals. And the Bible does include the festival of weeks among the מועדים (e.g. Lev. 23.2, 37; Num. 29.39). The author of *Jubilees* seized upon this possible sense of the term and concluded that Isaac was born on a festival. Yet, even if one granted that the biblical text could be construed as referring to a holiday in these passages one could still ask what warrant the writer found for selecting the festival of weeks as the occasion when so many other sacred times are also called מועדים. Again Genesis provides the answer. Gen. 18.10, 14 relate that the child was to be born כעת חיה (v. 14 identifies it with the מועד)—a phrase which *Jubilees'* author clearly understood as referring to springtime, the time of new life.[30] Weeks is celebrated, of course, in late Spring. He was hardly the only exegete who read the text in this way: Rashi, for example, interpreted it as connoting passover (see also *b. Rosh. Hash.* 10b).[31] Consequently, one may conclude theat the festival of weeks appears in *Jubilees* because the author saw hints of it in the text of Genesis.[32]

b. *The Festival of Tabernacles.* The scriptural authority for predating this holiday to patriarchal times is less transparent but it is there nevertheless. In its passages about the great festival of the seventh month. *Jubilees* highlights the joyous nature of the celebration. Biblical legislation stresses the same emotion (Lev. 23.40; Deut. 16.14, 15; Neh. 8.17; nominal and verbal forms of שמח are used). The happy circumstance to which *Jubilees* affixes the feast is the joy felt by Abraham after learning that he and his aged wife Sarah would become parents (*Jub.* 16.20, 25, 27, 29). Genesis does not employ forms of שמח in this context, but the same idea could be derived from the scriptural word for Abraham's reaction when he first heard the promise—ויצחק (Gen. 17.17; for Sarah's laughter, see 18.12; 21.3). More than one early exegete considered the laughter of Abraham to be different from that of Sarah. As Rashi commented:

> This word *wyṣḥq* Onkelos translated by *wḥdy* which signifies joy ('and he rejoiced') but *the similar verb* in the case of Sarah (*wtṣḥq* XVIII.12) *he translates* as meaning laughter. *From this* you may understand that Abraham had faith and rejoiced, and that Sarah

had no faith and sneered, and that is why God was angry with Sarah (when she laughed) but was not angry with Abraham.[33]

Jubilees is an earlier witness to this line of interpretation. Abraham's believing joy suggested to the writer that this auspicious occasion of happiness was the jubilant festival of tabernacles.

But why did he place Abraham's happiness and thus the holiday in the seventh month? This follows from the timing of Isaac's birth—3/15. If he was born at that time, then Sarah became pregnant in the sixth month of the preceding year (*Jub*. 16.12: 'in the middle of the sixth month'). *Jub*. 16.16 indicates that the angels who had earlier promised a son to the elderly couple returned in the seventh month and found Sarah pregnant. By the seventh month Sarah would have been aware of her condition; therefore, the expectant father and mother rejoiced greatly (16.19). A connection with the festival of tabernacles was not a difficult inference from these biblical givens.

c. *The Day of Atonement*. This solemn occasion appears to be under consideration in *Jub*. 5.17-18, although it is not mentioned by name. A fuller account appears in 34.12-19 where its origin is traced to the distress and grief experienced by Jacob when he was duped into thinking that Joseph had been killed. Genesis, of course, makes no reference to the day of atonement at this point, but the parallels between the situation in Gen. 37.31-35 and the description of the day in Leviticus 16 were too enticing for the author of Jubilees to resist associating them. On both occasions the biblical text speaks of the sins of Israel's sons (Gen. 37.18-28; Lev. 16.16, 19, 21); a goat is slaughtered (Gen. 37.31; Lev. 16.15; Num. 29.11); and the blood of the goat figures in the action (Gen. 37.31-33; Lev. 16.15, 18, 19).

Thus, in all cases in which *Jubilees* mentions a festival, it is named explicitly in the section of the *Torah* covered by the narrative of *Jubilees* (e.g. passover, unleavened bread in Exod. 12.1-20) or the writer was able to derive its existence in patriarchal times from data within this part of the biblical text (e.g. the festivals of weeks and tabernacles and the day of atonement). This entails that the absence of a religious holiday from *Jubilees* means only that the writer saw no warrant in Genesis–mid-Exodus for positing that it was known and practised by the fathers.

B. *The Festivals in the Temple Scroll*

The greater number of holidays in the scroll results from the fact that it builds upon those sections of the Torah which contain the calendars of festivals. Apart from the terse list in Exod. 23.12-17 and Ezekiel's unusual enumeration (45.18-25), all of the scriptural schedules of holidays are found in the latter parts of Exodus, in Leviticus, Numbers, and Deuteronomy. The author of the festal section of the scroll derived the rules for the days of ordination from Exodus 29 and Leviticus 8,[34] while most of his other festivals are drawn from the pentateuchal lists: passover, unleavened bread, the day for waving the omer, weeks, the first of the seventh month, the day of atonement, and tabernacles. Only the first of the first month, the first-fruits festivals of wine and oil, and the days of the wood offering remain to be explained.

That the first of the first month should be a special religious occasion could have been inferred from its position in the calendar; also, Num. 28.11, which mentions 'the beginnings of your months', could have contributed to its status. But, as Yadin has observed, the features of 1/1 as a holiday are drawn from the biblical descriptions of the first of the seventh month (see Lev. 23.23-25; Num. 29.1-6; Ezek. 43.18-19).[35] Consequently, the only holidays which are surprising for a composition based on the legal parts of the pentateuch are the two new festivals of weeks (wine and oil) and the days of the wood offering. Though they are not named in the *Torah*, it can be argued that at least the former two were derived from it by exegetical inference. The same is possible but less certain for the days of the wood offering.

1. *The Festivals of New Wine and Oil*

There is little doubt that the two new festivals of weeks are fashioned on the model of the original one of the third month (the method for dating them is exactly the same as for the holiday of the third month). The terms used in the scroll indicate what may have been the associative process that gave birth to the festivals of wine and oil. 11QT 43.3-10 employs the following words for the crops whose first-fruits are to be presented on each of the holidays: דגן (or דגן החטים), תירוש (or יין), and יצהר (or שמן). These nouns constitute a regular trio in the Pentateuch and elsewhere (Num. 18.12; Deut. 7.13; 11.14; 12.17; 14.23; 18.4; 28.51; 2 Kgs 18.32; 2 Chron. 31.5; 32.28; Neh.

5.11; 10.40 [Eng. v. 39]; 13.5, 12; Jer. 31.12; Hos. 2.10, 24 [Eng. vv. 8, 22]; Joel 1.10; 2.19; Hag. 1.11). דגן, תירוש, and יצהר are '. . . a conventional list of the basic products of Israelite agriculture and the staples of the people's diet'.[36] Some of the passages which mention these products could be read as implying that there were set times for presenting them. For example, Hos. 2.9 (Heb. v. 11) says: 'Therefore I will take back my grain in its time, and my wine in its season [במועדו];. . . ' Several passages also command that these be brought to the sanctuary (Deut. 18.4; Neh. 10.39 [Heb. v. 40]; etc.). It would have been a simple step to take if the author or his tradition had concluded that these scriptural notices entailed first-fruits holidays for wine and oil—those staples of agriculture and sacrifice—just as there was one for grain, the other member of the trio.

One of the contexts in which the scroll names these additional festivals is col. 43, where the writer treats the topic of the tithe. One of the biblical sections upon which he draws is Deut. 14.22-26. Within that pericope, one reads: 'Eat the tithe of your grain, new wine and oil. . . in the presence of the Lord your God at the place he will choose as a dwelling place for his name' (v. 23; cf. also 12.17-18). It appears likely that such scriptural givens and the natural harvest cycle in Israel—the grape harvest follows the grain harvest by approximately seven weeks and the olive harvest came some seven weeks after the grape harvest—provided the impetus for the new first-fruits festivals in the scroll.[37]

2. The Days of the Wood Offering

As Yadin indicated,[38] the biblical basis for the offering is Neh. 13.31; 10.35 (Eng. v. 34). In the former Nehemiah says: 'I provided for the wood offering, at appointed times, and for the first-fruits. Remember me, O my God, for good'. Yadin inferred from information in the scroll that it, unlike the other sources which mention bringing wood to the temple, bunches these 'appointed times' together from 6/23 (the day after the oil festival) through 6/29 (excluding the sabbath).[39] Nehemiah does not specify when the wood was to be furnished, but in the other reference to the practice one finds an intriguing note: 'We have likewise cast lots, the priests, the Levites, and the people, for the wood offering, to bring it into the house of our God, according to our fathers' houses, at times appointed, year by year, to burn upon the altar of the Lord our God, *as it is written in the law*' (10.34; italics added). It is not certain to how much of the verse the italicized words refer. They could be read as saying that burning upon the altar was in conformity with the divine law; or possibly they also intend the act of bringing wood. In the book of Nehemiah תורה should be the law of Moses, but if 10.34 claims that Mosaic legislation prescribes that wood be brought to the temple, then a problem arises because there is no pentateuchal command of this nature. Naturally, the elaborate sacrificial system presupposed that a large supply of wood was available, but no instructions are found for how and when it was to be transported to the sanctuary. Commentators often suggest that Lev. 6.5 (Eng. v. 12) is the nearest approximation: 'The fire on the altar shall be kept burning on it, it shall not go out; the priest shall burn wood on it every morning, and he shall lay the burnt offering in order upon it, and shall burn on it the fat of the peace offerings'. While the verse does refer to wood on the altar, it does not deal with the process of bringing it there.[40]

The exact authority in the *Torah* for the wood offering thus remains elusive. Yet it may be that the Judeans of Nehemiah's time thought they were bringing it in harmony with the law of Moses. Perhaps some other passages should also be considered in this context. Could those verses in which the Israelites are ordered to bring wood for the tabernacle have contributed to the idea of a wood offering and festival? Many parts of the tabernacle were constructed from wood, and when the people are told to supply building materials for them 'acacia wood' is named a number of times (see Exod. 25.5; 35.7—the wood is part of their תרומה [25.2-3; 35.5]).

In summary, then, the wood offering may be the only exception to the rule that the festivals in the Temple Scroll are derived from explicit or implicit statements in the material from mid-Exodus through Deuteronomy. It is intriguing that Nehemiah and his colleagues may have found it there, but where they might have located it cannot be determined now with any degree of certainty. In all other instances, however, a good case can be made that the author of *Jubilees* and the Temple Scroll include only those holidays that they found in the specific parts of the pentateuch with which they were dealing. For that reason it would be inappropriate to claim that, since the festivals which are cited in the two works are not all the same, their authors disagreed fundamentally. It is unlikely that the author of one drew directly from the work of the other, not because of conflicts between their views about festivals, but because they built upon different parts of the sacred text.

In concluding this section about the festival calendars in the two compositions, it is worth adding that the author of *Jubilees* may well have known of some of the additional holidays that figure in the scroll but not in his book. Yadin drew attention to the close similarities between 11QT 43.3-12 and *Jub.* 32.10-15. In both texts the cut-off points for eating the newly harvested products are the harvest periods for grain, wine and oil.[41] *Jubilees* does not designate specific times for these cut-off points, nor does it say anything about intervening periods of seven weeks; but the agricultural cycle of Israel reveals when these dates must have been. It is, therefore, likely that *Jubilees* knows of these first-fruits holidays. It is doubtful, however, that Yadin was correct in finding an echo of the wood offering in *Jub.* 21.13-14. The text does mention 'woods (that are used for) sacrifice' and that only certain kinds were to be brought onto the altar. But it lacks any reference to a wood offering or to times for bringing one.[42]

3. *The Festal Sacrifices*

In the first section of this paper it as noted that Schiffman has written the only truly systematic study of the relationship between the Temple Scroll and *Jubilees* in that he has analyzed all aspects of a single topic, namely, the laws about the sacrifices that were to be offered on the sundry cultic occasions of the sacred calendar. This is a natural subject for comparative study because both texts contain detailed statements about it. Moreover, as they agree about the calendar which underlies the schedule of religious holidays, one would expect agreement in this domain as well. Thus it comes as a surprise that Schiffman has found quite the opposite to be the case. From his study of the sacrificial laws for eleven cultic occasions he concluded that there are differences (partial or complete) in seven of them. The discrepancies and contradictions are of various kinds: sacrificial procedure, the number of animals offered on specific occasions, and the holidays celebrated.[43]

Before turning to the data, two remarks should be made about Schiffman's list. First, as he recognizes, there is simply too little evidence to justify firm conclusions in some areas that he compared.

That is, there may be insufficient information in *Jubilees*, or the text of the scroll may be too poorly preserved in the relevant places for making comparisons. He admits this for his third (sacrifice for the new month), eighth (wood offering), and tenth (day of atonement) items. It will be shown below that the first entry (the תמיד offering) should be added to this list. Second, some of the disagreements that he has isolated can be explained by the rule established above that the parts of the pentateuch with which *Jubilees* and the scroll work determine which festivals are named in each. Hence they should not be classified as disagreements. Items which fall under this heading are nos. 5 (the days of ordination), 7 (issues connected with the first-fruits festivals), and 9 (the day of remembrance). In the paragraphs that follow, these points will be elaborated briefly. Then a section will be devoted to those few remaining areas in which there is greater likelihood that Schiffman has spotted actual discrepancies or contradictions between the two documents.[44]

A. *Items for Which Too Little Comparative Evidence is Available*
Schiffman thinks there is in fact an adequate basis in the two works for determining whether the תמיד offering was financed from public or private funds (pp. 219-20). The Temple Scroll suggests that private funds were involved because in 13.14, a poorly preserved line,[45] it seems that the priest is allowed to keep the hide of the burnt offering—something that would be permissible only if he had contributed the animal. Yet, even if one accepts this as the proper reading (and that is uncertain), *Jubilees* should not be placed in opposition to it, since it does not address the issue. Schiffman adduces *Jub.* 6.14, which, through its use of plural pronouns, may imply that public funds were to meet the cost; there is no hint in the book, however, that private funding was thereby excluded. The question simply does not arise.[46]

The other three items which belong in this category can be treated briefly because there is no dispute about them. The new month festival appears in both works (11QT 14.2-8; *Jub.* 31.1, 3) but is handled differently. The *Jubilees* passage, which speaks only of 7/1, incorporates it into material from Genesis 35 and does not elaborate the rituals which might have been involved. The scroll follows Num. 28.11-15 and 15.1-3 and for that reason lists the sacrifices to be offered. The two are not sufficiently alike to compare (p. 221). It should be added that this is another instance in which *Jubilees* works with the first part of the *Torah* and the Temple Scroll with later sections.

The issue of the wood offering (no. 8) is also not in dispute. Schiffman correctly notes that 'it is difficult to compare this material [*Jub.* 21.12-13] with the laws in TS 23.1–25.1... since the two texts seem to be dealing with totally different matters' (p. 228). That is, as noted above, *Jubilees* does not mention a wood offering. Finally, his no. 10 (the day of atonement) fits here (pp. 229-30). The presentations of this day in the two sources are very different and are almost entirely conditioned by the parts of the pentateuch with which the authors are concerned.

B. *Different Festivals from Separate Scriptural Bases*

(No. 8 and to a certain extent no. 10 could be included here as well as in section A above.) If the four items in section A are subtracted from Schiffman's list, seven problem areas remain. Three of these may be eliminated, since they are products of the differing biblical foundations of *Jubilees* and the Temple Scroll, not of contradictions between the views of the authors.

No. 5 (the days of ordination) is a case in point. Schiffman compares 11QT 15.3–17.4 and *Jub.* 32.1-2. In the latter, Jacob ordains Levi in the seventh month; in the scroll, priestly ordination takes place in the first month. In *Jubilees* nothing is said about annual days of ordination, while the scroll prescribes a yearly observance. Moreover, the sacrifices which Jacob offers agree with neither the scroll's sacrifices for the days of ordination nor with the laws for the festival of tabernacles—the occasion to which Levi's investiture is tied (pp. 223-24). The differences are global, but the reason for this state of affairs is that *Jubilees*, like Genesis and the first part of Exodus, has no set days of ordination. Levi's case is unique. Here the writer makes no effort to remind the reader of the biblical passages which detail the process for ordaining priests—Exodus 29 and Leviticus 8—the very sections on which the scroll bases itself. *Jubilees*' narrative reaches neither of these chapters, and thus the occasion is not mentioned in it.

A second example is provided by the series of first-fruits holidays (no. 7). The scroll gives elaborate prescriptions for dating the three festivals of weeks and lists the sacrifices for them and for the omer ceremony in great detail. *Jubilees*, however, never alludes to the day for waving the omer and names only the festival of weeks as a holiday for first-fruits. The sacrifices which it does mention for this one celebration conflict with those of Lev. 23.18-20 (pp. 226-27). Schiffman writes: 'Comparison of the material in Jubilees with that of the *Temple Scroll* regarding this series of harvest festivals leaves one greatly in doubt as to any relationship' (p. 227). One can hardly dispute the facts, but the reason for them is again that the authors reproduced what they read or inferred from different parts of the pentateuch (see above, section 2.A.2.a and B.1).

The final example under this heading is the day of remembrance (no. 9; pp. 228-29). As explained above (2.A.1 and 2.B), the undeniable differences between *Jubilees* and the scroll regarding the first of the seventh month are caused by the fact that *Jubilees* attaches its treatment of it to the flood story which named or implied four days of remembrance, while the scroll follows the regulations of Num. 28.11-15; 29.1-6.

C. *Remaining Problems*
After the items in sections A and B are removed from Schiffman's list, difficulties remain in connection with nos. 4 (the first of the first month), 6 (passover), and 11 (tabernacles).

1. *The First of the First Month*
Schiffman has noticed a discrepancy between *Jub*. 7.1-2, in which Noah picks grapes from his vine in the seventh month of the fourth year of its growth but refrains from drinking the wine until 1/1 of the fifth year. The choice of 1/1 as the time from which new wine could be drunk conflicts, in his opinion, with the verdict of the Temple Scroll that new wine could be consumed only after the new wine festival on 5/3 (pp. 221-23). Nevertheless, it seems that two separate issues are involved here. *Jub*. 7.1-2 addresses the question of how long one should wait to enjoy wine from the fruit of a new vine, not with the annual issue of first-fruits. *Jubilees*' author, too, knows of the later cut-off date for new wine (32.12) which he places in 'the time for wine'. In Israel, this would hardly occur near the first of the first month. Noah's procedure, which does not serve as a precedent for an explicit law in *Jubilees*, simply indicates that what he did was in harmony with Lev. 19.23-25.[47]

A second problem in the same context has to do with the order in which the prescribed animals are sacrificed. *Jub.* 7.3-5 states that the goat is to be prepared first; some of its fat was to be placed on the meat upon the altar. Then that fat was offered with the bull, ram, and sheep. The texts agree about the animals involved, but for Schiffman *Jubilees* implies that although the goat was prepared first the others were actually offered before it. 11QT 14.11-18 is too filled with lacunae to allow certainty, but the general principle in the scroll is that the goat of the sin offering is first to be sacrificed completely. Only after this ritual is finished are the other animals offered (pp. 222-23). It is likely, however, that *Jubilees* intends the same arrangement. Nothing in 7.4-5 requires that the goat be handled in two stages, one before and one after the other victims. It is mentioned first in the account of the sacrifice and does not figure later in the section.

2. *Passover*
Here the specific issue on which Schiffman focuses is the segment of time during which the passover is to be sacrificed and eaten. He concludes from *Jub.* 49.10, 12, 19 that the lamb was slaughtered in the last third of Nisan 14 and eaten during the first third of the night of Nisan 15. Expressed in more familiar terms, the sacrifice took place between 2.00 and 6.00 p.m. and the meal between 6.00 and 10.00 p.m. After 10.00 p.m. the meat was considered נותר and was to be burned. The scroll differs in that it allows the passover to be eaten throughout the night (pp. 224-25). As a matter of fact, it may well be that *Jubilees* does not speak of the first third of the night but about the third part of the night (49.10, 12). Note v. 12: 'They will eat it during the evening hour(s) until the third part of the night. Any of its meat that is left over from the third part of the night and beyond is to be burned'. Also, 49.1 allows it to be consumed during the night at any time past sunset. Thus, *Jubilees* and the scroll appear to agree that the passover could be eaten at any time of the night (see 11QT 17.8).[48]

3. *The Festival of Tabernacles*
This is the only area in which Schiffman has uncovered incontrovertible differences between the festal sacrifices of *Jubilees* and the Temple Scroll. The two prescribe conflicting numbers of animals for

the sacrifices during this holiday. In order to make the evidence as clear as possible the victims listed in the two documents are given, as are the numbers for the same festival in the relevant parts of the Bible.

Jub. 16.22	*Jub.* 32.4	11QT 28.03-29.1	Num.29.13-34	Ezek.45.23-25
2 bulls	14 bulls	[13]-7 bulls	13-7 bulls	7 bulls
2 rams	28 rams	2 rams	2 rams	7 rams
7 sheep	49 sheep[49]	14 lambs	14 lambs	
1 goat	7 goats	1 goat	1 goat	1 goat

All of these texts also provide for cereal offerings, and all but Ezekiel mention libations. The first four texts also give rules for the sacrifices of the eighth day (see below). The numbers show that there is disagreement within *Jubilees* itself and that both of its sets of figures clash with those of the Temple Scroll which agrees with Num. 29.13-34. The Bible is also inconsistent in this regard, as the figures for Numbers and Ezekiel show.

The two lists in *Jubilees* are not so thoroughly different as they may appear. Furthermore, their disagreements with the numbers in the scroll are not large. The figures in *Jub.* 16.22 and 32.4 are, with one exception, related in a ratio of 1:7. The exception—the two rams of 16.22 and the 28 of 32.4—stand in a relationship of 1:14. Interestingly, the two rams of 16.22 agree with the numbers in the scroll and in Num. 29.13-34. This fact casts suspicion on the number *28* in *Jub.* 32.4. It appears that the higher figures in 32.4 are actually the totals for the seven days of the festival, not the sacrifices for each of the seven days. *Jub.* 32.6 is not inconsistent with this hypothesis because the statement that Jacob offered similar sacrifices every day is directly connected only to the supplementary peace offering. If it is the case that 16.22 gives the numbers of victims for each day while 32.4 provides the totals for the seven festal days, then the only problem in reconciling the two passages is the total of 28 rams in 32.4. The number is thus difficult in *Jubilees* and agrees with no other source. Hence, the numbers in *Jub.* 16.22 should be the ones compared with those of the Temple Scroll.

When one compares the figures in the two sources, the discrepancy in the numbers of bulls constitutes an obvious problem.[50] As a matter of fact, the number *14* in *Jub.* 32.4 is closer to what the scroll requires. The only other disagreement concerns the sheep or lambs. *Jubilees* calls for seven, but the scroll prescribes fourteen (*Jub.* 16.23

mentions seven sheep for the peace offering; 11QT 29.012 calls for seven on the eighth day). It is also possible that the numbers of animals sacrificed on the eighth day differ in *Jub.* 32.27 and 11QT 29.011-1. Nevertheless, *Jubilees* may not be saying that the very same numbers of animals as on the previous seven days were to be offered on the eighth day; it may be stating only that, as he had sacrificed animals on the first seven days, so Jacob engaged in the immolation of victims again on the eighth day.

Consequently, one must admit that a clear difference between *Jubilees* and the Temple Scroll exists in the one case of some of the numbers of animals to be offered during each day of the festival of tabernacles. In all other comparable passages in the two works, there are no differences of this kind. It may be that some numbers have been confused during the long history of transmission which *Jubilees* has endured, but there is no strong versional or manuscript evidence that errors occurred in the sections under discussion. One must also leave open the possibility that more such discrepancies would emerge if all parts of the Temple Scroll had survived and were legible (e.g. the animals to be slaughtered on the festival of weeks). But the most significant result of this section on the festal sacrifices is that, in the present state of our knowledge, the scroll and *Jubilees*, while not in perfect harmony, are extremely close to one another, as long as one recognizes that their authors were responding directly and primarily to different parts of the pentateuch.

Conclusion

Jubilees and the Temple Scroll operate with the same 364-day cultic calendar, never conflict with one another regarding festivals, and agree almost completely about sacrifices and procedures for their holidays. These conclusions demonstrate that the two are very closely related works, despite their sharply divergent character. Because of the nature of the scholarly discussion which has revolved about these issues, this paper has necessarily focused upon possible areas of conflict; but if one turned to the many specific instances in which the two compositions agree, the point would be further reinforced.[51] Does the evidence allow one to say, then, that they are related in the strict sense that one quotes from the other or borrows material directly from the other? It is not impossible, given their similarity in wording in some passages. But in general it seems more likely that, as exegetical works on two different parts of the *Torah*, they express the same line of thought. That is, the authors of the two are drawing upon the same exegetical, cultic tradition. The books are therefore related in the looser sense defined at the beginning of this paper.

In the first section of this essay it was noted that Wacholder has advanced the theory that Jubilees and the Temple Scroll are two parts of a single work—a second *Torah*, as it were. He observes that *Jubilees* 1, which provides the setting for the entire work—Moses on Sinai—builds upon Exodus 34, the very chapter from which the first column of the Temple Scroll quotes at length. Thus *Jubilees*, which covers the material in the first part of the pentateuch, ends (the latest scene in the book is the revelation to Moses at Sinai) where the Temple Scroll, which deals with the contents of the remaining parts of the *Torah*, begins. As a result, the two works recapitulate the five books of Moses.

While his theory has a certain appeal, it is not consistent with all of the evidence at hand and encounters some major problems. First, the pseudepigraphic situation is not the same in the two books. In *Jubilees* God speaks directly to Moses only in the first chapter; then, in chs. 2–50 an angel of the presence reveals the stories and laws to him. In the Temple Scroll, God speaks to Moses face to face and addresses him in the second person, unless the person of the biblical passage quoted is left unchanged.[52] This formal difference constitutes a telling objection to the unity of the two works. Second, Yadin is correct in arguing that the temple of the scroll (11QT 29.8-10) is one that the Israelites are to build; it is not the eschatological temple which God himself will construct. *Jub.* 1.17, 27, 29 also speak of the eschatological temple made by God, and it is, for that reason, not the one described in much of the remainder of the scroll.[53] And third, a discrepancy such as the one about the number of animals to be sacrificed during the festival of tabernacles serves as another indicator that the two compositions are not from the hand of the same author.

The data permit one to say that *Jubilees* and the Temple Scroll are indeed very closely related, but it is quite unlikely that the same priest composed both. The authors of the two books belonged to the same legal and exegetical tradition, but, not surprisingly, they disagreed about some details.

NOTES

1. *The Temple Scroll*, II, p. 478 (Heb.: II, p. 315).

2. *The Temple Scroll*, I, p. 398 (Heb.: I, p. 304). He then refers to 11QT 43.4-10 and *Jub.* 33.10-11 (an error for 32.10-11).

3. *The Temple Scroll*, I, p. 99 (Heb. I, p. 81).

4. *The Dawn of Qumran: The Sectarian Torah and the Teacher of Righteousness* (MHUC, 8; Cincinnati: Hebrew Union College, 1983), p. 62.

5. *The Dawn*, pp. 41-62.

6. *The Dawn*, pp. 53-60.

7. 'The Relationship Between 11Q Torah (The Temple Scroll) and the Book of Jubilees: One Single or Two Independent Compositions?', *SBLSP* (1985), pp. 205, 207-16.

8. 'The Relationship', p. 213.

9. The Sacrificial System of the *Temple Scroll* and the Book of Jubilees', *SBLSP* (1985), pp. 217-33.

10. 'The Sacrificial System', p. 233.

11. 'Literary Sources of the *Temple Scroll*', *HTR* 75 (1982), pp. 275-88.

12. *The Temple Scroll*, I, p. 117. Apart from a minor change or two and insertion of the word *fortunately*, the English simply reproduces the original Hebrew statement (Heb.: I, p. 95). For the text of the fragment to which Yadin refers, see J.T. Milik, 'Le travail d'édition des manuscrits du Désert de Juda' (VTSup, 4; Leiden: Brill, 1957), p. 25.

13. 'The Temple Scroll: Aspects of its Historical Provenance and Literary Character', *BASOR* 232 (1978), pp. 5-23. His calendrical discussion occupies pp. 7-11.

14. 'The Temple Scroll', p. 7.

15. 'The Temple Scroll', p. 9.

16. 'The Temple Scroll', pp. 9-10.

17. 'The Temple Scroll', p. 11.

18. *The Dawn*, pp. 53-55.

19. '"Sabbath" and "Temple City" in the Temple Scroll', *FASOR* 232 (1978), pp. 25-27.

20. '"Sabbath" and "Temple City"', p. 26. Yadin (*The Temple Scroll*, I, pp. 103-104 [Heb.: I, pp. 84-85]) had suggested that the phrase was used in the lost upper part of col. 18 in the section about the omer ceremony and that the author therefore felt no need to repeat it here. J. Baumgarten ('The Calendar of the Book of Jubilees and the Temple Scroll', *VT* 37 [1987], pp. 71-78) has also opposed Levine's conclusion. He adduces three considerations which, on his view, make it unlikely that the count for the dating of the first-fruits festivals in the scroll duplicated the rabbinic procedure of beginning on the first day of the festival of unleavened bread. First, the scroll

deals with the omer ceremony after the seven days of passover. Second, the later Christian groups which adhered to a similar pentecontad scheme for the first-fruits festivals ended their counts on Sundays. And third, it would be difficult to account for the high esteem in which the scroll was held at Qumran if it reflected a divergent practice in this important area. He agrees with Yadin that the *Jubilees*/Qumran calendar is presupposed in the scroll and thinks the author of *Jubilees* was aware of the pentecontad arrangement. The fact that *Jubilees* does not elaborate the details of the 49-day counts is related to the purpose of the work (promotion of the writer's solar calendar and strict observance of the sabbath). Baumgarten has rightly noted that the differing purposes of the authors of *Jubilees* and the scroll are important for evaluating the relationships between the compositions. This is a point that has not been properly appreciated.

21. 'Is the Temple Scroll a Sectarian Document?', in G. Tucker and D.A. Knight (eds.), *Humanizing America's Iconic Book: Society of Biblical Literature Centennial Addresses 1980* (SBL Biblical Scholarship in North America, 6; Chico, California; Scholars Press, 1982), pp. 153-69. His discussion of the calendar is found on pp. 162-67.

22. 'Is the Temple Scroll a Sectarian Document?', p. 163.

23. 'Is the Temple Scroll a Sectarian Document?', pp. 166-67. Levine did mention the fragment in question once ('The Temple Scroll', p. 8) without elaborating on it. He also cited the Hebrew for it in p. 21 n. 6, again without comment. For a similar but shorter statement from Yadin, see *The Temple Scroll*, I, p. 407.

24. If one doubts the validity of using an unpublished fragment from one document in identifying the calendar of another (here, the Temple Scroll), it may be helpful to recall that something similar led to the correct understanding of the calendar in *Jubilees*. Though its system is now crystal clear, none of the scholars who worked with the problem before the Qumran discoveries was successful in unraveling all its details. Information from the scrolls that were known in the late 1940s and early 1950s provided the impetus for understanding the full arrangement. See A. Jaubert, 'Le calendrier des Jubilés et de la secte de Qumrân', *VT* 3 (1953), pp. 250-64; contrast he ' sure grasp of the data with an earlier attempt such as that of L. Finkelstein, 'The Book of Jubilees and the Rabbinic Halaka', *HTR* 16 (1923), pp. 40-45.

25. This was Yadin's suggestion (*The Temple Scroll*, I, pp. 99-100 [Heb.: I, p. 82]).

26. All citations from *Jubilees* are taken from my forthcoming edition and annotated translation of the book. Biblical quotations are from the RSV.

27. Rashi interpreted Gen. 8.22 as referring to six seasons, beginning with the second half of Tishri. See M. Rosenbaum and A.M. Silbermann, *Pentateuch with Targum Onkelos, Haphtoroth and Rashi's Commentary*, Vol.

I: *Genesis* (London: Shapiro, Vallentine, 1929), p. 36.

28. The date of 3/15 for the festival of weeks can also be deduced from 44.1-5. Cf. 14.17-20; 17.1; 22.1.

29. BDB, p. 417.

30. See, too, BDB, p. 312; '*at the time* (when it is) *reviving*, the spring'. The editors also cite 2 Kgs 4.16-17, where the same phrase is used twice, both times with מוֹעֵד.

31. Rosenbaum and Silbermann, *Pentateuch*, p. 72. Rashi is here explicating Gen. 18.10.

32. The author of *Jubilees* dates two other covenants to the third month (not to 3/15 specifically) on the basis of scriptural indications. The sinaitic covenant (see *Jub.* 1.1) became associated with the third month and thus with the festival of weeks because of the notice in Exod. 19.1 that the Israelites had entered the wilderness of Sinai at this time. Biblical dates also seem to have implied the third month for Noah's covenant, since he and the other survivors left the ark on 2/27 (or possibly shortly thereafter; see Gen. 8.14-19; *Jub.* 6.1 has the humans debarking on 3/1). The pact with Noah was concluded just after this (Gen. 8.20–9.17; *Jub.* 6.4-22).

33. Rosenbaum and Silbermann, *Pentateuch*, p. 68.

34. Yadin, *The Temple Scroll*, I, p. 93 (Heb.: I, p. 77).

35. *The Temple Scroll*, I, pp. 89-90 (Heb.: I, pp. 74-75). Note also Exod. 40.2

36. F.I. Andersen and D.N. Freedman, *Hosea* (AB, 24; Garden City: Doubleday, 1980), p. 242.

37. Yadin (*The Temple Scroll*, I, p. 86 [Heb.: I, p. 72]) seems to think that these additional holidays were known to Nehemiah and deduced from divine law. Milgrom ('First Fruits, OT', *IDBSup*, p. 337) makes the same suggestion. For Neh. 10.33-35 and 13.31, see section 2.B.2 in this paper. Cf. also Baumgarten, '4Q Halakah[a] 5, the Law of Ḥadash, and the Pentecontad Calendar', *JJS* 27 (1976), pp. 36-46 (reprinted in his *Studies in Qumran Law* [SJLA, 24; Leiden: Brill, 1977], pp. 131-42). He points to Exod. 22.28 (Eng. v. 29) as a possible biblical base. In the rendering of Targum Pseudo-Jonathan to this passage, wine is a legal kind of first-fruit offering.

38. *The Temple Scroll*, I, pp. 124, 128 (Heb.: I, pp. 100, 103).

39. *The Temple Scroll*, I, pp. 122-124, 130-31 (Heb.: I, pp. 99-100, 105-106).

40. See L.W. Batten, *The Books of Ezra and Nehemiah* (ICC: New York: Charles Scribner's Sons, 1913), p. 378; J.M. Myers, *Ezra–Nehemiah* (AB, 14; Garden City: Doubleday, 1965), pp. 179-80. Note also R. North's comment: 'The wood offering is indeed unusual, but sufficiently virtual in Lv 6.12' (*JBC*, p. 438). Cf. also Yadin, *The Temple Scroll*, I, pp. 128-30 (Heb.: I, pp. 103-105), where he cites later sources which deal with the wood offering.

41. *The Temple Scroll*, I, pp. 114-15 (Heb.: I, pp. 92-93). See also Baumgarten, 'The Calendar of the Book of Jubilees and the Temple Scroll', p. 75.

42. *The Temple Scroll*, I, p. 124 (Heb.: I, p. 100). Wacholder (*The Dawn*, p. 53) likewise saw a reference to the wood offering in *Jubilees* 21.

43. 'The Sacrificial System', pp. 217-33.

44. In this section, the page numbers in Schiffman's essay will be indicated within parentheses in the text.

45. See Yadin, *The Temple Scroll*, II, pp. 52-54 (Heb.: II, p. 40-41).

46. Schiffman himself is uncertain ('The Sacrificial System', p. 220) because, as he notes, 13.17 uses a plural verb.

47. Cf. the discussion of the *Jubilees* passage in Finkelstein, 'The Book of Jubilees', pp. 52-53.

48. For the text, see Yadin, *The Temple Scroll*, II, p. 74 (Heb.: II, p. 55). All of the letters of בלילה are uncertain.

49. In both passages in *Jubilees*, the lists of victims are supplemented by specifications for peace offerings. The biblical passages do not mention anything similar. The peace offering in *Jub.* 16.22-23 includes the same numbers and kinds of animals as the sin offering of Hezekiah in 2 Chron. 29.21. *Jub.* 32.4, whose numbers may in some way be affected by the fact that tithes are under discussion, reports that Abraham also sacrificed twenty-one he-goats. Their function is not clear, and they are named in no other list. The numbers *7* (goats) and *21* (he-goats) in *Jub.* 32.4 are actually emendations from *60* and *29* respectively. The emendations are, however, almost certainly correct, since they follow the readings of the Latin version and involve simple confusions (see H. Rönsch, *Das Buch der Jubiläen oder die Kleine Genesis* [Leipzig: Fues (R. Reisland), 1874 (reprinted: Amsterdam: Rodopi, 1970)], p. 147). The numbers of bulls given for the Temple Scroll (the *13* is reconstructed) and Numbers 29 indicate that the total is lowered by one for each succeeding day of the first seven days in the festival of tabernacles.

50. MS 20, one of the oldest and best Ethiopic copies of *Jubilees*, reads *seven* rather than *two* bulls.

51. As examples, mention may be made of the fact that both texts, unlike the pentateuch, legislate that all males of twenty years and above celebrate the passover. The scroll's comments about the eschatological temple (not the structure described in the second half of the text) are helpful for understanding what *Jub.* 1.17, 27, 29 say about the sanctuary of the new age. There are many more examples of this kind.

52. Cf. Yadin, *The Temple Scroll*, I, pp. 71-73 (Heb.: I, pp. 60-62).

53. *The Temple Scroll*, I, pp. 182-87 (Heb.: I, pp. 140-44).

PART IV

THE LAW, THE LEVITES AND THE SADDUCEES

THE TEMPLE SCROLL
AND THE SYSTEMS OF JEWISH LAW
OF THE SECOND TEMPLE PERIOD

Lawrence H. Schiffman

New York University

The discovery of the Temple Scroll and its subsequent publication by the late Professor Yigael Yadin[1] has provided us with a gold mine of information pertaining to the views of its author(s) on Jewish law, what the Rabbis later termed *halakhah*. This scroll of sixty-six columns, larger than the great Isaiah Scroll (fifty-four columns), covers numerous topics in Jewish law. When first unrolled, and in the publications of Professor Yadin, it was assumed that this text testified to the traditions of the same group usually termed the Qumran sect, identified by most scholars with the Essenes (a matter about which we have elsewhere raised questions).[2] Beginning soon after publication, a series of articles, to which this writer also contributed, took issue with this point, arguing that the Temple Scroll did not accord with various teachings of the better-known Dead Sea sect and that it had to be considered as emerging from a closely related, but different group.[3] It was also argued that the existence of a text in the sect's library did not indicate its provenance. In fact, we are only now realizing the extent to which the library at Qumran was eclectic. At the meeting of the International Organization for the Study of the Old Testament in Jerusalem, Israel, Professor Hartmut Stegemann masterfully laid to rest the claim of Qumran sectarian authorship for the Temple Scroll.[4]

The Redaction of the Text

There can be no question that the Temple Scroll was created by an author/redactor who incorporated certain preexistent sources into his composition. Certainly among these sources is the sacrificial calendar of 11QT 13-29 and the Law of the King of 11QT 56-59. A.M. Wilson and L. Wills have also argued for the separate origin of the purity laws of 48-51, a proposal as yet unconfirmed by our research,[5] but supported by H. Stegemann. The author/redactor sought to compose a complete *Torah* which would expound his views of the sanctity of the Temple, land and people, as well as of the ideal government and society. He began with the command to build a sanctuary in Exodus 34-35 and worked through the *Torah*, arranging all the pertinent material around the first occurrence of a topic. In this way he reedited and reredacted the pentateuchal legislation, often making use as well of material from the Prophets and the Writings. At the appropriate places he inserted the preexistent collections at his disposal. To give the impression that his *Torah* was a complete Law, he appended at the end a selection of laws from Deuteronomy, some of which deal only tangentially with the theme of his scroll. This collection is simply a paraphrase of Scripture. It may itself stem from an 'expanded *Torah* scroll' or Deuteronomic scroll, as suggested by Stegemann.

Yet this final author/redactor was not just a collector of scattered traditions. On the contrary, despite a few lapses, such as his treatment of the laws of war from Deuteronomy 20 in both the Law of the King (11QT 58.3-21) and in the Deuteronomic paraphrase (11QT 61.12-62.16), the redactor is both organized and consistent. He has carefully integrated his sources into his own composition. He presents materials which embody a consistent method of biblical exegesis, itself based on a particular 'theology' of law, as well as a consistent view of holiness and sanctity. Further, the nature of his subtle polemic is such that it runs like a thread throughout the entire composition. This consistency of approach means that we can examine his final product to determine what circumstances would have led him to include various materials in is work, just as we may ask what conditions may have led the author of these sections to have composed them. It goes without saying that we may ask similar questions regarding those portions of the scroll which are the compositions of the author/redactor.

'Theology' of Law

One of the fundamental issues in Second Temple Judaism was that of how to incorporate extra-biblical traditions and teachings into the legal system, and how to justify them theologically. Despite the fact that in antiquity and late antiquity there was little theoretical theological inquiry in Judaism (except in the Hellenistic Diaspora), issues of theology were of central importance and often lie behind other more clearly expressed disputes.

All Jewish groups in the Second Temple period endeavored to assimilate extra-biblical teachings into their way of life. Our detailed examination of the writings of the Dead Sea (Qumran) sect has led us to determine that they did so through the concept of the נגלה ('revealed') and נסתר ('hidden'). That which was revealed was the simple meaning of Scripture and the commandments which were readily apparent from it. These were known to all Jews. Only the sect possessed the hidden knowledge, discovered by it through what it saw as inspired biblical exegesis, regularly conducted by members of the sect. Tradition is regarded as having no authority, since all Israel has gone astray and the true way has only been rediscovered by the sect's teacher. The laws which emerged from this interpretation were eventually composed in סרכים, lists of sectarian laws. These were then redacted into such collections as the Zadokite Fragments (Damascus Document) or the less organized 'Ordinances' (4Q 159, 513, 514). These rules and the interpretations upon which they were based served to make clear the application of the Law of the *Torah* to the life of the sect, and to make possible life in accord with the 'revealed' *Torah* in the present, pre-Messianic age.[6]

Although we do not have Pharisaic texts from this period, we can suggest the general lines of the approach of this group based on later accounts in the New Testament, the writings of Josephus and on the reports in the even later tannaitic corpus. Apparently, the Pharisees possessed traditions 'handed down by the fathers' and 'unwritten laws'. These included various legal traditions of great antiquity as well as interpretations of the biblical texts. Indeed, the Pharisees were known as expounders of the *Torah* and seem to have excelled in the application of the laws of the Pentateuch to their own circumstances and times. Somewhat later, the successors to the Pharisees, the *tannaim* (teachers of the *Mishnah*) would develop the notion that these traditions had been revealed by God to Moses on Sinai as a second *Torah*. The Rabbis asserted that God had given two *Torot* to Israel, the written and the oral. For the Rabbis, this view essentially elevated tne oral *Torah* to a sanctity and authority equal to that of the written. Yet evidence does not point to such an assertion on the part of the Pharisees themselves, although our sources do not allow us to be certain.[7]

The Sadducean approach has yet to be properly investigated. The general claim that the Sadducees were strict literalists represents a misunderstanding of their approach often predicated on late rabbinic sources and on a parallel misunderstanding of the medieval Karaite movement. In any case, we should note that the Sadducees apparently saw only the written Law as authoritative, although they admitted the need to interpret it. Their interpretations attempted to adhere as closely as possible to the plain meaning (what the Rabbis later called פשט) of Scripture. We will return below to the question of whether certain Sadducean views can be culled from the Qumran corpus.

Against this background we can now understand the approach of the author/redactor of the Temple Scroll. He seeks to assimilate extra-biblical traditions by the contention that his new, rewritten *Torah* properly expresses the will of God as revealed in the original document. He asserts that the correct meaning of the divine revelation at Sinai, apparently left vague in the canonical *Torah*, is to be found in the Temple Scroll. This means that like the sectarians of Qumran he has no dual *Torah* concept. Unlike this group, he does not accept the notion of a continuous, inspired revelation through biblical exegesis. He maintains only a one-time revelation, at Sinai. In this respect he agrees with the later *tannaim*, except that for them the one-time revelation is of two *Torot*, yet for him it is of a single *Torah*, the true contents of which are expressed in the scroll he authored and redacted.

Dating and Historical Background

The key to the dating of the Temple Scroll as a whole must be the Law of the King (11QT 56.12–59.21). This section, one of the sources used by the author/redactor, represents the most sustained example of original composition, as opposed to the rewriting of Scripture, in the entire document. Here are found the clearest references to specific historical events.

Elsewhere, in a detailed study of the Law of the King, we have concluded that both the legal and historical aspects of this material all point to a Hasmonean dating.[8] At this time, the author of the Law of the King sought a complete reformation of the existing structures of the temple and its cult, as well as of the governmental system. Both extant copies of the Temple Scroll are Herodian. Yet the scroll in the hands of J. van der Ploeg should be dated to the mid-first century BCE. We must, of course, allow for composition. The palaeographic evidence, therefore, supports the notion that the scroll was composed in the Hasmonean period. Since the text reflects the historical experience of the Hasmoneans Jonathan (160–143 BCE) and John Hyrcanus (135–104 BCE), we must see the composition of the Law of the King as taking place no earlier than the second half of the reign of John Hyrcanus, termed king by Josephus.[9] He is the first of the Hasmoneans to have consolidated a stable empire.

Yet we must account for two levels of composition: (1) that of the Law of the King, and (2) its redaction into the complete scroll. The completed scroll had to be composed either at the end of the rule of John Hyrcanus, or early in the reign of Alexander Jannaeus. We would accordingly date the composition of the scroll as it now survives to c. 110–90 BCE, a date closely agreeing with that proposed by a number of distinguished colleagues.[10]

The Scroll and Contemporary Jewish Law

In a paper delivered at the Dead Sea Scrolls Conference sponsored by the Polish Academy of Sciences, held in June 1987 in Mogilany, near Krakow, we systematically explored the relationship of the Temple Scroll to four major corpora of Jewish legal tradition, the group of sectarians from Qumran, the circles which produced the book of *Jubilees*, the Sadducees, and the Pharisaic-rabbinic tradition. For each corpus to be compared, one representative area of law was selected.

The laws of oaths and vows which occur in both the Temple Scroll (53.9-54.7) and in the Zadokite Fragments (16.6-13) were studied to test the relationship of the Qumran corpus to the Temple Scroll. What emerged is the complete incongruity of the treatments so that it is almost superfluous to ask if the texts agree or not. What we observe is a totally different agenda, a different literary form and exegetical method, and results which disagree. At the same time, some few details, often of great importance, are found to agree. An example is the discouragement of vows by both texts. But let us not forget that vows were discouraged also by rabbinic tradition later on.[11] This example, we may add, is typical for the few areas of law in which sustained comparisons are possible between the Temple Scroll and materials attributed to the Qumran 'sect'.

The comparison of *Jubilees* and the Temple Scroll was undertaken by studying the sacrificial festival calendar of the Temple Scroll (13.10–29.10).[12] This section of the scroll reviews all the required sacrifices for the daily and festival offerings, including some festivals not explicitly known from other sources. One cannot speak of consistent agreement in matters of Jewish law between the Temple Scroll and the book of *Jubilees*. When the texts agree, it may be because of commonly held traditions, or because the authors or their teachers followed similar exegetical techniques regarding the same biblical texts.

The calendar found in the book of *Jubilees*[13] has often been identified with the Sadducees. Actually, tannaitic sources attribute this calendar to the Boethusians[14] who were in some way related to the Sadducees, although our sources are not clear regarding this sect. Apparently the Boethusians, like the Qumran sect, began counting the fifty-day *'omer* period on the Sunday after the last day of the festival of Passover, so that Shavuot fell in their calendar on a Sunday, in accord with the literalist interpretation of Lev. 23.11, ממחרת השבת. This calendar was also used by the Qumran sect. The text of the Temple Scroll, when understood properly, is here in accord with the later rabbinic calendar, also attested in certain prayer texts from Cave 4, and does not agree with the Boethusian calendar nor that of the Qumran sect.[15]

By the destruction of the Temple in 70 CE, the Pharisees had passed their legacy on to the tannaim, the teachers of the *Mishnah*. It is therefore instructive to compare the *halakhah* of tannaitic sources with the laws of the Temple Scroll. The Temple Scroll lists various classes of people excluded from the temple and its precincts (11QT 35.1-8; 39.5-9; 45.7-18). A similar classification is undertaken by the *tannaim*. Regarding several classes of people, the Temple Scroll maintains stringent rulings unknown in tannaitic legislation. Some of those allowed by the tannaim into the Levitical camp, are here excluded from the middle court of the temple.

On the other hand, there is substantial agreement with the tannaitic sources about those excluded from the scroll's inner court, parallel to the tannaitic camp of the Divine Presence.[16] The author of the Temple Scroll sought to extend the sanctity of the sanctuary by extending the rules for the Levitical camp, the Temple Mount, to his entire sanctuary. Thus, he expanded the stringency of the purity laws along with the architectural plan of the *temenos*.

This brief survey has demonstrated that it is impossible to show direct correspondence between the Temple Scroll and the other systems of Jewish law as known from the available sources. Yet new data may allow us to suggest a possible provenance for some of the laws included in the Temple Scroll.

The 4Q Miqṣat Maʿaseh Ha-Torah

Recently, there has come to light the so-called 'halakhic letter', 4Q *Miqṣat Maʿaseh Ha-Torah*, abbreviated as 'MMT'.[17] This text has opened up a valuable window on the sectarian constellation of the period immediately following the Maccabean revolt. (I thank Professor John Strugnell for allowing me the opportunity to read it and to comment on the draft of the commentary he and Dr Elisha Qimron are preparing.) The text is preserved in six manuscripts. It is essentially a letter, either actual or 'apocryphal', which purports to be from the leaders of the sect to the leaders of the priestly establishment in Jerusalem. The author lists some twenty laws in which the writers disagreed with the temple priests and their procedures. The views of the authors are usually introduced with אנחנו חושבים, 'we are of the view that. . . ', and the polemical nature of the material is evident in the use of ואתם יודעים, 'and you well know'. We shall examine here the various regulations of this text in some detail, paying close attention to those sections where the text of MMT may be compared with that of the Temple Scroll. The following is a catalogue of the 'halakhic' regulations contained in this document.

B 3-5	Prohibition against non-Jews bringing תרומה to the temple
B 5-8	Prohibition of cooking חטאת offerings in copper vessels, with additional fragmentary provisions
B 8-9	Prohibition of accepting sacrifices from non-Jews
B 9-13	Prohibition on leaving the תודה offering of שלמים to be eaten on the following day

B 13-17 Purification of those who prepare the red heifer, including rejection of the concept of טבול יום

B 18-20 Prohibition of bringing skins of animals to the temple

B 21-22 Law referring to skins and bones of unclean animals

B 22-23 Impurity of one who carries skin and bones of the carcass of a clean animal

B 23   Prohibition of שחיטת חולין in Jerusalem

B 23-29 Definition of מחנה

B 30-33 Prohibition of the slaughter of pregnant animals

B 34-44 Prohibitions on 'entering the congregation'

B 44-49 Prohibition on entering the temple by blind and deaf

B 50-53 The law of נצוק (liquid streams)

B 53-57 Prohibition of bringing dogs to Jerusalem, with definition of the מחנה

B 57-58 Fruit of the fourth year to be given to priests

B 58-59 Tithes of cattle and sheep to be given to priests

B 59-67 The purification of the מצורע, including rejection of the concept of טבול יום

B 67-69 Impurity of human bones

B 70-77 Marriage of priests

Of these regulations, a few have no parallel in the Temple Scroll. B 3-5 and 8-9 deal with limitations on the acceptance of תרומה and other sacrifices from non-Jews. This matter is not even alluded to in the extant portions of the Temple Scroll. The *tannaim* did permit non-Jews to bring such offerings. The use of copper vessels in the preparation of חטאת offerings is not raised in the Temple Scroll.

J.T. Milik has published a sentence from a purity law he termed 4Q Mišn[a].[18] This is actually a quotation from the MMT. It provides that if a liquid is poured from a pure vessel into an impure vessel, the impurity can flow back through the stream of liquid so as to render the vessel from which it is being poured impure. This is termed נצוק (literally 'that which is [or was] poured out') in tannaitic terminology. Indeed, the very same view is attributed to Sadducees in tannaitic sources and is disputed by the Pharisees (*m. Yad.* 4.7). This law, however, has no parallel in the Temple Scroll.

The rule of MMT B 70-77 which prohibits priests from marrying women who are not daughters of priests has no parallel in the Temple Scroll. Yet the use of וא[תם יודעים] makes this appear polemical. We know that the *tannaim* would not have agreed with this law.

In a number of cases the Temple Scroll provides a partial parallel to the MMT. B 9-13 is a prohibition on leaving the meat of a שלמים sacrifice offered as a תודה, for thanksgiving, over to the next day. Rather, the meal offering, fats (חלבים) and meat must all be offered on the same day it is sacrificed. This law is derived from Lev. 7.15. The Temple Scroll does not contain a direct reference to this offering. The closest parallel is a passage in the sacrificial calendar, 11QT 20.11-13. Yet it must be noted that the entire sacrificial calendar avoids the term שלמים, 'presentation offering', although it appears elsewhere in the scroll. This passage refers to the sacrifices for the festival of new oil. From the text it is clear that this is, in procedural terms, a שלמים offering.

The Temple Scroll states, ביום ההוא תא[כל] [ולוא תבו]א ע]ליו[השמש (20.12-13). Rabbinic law understood the *Torah* to permit the eating of such offerings until morning, but the *tannaim* added the restriction that they be eaten before midnight to make sure that accidental transgression would not occur (*m. Ber.* 1.1; cf. *m. Zebah* 6.1). How, then, do we understand the Temple Scroll? Apparently the scroll understood the verse as providing that the offering had to be eaten by sunset, but then (in accord with the rest of Lev. 7.15) there was a grace period for disposing of the נותר, the leftover offering, and this was until the following dawn. MMT, as noted by the editors, takes the same view. The authors' opponents were postponing the eating, believing it could continue until morning. The authors (אנחנו חושבים) call for observance of the same view found in the Temple Scroll.

Twice, in B 13-17 and 59-67, the MMT rejects the idea of טבול יום. The Temple Scroll requires that those who have undergone purification rituals, including immersion, be considered totally impure on the last day of their impurity until sundown. This ruling, repeated several times (11QT 45.7-8; 49.19-21; 51.4-5), is in accord with the view of the Sadducees who denied the Pharisaic category of טבול יום.[19] The Pharisees allowed one who has already immersed and performed all necessary purification rituals to come into contact with pure food outside of the sanctuary before the end of his purification period at sunset. In this case, MMT, the Temple Scroll and the Sadducean view coincide.

But what of the details of these very same laws? The Temple Scroll does discuss the requirement of waiting until sunset (49.19-21) but it does not discuss the laws pertaining to those who prepare the ashes of the red heifer (B 13-17). Regarding the מצורע, MMT and the Temple Scroll agree that they are excluded from the entire temple complex (מחנה). Tannaitic law agreed with that of the Temple Scroll and MMT that they were to be kept outside of the city.[20] Yet MMT claims that in actual practice they were being permitted to enter the temple (בית). Perhaps what is at stake here is some detail of the law, according to which the authors considered a disease to be צרעת while their opponents, the Jerusalem establishment, did not. The MMT goes on to argue (ואתם יודעים) that the opponents allow those who had contracted צרעת to touch pure food. No parallel to this exists in the Temple Scroll.

MMT B 18-23 contain laws regarding skins of animals. Regulations regarding skins appear in 11QT 51.1-6. The text of MMT may prohibit the bringing of the skins of clean animals slaughtered outside into the temple. Yet no such law is preserved in the Temple Scroll. Nor is there any reference in the Temple Scroll to making handles for vessels out of skins and the ramifications for impurity. MMT states that even the skins of a נבלה (the carcass of a clean animal) render one who carries them impure. In this case, the Temple Scroll agrees fully with this law. Perhaps, *m. Yad.* 4.6 indicates that the Sadducees agreed with the MMT and the Temple Scroll, while the Pharisees, like the later Rabbis, applied this law only to the flesh of animals. This controversy is based on the exegesis of Lev. 11.39 (cf. Deut. 14.8).[21]

Two laws are based on the concept of the מחנה, literally 'camp'. In MMT B 23, the writer complains that his opponents slaughter animals outside of the 'camp'. This may be parallel to the ruling of 11QT 52.13-16 prohibiting שחיטת חולין, 'non-sacral slaughtering', to those who lived within three days journey of the temple.[22] Yet MMT provides no such geographical limitations on its prohibition. The text (ואנחנו חושבים), like the Rabbis, defines the מחנה as Jerusalem. This מחנה is what the *tannaim* called מחנה ישראל. In this respect MMT disagrees with the Temple Scroll which places the מחנה ישראל within the expanded *temenos*.[23] This text does not assume expanded temple precincts.

MMT B 53-57 prohibits bringing dogs into the 'holy camp', the city of Jerusalem. Here it is emphasized that Jerusalem is the מחנה. This again refers to what the *tannaim* termed the מחנה ישראל in which the offerings of שלמים might be eaten. The text of MMT tells us that the fear was that such bones might be found by dogs and then the flesh of the sacrifices eaten by them. Again, we must note the differing approaches of MMT and the Temple Scroll to the interpretation of the 'camp'.

MMT B 30-33 prohibits slaughtering a pregnant animal. This passage takes it as a violation of Lev. 22.28. The use of אנחנו חושבים and הם יודעים signal the polemical character of the passage. It must have been directed against a view like that of the *tannaim* (*m. Ḥul.* 4.5) which permits the eating of an embryo after the ritual slaughter of its mother. The very same prohibition is found in 11QT 52.5-7, except that it refers only to sacrificial practice.[24] We cannot know whether the author of the Temple Scroll also considered such slaughter forbidden for other purposes.

The prohibition of certain classes 'entering the congregation' is discussed in MMT B 34-44. These classes are derived from Deut. 23.2-4. MMT takes the expression בוא בקהל to refer to both marriage and entering the sanctuary. Note that the authors must not have expected celibacy. Again we have the wording חושבים אנחנו . . . ואתם יודעים indicating the polemical nature of the passage. 4Q Florilegium clearly sees Deut. 23.2-4 as a reference to entering the temple.[25] The Temple Scroll does not present a parallel to this passage.

MMT B 44-49 forbids entry to the temple to the blind and the deaf. The text is concerned lest without the advantages of sight and hearing they accidentally defile something. Again the polemic is clear. Current temple practice is regarded as illegitimate. The Temple Scroll in 45.12-14 forbids the blind, but it appears that there the problem relates to 'blemishes'. The Temple Scroll has appropriated the rules for priests regarding disqualification from temple service (Lev. 21) and has applied them to Israelites as well.[26] No mention of the deaf is found in the Temple Scroll.

In a few cases, the laws of MMT and the Temple Scroll are in complete agreement. In MMT B 57-59 the fruit of the fourth year (נטע רבעי) and the cattle tithe are assigned to the priests. The exact same rulings appear in 11QT 60.1-5 (fragmentary). This law is in distinction to the tannaitic ruling requiring them to be eaten in Jerusalem by the owners, in the case of animals after the blood and certain parts are offered on the altar.

MMT B 67-69 states that the authors (אנחנו אומרים) take the view that any human bone, regardless of completeness, renders one who comes in contact with it impure as would a corpse itself. 11QT 50.4-6 recapitulates Num. 19.16-19 although a small change is made to make the point that even contact with a bone will render impure, in this way agreeing with our passage.[27] However, the Temple Scroll does not deal with the problem of a bone fragment. While it is possible that the author of the Temple Scroll would agree on this point with MMT, there is no evidence.

What this comparison has shown is that MMT and the Temple Scroll have much in common, while exhibiting some incongruities. A large number of points at which the extent of agreement cannot be determined must remain open.

Mishnah Yadayim

The *Mishnah*, in tractate *Yadayim*, reports a number of disagreements between the Pharisees and Sadducees. These disagreements are said there to have led to face-to-face disputes between some members of the two groups. (The historicity of these events is not revelant to our argument.) Since a number of these same issues seem to come up in MMT, a brief discussion of this passage is in order.

The following is a list of the disputes recorded there:

4.6
Pharisees: Scriptures defile the hands, but secular books do not.
Sadducees: All books (written on skins) defile.
Pharisees: Bones of donkey do not render impure, but bones of human being do.
Sadducees: (derived from words of Rabban Yohanan ben Zakkai) All bones render impure.

4.7
Pharisees: Impurity cannot travel back from a receptacle along a liquid stream.
Sadducees: Impurity does travel back from a receptacle along a liquid stream.
Pharisees: According to Sadducean view, water in a stream which flows through a cemetery should be rendered impure.
Sadducees: Water in a stream which flows through a cemetery is not rendered impure.
Pharisees: A master is exempt for the damages done by his servants.
Sadducees: A master is obligated for damages caused by his servants.

The remaining dispute found in *m. Yad.* 4.8 is, according to the manuscripts, between a Galilean heretic, or perhaps Jewish Christian (מין), and the Pharisees. We therefore have five disputes recorded here. Of these five disputes, four have echoes in MMT. The Sadducean view that all books render the hands impure may be derived from the view that skins slaughtered outside the Temple may not be brought in, and that skins, like flesh of carcasses of animals, render the one who carries them impure. The MMT, likewise, saw the bones of unclean animals as impure, hence the objection to using them as handles. The view of the Sadducees regarding the נצוק, the flowing of impurity back along a stream of water, corresponds exactly to the ruling in MMT. The dispute regarding the stream which passes through a cemetery is presented only because the Pharisees sought to point out the alleged inconsistency of the Sadducean position. The issue of damages brought about by servants could not be expected to appear in MMT since it is a catalogue of the improper sacrificial and purity practices of the Jerusalem Temple and priesthood.

In four out of the five Pharisee–Sadducee debates reported in *m. Yad.* 4, the author of MMT takes the view of the Sadducees, and polemicizes against the view ascribed in tannaitic sources to the Pharisees. At the same time, there is agreement or near agreement in a number of other regulations with MMT and the Temple Scroll. Yet here also, a number of minor points of disagreement or incongruity can be observed. In the Temple Scroll and in the so-called letter, 4Q MMT, various views previously attested to as Sadducean are found.

Conclusions

The Temple Scroll has a particular approach to the derivation of Jewish law from Scripture which is based on theological conceptions regarding the nature of God's revelation to Israel. This approach must be distinguished not only from that of the Pharisees and the later *tannaim*, but also from that of the Qumran sect as known from its documents. In addition, the content of the law of the Temple Scroll often can be shown to be inconsistent with that known from the other sectarian texts. Attempts to link the Temple Scroll to the book of *Jubilees* are likewise unsuccessful. Despite a number of parallels in legal details, the large number of disagreements which have been identified makes it impossible to postulate any direct link. Although in some areas the Temple Scroll is in agreement with the Pharisaic or later tannaitic teachings, the overwhelming differences between these corpora must be emphasized.

On the other hand, when attention is turned to the still unpublished 4Q *Miqṣat Ma'aseh Ha-Torah* the situation is very different. A series of parallels can be identified between this text and the Temple Scroll. Further, the disagreements between these texts are minor.

Comparison of the content of the MMT leads to the conclusion that in a number of laws it takes positions previously known as Sadducean. For some of these, with the help of tannaitic material, we can identify the opposing views, those the 'letter' claims were being practised in the Jerusalem Temple, as those attributed to the Pharisees.

If this 'halakhic letter' dates from a period close to the founding of the sect, as all evidence so far indicates, the views attributed to the Pharisees in tannaitic sources were indeed being practised in the temple in Hasmonean times. Further, from the MMT it can be gathered that many laws found in tannaitic sources were being practised. It has been claimed that rabbinic assertions of Pharisaic domination of the temple practices in Second Temple times are merely an anachronistic retrojection. This study requires us to give much greater credence to the claims of Pharisaic authority in the temple, at least for certain periods.

Once we realize that the MMT text takes the 'Sadducee' position, and that it, in turn, is closely related to the Temple Scroll, we must reopen the question of the relationship of the Sadducees to our sect. It is most likely that the sect was founded by disaffected priests who left the Jerusalem Temple after the Maccabean revolt when the Zadokite High Priests were displaced by the Hasmoneans.[28] If so, Qumran may provide us with some Sadducean documents. This possibility is heightened by the additional parallels in matters of Jewish law cited by J.M. Baumgarten.[29] The Sadducean connection may also be a clue to the provenance of the Temple Scroll. Indeed, these texts raise anew the need to reevaluate our views on the Sadducees and to determine if we can recover further evidence of their beliefs and practices with the help of the manuscripts of the Qumran corpus.

It is too early to draw any definite conclusions. After all, we still await the publication of many texts of great relevance from Cave 4. It is certain, though, that as we continue to evaluate the relationship of the Temple Scroll to the systems of Jewish law of the Second Temple period, we shall have to look most closely at the Sadducees and their priestly traditions, for it is here that in light of the *Miqṣat Ma'aseh Ha-Torah* we need to look further.

NOTES

1. Y. Yadin, *Megillat ham-Miqdaš* (3 Vols.; Jerusalem: The Israel Exploration Society and the Shrine of the Book, 1977); English trans. *The Temple Scroll* (3 Vols.; Jerusalem: The Israel Exploration Society and the Shrine of the Book, 1983).

2. L.H. Schiffman, *The Halakhah at Qumran* (SJLA, 16; Leiden: Brill, 1975), p. 135.

3. See L.H. Schiffman, 'The Temple Scroll in Literary and Philological Perspective', *Approaches to Ancient Judaism* II (BJS, 9; ed. W.S. Green; Chico, Calif.: Scholars Press, 1980), pp. 143-58, and especially B.A. Levine, 'The Temple Scroll: Aspects of its Historical Provenance and Literary Character', *BASOR* 232 (1978), pp. 5-23. Note the reactions to Levine in J. Milgrom, '"Sabbath" and "Temple City" in the Temple Scroll', *BASOR* 232 (1978), pp. 25-27 and Y. Yadin, 'Is the Temple Scroll a Sectarian Document?', *Humanizing America's Iconic Book* (ed. G.M. Tucker & G.A. Knight; Chico: Scholars Press, 1980), pp. 153-69. For bibliographic surveys on the *Temple Scroll*, see L.H. Schiffman, Review of Y. Yadin, *The Temple Scroll, BA* 48 (1985), pp. 122-25 and F. García Martínez, 'El Rollo del Templo (11Q Temple): Bibliografia sistematicà, *RevQ* 12 (1985-87), pp. 425-40.

4. A summary appears in H. Stegemann, 'Is the Temple Scroll a Sixth Book of the Torah Lost for 2,500 years?' *BAR* 13/6 (1987), pp. 28-35. The full article appeared as 'The Origins of the Temple Scroll', *Suppl. to VT* 40 (1988), pp. 235-56.

5. 'Literary Sources in the Temple Scroll', *HTR* 75 (1982), pp. 275-88.

6. Schiffman, *Halakhah at Qumran*, pp. 22-76.

7. Cf. J.M. Baumgarten, 'The Unwritten Law in the Pre-Rabbinic Period', *JSJ* 3 (1972), pp. 7-29; J. Neusner, 'Rabbinic Traditions about the Pharisees before A.D. 70: The Problem of Oral Transmission', *JJS* 22 (1971), pp. 1-18.

8. For a detailed discussion see L.H. Schiffman, 'The King, his Guard, and the Royal Council in the *Temple Scroll*', *PAAJR* 54 (1987), pp. 237-59.

9. *Ant.* 13.249, 288.

10. Cf. M. Hengel, J.H. Charlesworth, & D. Mendels, 'The Polemical Character of "On Kingship" in the Temple Scroll: An Attempt at Dating 11Q Temple', *JJS* 37 (1986), pp. 28-38.

11. *Sifre Devarim* 265; *b. Ned.* 22a and 77b.

12. See L.H. Schiffman, 'The Sacrificial System of the *Temple Scroll* and the Book of Jubilees', *Society of Biblical Literature 1985 Seminar Papers* (ed. K.H. Richards; Atlanta: Scholars Press, 1985), pp. 217-33.

13. See S. Talmon, 'The Calendar Reckoning of the Sect from the Judaean Desert', *Aspects of the Dead Sea Scrolls* (ed. C. Rabin, Y. Yadin; Scripta Hierosolymitana, 4; Jerusalem: Magnes, 1958), pp. 162-99.

14. *M. Menaḥ* 10.3; a *baraita* in *b. Menaḥ* 65a-b; *Megillat Ta'anit*, beginning.

15. Contrast Yadin, *The Temple Scroll*, I, pp. 116-19 (Heb.: I, p. 95). The view adopted here is argued by my colleague B.A. Levine in 'A Further Look at the Mo'adim of the Temple Scroll', to appear in *Archaeology and History in the Dead Sea Scrolls, The New York University Conference in Memory of Yigael Yadin*, ed. L.H. Schiffman. Levine proves his point by allusion to the omission of the phrase ממחרת השבת in the Temple Scroll's repeated reformulation of the biblical material. See now J.M. Baumgarten, '4 Q 503 (Daily Prayers) and the Lunar Calendar', *RevQ* 12 (1986), pp. 399-407.

16. See L.H. Schiffman, 'Exclusion from the Sanctuary and the City of the Sanctuary in the Temple Scroll', *HAR* 9 (1985), pp. 301-20.

17. See E. Qimron & J. Strugnell, 'An Unpublished Halakhic Letter from Qumran', *Biblical Archaeology Today* (ed. J. Amitai; Jerusalem: Israel Exploration Society, 1985), pp. 400-407.

18. M. Baillet, J.T. Milik, & R. de Vaux, *Les 'petites grottes' de Qumran* (DJD, 3; Oxford: Clarendon, 1962), p. 225, in his commentary to the Copper Scroll.

19. J.M. Baumgarten, 'The Pharisaic-Sadducean Controversies about Purity and the Qumran Texts', *JJS* 31 (1980), pp. 157-70; further material associating 11QT with Sadducean *halakhah* can be found in M.R. Lehmann, 'The Temple Scroll as a Source of Sectarian Halakhah', *RevQ* 9 (1977-78), pp. 579-87 and in M.R. Lehmann, 'The Temple Scroll as a Source for Sectarian Halakhah', *Beth Mikra* 25 (1980), pp. 302-308 (Heb.).

20. Schiffman, 'Exclusion from the Sanctuary', pp. 312-14.

21. Yadin, *The Temple Scroll*, I, pp. 338-41 (Heb.: I, pp. 261-62).

22. Cf. Yadin, *The Temple Scroll*, I, pp. 318-20 (Heb.: I, pp. 246-47).

23. Cf. Schiffman, 'Exclusion from the Sanctuary', pp. 307-309.

24. Cf. Yadin, *The Temple Scroll*, I, pp. 312-14 (Heb.: I, pp. 242-43).

25. Cf. J.M. Baumgarten, *Studies in Qumran Law* (SJLA, 24; Leiden: Brill, 1977), pp. 75-87.

26. Cf. L.H. Schiffman, 'Purity and Perfection: Exclusion from the

Council of the Community in the *Serekh Ha-'Edah', Biblical Archaeology Today* (ed. J. Amitai; Jerusalem: Israel Exploration Society, 1985), pp. 377-81.

27. Cf. Yadin, *The Temple Scroll*, I, pp. 334-36 (Heb.: I, pp. 257-59).

28. F.M. Cross, 'The Early History of the Qumran Community', *New Directions in Biblical Archaeology* (ed. D.N. Freedman & J.C. Greenfield; Garden City, N.Y.: Doubleday, 1971), pp. 70-89.

29. See n. 19.

11QT: THE SADDUCEAN *TORAH*

Hans Burgmann

Offenburg

The argument of this paper can be found in a somewhat different and more detailed form in my book *Die essenischen Gemeinden von Qumrân und Damaskus in der Zeit der Hasmonäer und Herodier*.[1]

Apart from many of the contributors to the present volume, there seems to be a general consensus that the Temple Scroll is a composition of the Qumran community. Three arguments are commonly cited in favour of this view. The first is that 11QT was found in a cave in the Qumran region. The second is that 11QT's calendar is the solar calendar of 364 days which is known to have been used by the Qumran community. The third is that particularly in 11QT 29.7-10 there is a kind of apocalpytic thought: God will appear on earth and personally erect his own temple. These arguments have resulted in the common opinion that 11QT is a product of the Qumran community.

But this consensus seems to me to be wrong; it is really not possible that the members of the Qumran community could have written such a scroll. As for the first argument, it seems that in later times several non-Essene groups found sanctuary at Qumran. These groups brought their manuscripts with them. It was customary at Qumran to assign particular caves for the depositing of the documents belonging to these groups. It is remarkable that the scrolls that are specifically products of the Qumran community have been found only in Cave 1 and in Cave 4. Only Greek papyri were discovered in Cave 7. And in Cave 11 no specifically Qumran scroll has been found: the psalms are not sectarian, but very close to the canonical psalms; the *targum* refers to the Pharisees amongst whom *targumim* were very popular at this time. Since the Temple Scroll was found in Cave 11 together with other non-Qumran scrolls, it is very improbable that it was the product of the Qumran community.

With regard to the solar calendar, this seems to me to have been the very carefully worked out product of the scholar-priests of the temple. They could not risk publishing or using it for fear of provoking a popular revolt against such innovation. As a result this calendric masterpiece was simply left in the temple archives to gather dust. Only a few people had access to the archives and to this brilliant understanding of the calendar. In any case only a few men knew about the solar calendar. They were probably Zadokites, not all of whom were Essenes. For example, among those who knew the solar calendar were the authors of the books of Daniel, of *Jubilees*, of *Enoch*; none of them was an Essene. Likewise the author or authors of 11QT were familiar with the solar calendar, but that does not force on us the assumption that they were necessarily Essene. As with its provenance in Cave 11, so with its use of the solar calendar, neither show that 11QT was an Essene product of the Qumran community.

As for 11QT 29.7-10, a mere thirty-three letters there speak of the eschatological coming of God. In a scroll of more than eight metres in length this is quite remarkable. It is only in this short passage that we learn that God will come and build his temple with his own hands. This section seems strange and does not appear to match the contents of the remaining sixty-six columns of the scroll. Indeed, a closer look at 29.7-10 in its context shows clearly that it is in between two major sections of material, the section on the feasts and the section on the building of the temple. At this point in the scroll it seems as if an interpolator has inserted a piece containing his own opinions, opinions which do not conform with the overall intention of the Temple Scroll and which have come under the influence of contemporary apocalyptic tendencies. While some modern scholars express bewilderment at the likely function of 11QT 29.7-10,[2] its complete dissimilarity from the rest of 11QT strongly suggests that it is an interpolation. As an interpolation 29.7-10 provides no evidence for 11QT being a product of the Qumran community.

In addition to these arguments against seeing a member of the Qumran community as author of 11QT there must be some consideration of that community's own self-understanding. A key issue in the community was the relationship of the members with each other; nowhere in 11QT is this mentioned in any way. Furthermore, the members of the community are themselves 'the temple of God'[3] and to that extent they had no need of any other temple. Thus these matters also point us away from thinking that the author of 11QT must be found amongst the Qumran community.

But, if the Qumran community did not produce the scroll, who did? The answer to this crucial question rests in identifying the group that is especially favoured in the scroll. That group is clearly the Levites. Concerning several matters Professor Milgrom has demonstrated that the Levites are favoured indeed.[4] The Levites are particularly privileged in the architectural layout of the temple and the number of rooms allocated to them; indeed they have more rooms than the priests. The Levites are accorded rights that the canonical *Torah* does not give them; to that extent 11QT stands as something of an anti-canonical *Torah*. The most surprising Levitical privilege described in 11QT is the 'shoulder'; while the priests are allotted the metapodes, the parts from the knees to the feet, mostly skin and bones with little meat, the Levites receive the shoulder, a very meaty part of the offering. This favouritism justifies the conclusion that the Levites must be the authors of the Temple Scroll.

From this conclusion it is possible to answer many of the seeming difficulties concerning how 11QT is to be understood. Moreover, this thesis, that 11QT was written by Levites, is supported by the hostile attitude of 11QT towards other groups. In German this attitude might be best expressed by *Rundumschlag* which can be weakly translated as 'all-round attack'. The Levites fought such an all-round attack against three groups: the priests, the Pharisees and the Essenes.

Firstly, 11QT is an important document from the late Second Temple period for what it tells us about the struggle between priests and Levites, a struggle which lasted for many centuries. The Levites considered their office in the temple as little better than slavery, and they hated the dominant priests.

Secondly, the Levites also disliked the Pharisees. The hostility between these two groups was deeply rooted. The Levites considered themselves to be the mediators between the temple and the people; as such, they sometimes functioned as teachers of the people. But nobody listened to the Levites; rather they paid attention to the Pharisees and their promises. The Pharisees had the ear of the people because their promises seemed to the lowly and poor to be the solution they were looking for. The Pharisees prophesied apocalyptic events in the end-time, for example, the coming of the prophet Elijah, the coming of the Messiah, the coming of God, who would establish his own kingdom on earth, the resurrection of the dead and eternal life for the pious in communion with God in bliss. Such promises were not part of the teaching of the Levites for they did not believe in such apocalyptic events. The Levites were Sadducees like the priests and so had the same beliefs as the priests. For the Sadducees there were no angels, no eschatological figures such as Elijah or the messiah, no establishment of God's kingdom, and no resurrection of the dead. It is worth mentioning in this respect that in 11QT there are no angels, no apocalyptic figures, no messiah or eschatological prophet, no establishment of God's kingdom, nor the resurrection of the dead. This is firm evidence in support of seeing 11QT as the Sadducean *Torah*. The Temple Scroll is the only extant document from the Sadducees; to my knowledge, there is no other.

The lack of apocalypticism was a great disadvantage for the Levites. The overwhelming popularity of the Pharisees based on their consoling promises, which the Levites could not match, led directly to the Levites detesting the Pharisees. Their hatred was so vehement that for them the common rules of the *Torah*[5] did not apply. For example, the high priest/king Alexander Jannaeus crucified 800 Pharisees on one day. Such an action was strictly forbidden according to the *Torah*. In the *Antiquities* (13.381) Josephus mentions that 'the penalty he exacted was inhuman', but in the *War* (1.97) he explicitly describes it as 'impiety' (ἀσέβεια). Only stoning and burning were the permitted death penalties in the time of free Israel. 11QT defends Jannaeus's brutal and godless action. The Levites justified crucifixion as a legitimate sentence for the crimes of the Pharisees who had rebelled against the high priest/king, who had called upon a foreign Gentile king to enter the land by force, and who had then fought a real war against the high priest. Many Pharisees fled into neighbouring territories, an action itself capable of being considered a capital offence.

Because the Levites had legitimated crucifixion as a means of execution, they effectively defended Alexander's inhuman and godless action. No doubt they also hoped that he would obey the rest of the direct speech of God in the Temple Scroll and would erect the new temple according to the plan which had been written there by a Levitical group. It had always been considered the king's duty to build the temple. King Solomon had erected the first temple, his Davidic descendant Zerubbabel had built the second; now it was the turn of Alexander Jannaeus to build a third. If he did this, 11QT, the Sadducean *Torah*, promised him victory over all his enemies, prosperity and the blessing of God.

Thirdly, the *Rundumschlag*, the all-round attack, was directed against the Essenes as well. But here it is more difficult to detect the offensive because the charge is hidden. Nevertheless such concealed attacks against the Essenes are detectable most especially in the formulations of law in 11QT which are either particularly long, or which repeat a point to stress some special detail, or which reflect the overall dominant redactional concerns of the scroll.

Three points in particular are worth describing in more detail. To begin with, there is no doubt that the passages concerning the feast of oil and the feast of new wine protrude in as much as these feasts are discussed in such detail and at such length. Together they appear to be the most important feasts in 11QT, but they are not mentioned in the *Torah* as it now stands. This seems quite remarkable and I would argue that they are offensively directed against the monks at Qumran. Josephus reports that the pious Qumran community did not use oil (*War* 2.123). This should be taken seriously. Apparently oil was impure and taboo and therefore forbidden in the community. But in 11QT the whole people, young and old, were delighted by using oil and olives: 'Afterwards they shall eat and anoint themselves from the new oil and from the olives, for on this day their sins are atoned for [with respect to all the fresh] oil of the land before YHWH, once a year, and they shall rejoice...' (11QT 22.14-16).[6] 11QT describes the participation of the people at the feast of new wine in a similar way: '...and after them the whole people both grea[t] and [small] and they shall begin to drink new wine]...... [On this day this shall make atonement for the] wine and the Israelites shall rejoice be[fore YH]WH' (11QT 21.6-8).[7] That is certainly not the spirit of the Qumran community.

In the second place it is clear that 11QT customarily puts together any two texts in the *Torah* which have a similar content. But it is remarkable that the theme of 'fortune-teller' or 'false prophet' is worked out in detail in two different columns. This is extraordinary and uncustomary. It seems to me that this can be explained in relation to a particular event in the history of the sect. The founder of the Qumran community, the 'Teacher of Righteousness', was attacked by the 'Wicked Priest', the high priest then officiating in the temple of Jerusalem. A clerical tribunal was summoned and the 'Teacher' was accused. The cause of the accusation could have been the reproach that the 'Teacher' was a 'fortune-teller', a 'false prophet'.[8] The high priest sentenced him to be flagellated. But the Levites condemned him to death according to the severe decrees of the *Torah*. This sentence is written in two distinct and separate passages in 11QT (54.8-13; 60.16-61.5). This severe judgment by the Levites seems to be a clear attack on the 'Teacher' and his community.

In the third place it is well known that there were many problems in the late Second Temple period concerning matters of jurisprudence, cultic practice and the interpretation of the authoritative biblical texts. Different groups offered different solutions to these problems. The hasidic group (i.e. both Pharisees and Essenes) solved the problems through their expectation of the eschatological prophet: Elijah would come and decide all the accumulated questions and problems and would put an end to all these difficulties through his authoritative declarations.

But this was not a possible solution for the Sadducean Levites because they looked neither for the eschaton nor an eschatological prophet. It was their belief that their service at the altar would be performed without a break for ever. In fact it was unthinkable that there might be a break in their continual duty, and yet there were problems of interpretation for the Levites as well. They were forced to propose another solution, and this can be found in 11QT. Yigael Yadin has stated that one intention runs through the whole scroll, 'harmonisation';[9] this is visible in many places in the scroll. All the differences between texts in the *Torah* are eliminated through harmonization. In this way one can say that for the Levites 11QT is the substitute for the eschatological prophet: Elijah is replaced by this harmonization. Through their editorial work the Levitical authors of 11QT deal a final blow to the beliefs of the Pharisees and the Essenes.

In this way 11QT is a *Rundumschlag,* an all-round attack against the three enemies of the Levites. This paper is also something of a *Rundumschlag* against many friends working in Qumran studies.[10]

NOTES

1. Chapter 7 of this book is entitled 'Die sadduzäische Tora 11QT: Der Auftrag Gottes an Alexander Jannai, ein vorbildliches Königtum zu errichten, die Leviten in ihren materiellen Ansprüchen und in ihren ultratorakratischen Erwartungen zu unterstützen und endlich den Tempel in den idealen Abmessungen zu bauen'. It is to be published shortly by Peter Lang, Frankfurt.

2. E.g. P. Callaway, 'Exegetische Erwägungen zur Tempelrolle XXIX, 7-10', *RevQ* 12 (1985-87), pp. 95-104.

3. Cf. J. Maier, *Die Texte vom Toten Meer,* München-Basel: E. Reinhardt, 1960, Vol. II, pp. 22, 30, 89-91; B. Gärtner, *The Temple and the Community in Qumran and the New Testament* (SNTSMS, 1; Cambridge: Cambridge University Press, 1965), pp. 16-46.

4. 'Studies in the Temple Scroll', *JBL* 97 (1978), pp. 501-506.

5. I.e., the *Torah* as now preserved in the MT.

6. J. Maier, *The Temple Scroll: An Introduction, Translation & Commentary* (JSOTS, 34; Sheffield: JSOT, 1985), p. 29.

7. J. Maier, *The Temple Scroll: An Introduction, Translation & Commentary,* p. 28.

8. Josephus mentions three instances of Essene predictions, those of Judas (*War* 1.78), Simon (*War* 2.113), and Menahem (*Ant.* 15.373-79).

9. *The Temple Scroll,* I, pp. 73-77 (Heb.; I, pp. 62-65).

10. Though I am pleased to acknowledge that in this volume the contributions by L.H. Schiffman and M.R. Lehmann are very relevant to my theme. M.R. Lehmann's earlier studies also draw attention to the possible Sadducean connections of 11QT: 'The Temple Scroll as a Source of Sectarian Halakhah', *RevQ* (1977-78), pp. 579-87; 'The Temple Scroll as a Source for Sectarian Halakhah', *Beth Mikra* 25 (1980), pp. 30?-308.

THE BEAUTIFUL WAR BRIDE (יפת תאר) AND OTHER *HALAKHOTH* IN THE TEMPLE SCROLL

Manfred R. Lehmann

New York

When the Temple Scroll was first published, in Hebrew, by the late Professor Yigael Yadin,[1] I realized that, more than any other scroll yet discovered, it was of the greatest importance both for the study of the attitude of the Qumran community to the *halakhoth* which form the body of traditional Judaism, and also for the study of the history of *halakhoth* in themselves. My paper entitled 'The Temple Scroll as a Source of Sectarian Halakhah' appeared in *Revue de Qumrân* already in 1978.[2] I had the privilege of showing my paper to Professor Yadin at a symposium which he chaired in Jerusalem, and he expressed his enthusiasm for approaching the Temple Scroll as a source for the study of *halakhoth*.

My conclusion then was that we may see in the Temple Scroll a body of Sadducean *halakhot* of which we have previously had testimony in *Megillath Ta'anith*[3] and in parts of the *Talmud*.[4] We know, generally, that the Sadducees had *halakhot* of their own, which, although apparently representing an oral tradition, were recorded at some time. This is an apparent contradiction to the traditional view that the Sadducees, like the Karaites and other heretical sects throughout Jewish history, disavowed oral laws, accepting only the written laws of the *Torah*. I believe that this problem can be solved. What happened, I suggest, is that the Sadducees had oral traditions on laws, which, in order to give them the status and impelling force they needed, were interpolated into the biblical text, in order to make them *appear* as written law. That was, in many cases, the function of the Temple Scroll; it was 'edited' to accommodate the inclusion of such oral laws.

A few examples should illustrate this point. We shall first mention briefly a few purity laws and then concentrate on the laws of the יפת תאר, 'the beautiful war bride'.

The ritually impure according to the Temple Scroll (45.15-17) may not enter the city of the sanctuary (עיר המקדש) until seven days of purification have passed. This is a more stringent rule than can be found in rabbinic *halakhah* which excludes the impure only from the inner Temple itself, but not from the entire city of Jerusalem, nor even from the outer courts of the Temple.[5] This was legislated in the *Mishneh Torah* by Maimonides: טמא מת אפילו המת עצמו מותר להכנס להר הבית;'It was permissible for one unclean by the dead, and even the dead corpse itself, to enter into the Temple Mount'.[6] In this case, the covenanters imposed on themselves a more stringent application of the laws of the *Torah* (חומרא). The application of such stringent versions of the law is in itself not unusual. It has been the aim of many rabbis and rabbinic schools. For example, a rule ascribed to the 'Men of the Great Synod' (אנשי כנסת הגדולה) who functioned in the fourth and third centuries BCE is given as עשו סייג לתורה, 'Make a fence around the *Torah*', i.e., 'Remove yourselves from violating the law itself, by imposing stringent "fences" around it'.[7] The entire school of Shammai is known for its stringent application in almost all legal matters. These were recognized as rabbinic restrictions, clearly set aside from the biblical laws themselves. By contrast, in the Temple Scroll, the stringencies are elevated to the standing of biblical laws, by being given scriptural authority, having been inserted into the written biblical text itself.

The laws of purification of defiled implements and vessels also show the more stringent form of *halakhah* in the Temple Scroll. In rabbinic law stone implements cannot become ritually impure. For example, Maimonides writes: כלי אבנים . . . לעולם טהורין ואין מקבלין טומאה מן הטומאות ולא טומאת מדרס לא מן התורה ולא מדברי סופרים; '. . . vessels of stone. . . are always clean, and they are not susceptible to any of the uncleannesses nor to *midras* uncleanness, whether on the authority of Scripture or on the authority of the Scribes'.[8] This is no doubt also the reason for the reference in the New Testament to the use of stone jars.[9] Likewise, archaeologists have recently unearthed a prevalence of stone vessels and household implements in the ruins of private houses in Jerusalem of the Second Temple period.[10] They were preferred because they were immune to טומאה,

ritual impurity. However, in the Temple Scroll (49.14), it seems that even stone implements were considered capable of attracting ritual impurity and therefore had to be purified just as clay vessels when found in the house of a dead person.

In 11QT 45.12-14 we learn that a blind person was banned from the entire city of Jerusalem. In rabbinic *halakhah* only priests can be barred, if they have a bodily blemish, including blindness, but only from the Temple itself, not from the city as a whole. Of course, we may agree with Yadin that the scroll by and large addresses itself to priests only,[11] since it is concerned with the temple service. In this case, כול איש עור in the Temple Scroll passage just cited may refer to priests. Nevertheless, even in this interpretation, the scroll is more stringent than rabbinic *halakhah*.

Let us now turn to an interesting *halakhah* which clearly shows the method of interpolation of an oral law into the written scripture. I refer to the laws of the יפת תאר, the beautiful war bride. This law, found in Deut. 21.10-14, is frought with many complications. The Talmud has innumerable discussions on this subject. The questions raised are, for example, whether more than one intercourse is permitted with a pagan woman captured in battle before she goes through the requirements listed in the biblical text, at what point she can be considered a married Jewish woman, and since she needs conversion, whether a priest can marry such a woman.

The Temple Scroll (63.14-15) follows the biblical text, but at the end adds words of strictly *halakhic* nature: ולוא תגע לכה בטהרה עד שבע שנים וזבח שלמים לוא תואכל עד יעבורו שבע שנים אחר תואכל, 'she may not touch any purity till seven years have passed, nor may she eat of any peace offerings for seven years; thereafter she may eat (therefrom)'.

As the Temple Scroll addressed itself basically to priests, we may assume that this law too applies to priests, especially as the purity of תרומה 'heave offerings', and the eating of שלמים, 'peace offerings', are referred to, which are in the priestly realm. In the Talmud[12] the Amoraic authors Rav and Shemuel disagree whether a priest may marry a יפת תואר. Shemuel argues that since the יפת תואר requires conversion before she may marry her captor, a priest is disqualified since he may not marry a convert. Rav, however, holds the view that the whole law is an extraordinary dispensation from the normal legal restrictions, and therefore the restrictions imposed on the priesthood

are also suspended, and a priest may consequently also marry a
יפת תואר. The codified law follows the opinion of Shemuel, according
to which a priest is barred from marrying a יפת תואר. The Temple
Scroll would therefore appear to vary from the accepted *halakhah*,
although the rabbinic minority opinion, held by Rav, does agree with
the scroll.

However, the main problem arises around the limitation of seven
years. There is no apparent parallel to any such limitation in rabbinic
halakhah. In the words of the medieval work *Sefer ha-Hinukh*[13] the
יפת תואר, after conversion, must be married according to all the usual
marriage laws, and thereafter 'all the laws are those which apply to
Jewish women' (דינה כדין בנות ישראל), and none of her privileges and
rights is further delayed.

As to the Temple Scroll, Professor Yadin sees here a delay, not of
seven years, but a waiting period of fourteen years, since twice seven
years are mentioned.[14] Yadin sees in this limitation an application of
the usual period of probation imposed by covenanters on any new
application for membership. The seven-year waiting period would,
therefore, not be directly connected with the particular laws of the
יפת תואר, but would coincide with the usual membership rules of the
sect. In this case, certainly the inclusion of this restriction in the
biblical text represents a rather crude attempt to tamper with
scripture in order to be consistent with the particular rules of the
Qumran community.

However, I would suggest a different interpretation of the scroll
text. I would draw your attention to a little known *Midrash, Midrash
Shemuel*, which is of Palestinian origin from the Amoraic period, but
which quotes much earlier authorities. On the subject of the יפת תואר
this *Midrash* states: לא התירו אשה יפת תואר אלא לאחר ארבע עשרה שבע
שכיבשו ושבע שחילקו, 'the laws of the יפת תואר were only applicable
after 14 years—7 years of conquest (of the land) and 7 years of
division (of the tribal districts)'.[15] We can now see that the seven plus
seven years of the scroll have a perfect parallel in the *Midrash* just
quoted. This parallel could be used to suggest that the Temple Scroll
might only refer to the initial fourteen years of occupation of the
land, with the result that we could read the text of the scroll as
follows: 'She may not touch any purity till seven years (of occupation
of the land) have passed, and may not eat of peace offerings for a
further seven years (of division of the tribal districts); thereafter she
may eat therefrom'.

Under the rule of the *Midrash* no part of the law of the יפת תואר could be practiced until fourteen years of initial occupation had passed. Under the law of the Temple Scroll, however, the marriage to the war bride can in fact take place under the rules of the יפת תואר immediately upon entering the land, with the only restriction against touching the heave offering during the initial seven years of occupation, and fourteen years against the eating of the peace offerings, to include the seven years of distribution of the tribal districts. In other words, both traditions were aware of a restriction for seven plus seven years, together fourteen years. The *Midrash* states that the restriction of these fourteen years applies to the entire body of laws covering the יפת תואר, and that no marriage can take place till these fourteen years have passed, while the Temple Scroll permits the marriage within these fourteen years, but uses the element of fourteen years only as a prohibition against the priest's bride touching the heave offering, and her eating the peace offering, during the initial fourteen years.[16]

The Temple Scroll implies that the captor may be a priest, since the main portions of the שלמים, the peace offerings, 'belong to the priests, their wives, their children and their slaves': שלמים ... המורם נאכל לכהנים לנשיהם ולבניהם ולעבריהם.[17] Furthermore the reference in *m. Zeb.* 5.7 to touching the 'purities', תרומה, 'heave offerings', again implies that the captor in the Temple Scroll is a priest to whom the heave offerings are rendered. This *halakhah* agrees with the minority opinion of Rav, as stated above, but deviates from the accepted *halakhah* which follows the opinion of Shemuel to the effect that a priest must not marry a pagan captive.

As we have seen, all these refinements in the law of the beautiful war bride are in the realm of oral law in the Jewish tradition. In the Temple Scroll, however, they have, at least partially, been inserted into the written text of the pseudo-biblical text, no doubt in order to avoid relying on oral law and, instead, elevating the oral law to the status of written law.

A continued study of the Temple Scroll will undoubtedly yield many more similar examples of deliberate interpolations into the biblical text. This method of tampering with the biblical text for the sake of sectarian laws was, of course, annoying to those Jewish authorities who recognized the canonized biblical text, alongside the legal traditions handed down orally, as binding law. No wonder that, as *Megillath Ta'anith* 4 reports, the ultimate destruction of 'Sadducean' written legal works was celebrated as an important historical accomplishment for the maintaining of the traditional concept of Jewish law.

NOTES

1. *Megillat ham-Miqdaš* (3 Vols.; Jerusalem: The Israel Exploration Society and the Shrine of the Book, 1977); English trans. *The Temple Scroll* (3 Vols.; Jerusalem: The Israel Exploration Society and the Shrine of the Book, 1983).

2. *RevQ* 9 (1977-78), pp. 579-87; 'The Temple Scroll as a Source for Sectarian Halacha', *Beth Mikra 25* (1980), pp. 302-308 (Heb.).

3. E.g. *Meg. Ta'an.* 4: בארבעה עשר בתמוז עדא ספר גזירתא דלא למיספד. See also S. Zeitlin, 'Nennt Megillat Taanit antisadduzäische Gedenktage?', *MGWJ* 81 (1937), pp. 351-55.

4. E.g. *b. Mak.* 5b; *b. Nid.* 33b; *b. Sanh.* 52b; *b. Sukk.* 43b, 48b; *b. Yoma* 4a, 19a, 19b, 40b, 53a, 56b; cf. *m. Yad.* 4.8.

5. See *m. Kelim* 1. On the scholarly debate concerning the definition of עיר המקדש, see especially J. Milgrom, '"Sabbath" and "Temple City" in the Temple Scroll', *BASOR* 232 (1978), pp. 25-27.

6. *Hilkhoth Bi'ath Miqdash* 3.4; English trans. by M. Lewittes, *The Code of Maimonides VIII: The Book of Temple Service* (New Haven: Yale University, 1957), p. 93.

7. *M. 'Abot* 1.1.

8. *Hilkhoth Kelim* 1.6; English trans. by H. Danby, *The Code of Maimonides X: The Book of Cleanness* (New Haven: Yale University, 1954), p. 398. Cf. Yadin, *The Temple Scroll* (Heb.), Vol. I, p. 255.

9. Jn 2.6.

10. See e.g. B. Mazar, *The Mountain of the Lord* (Garden City, N.Y.: Doubleday, 1975), pp. 85-86; N. Avigad, *Discovering Jerusalem* (Oxford: Blackwell, 1984), pp. 132, 174-176, 181-83, especially p. 183 where Avigad refers to *m. Kelim* 10.1 and *m. Para* 3.2 to explain the great number of stone vessels in Jerusalem in the late Second Temple period.

11. E.g. Yadin, *The Temple Scroll*, I, p. 399 (Heb.: I, p. 305).

12. *B. Qidd.* 21b.

13. *Sefer Hahinuch. English and Hebrew. The Book of (Mitzvah) Education* ascribed to Rabbi Aaron HaLevi of Barcelona, 13th cent. (with translation and notes by C. Wengrove), New York: Feldheim, 1978.

14. *The Temple Scroll*, I, p. 367 (Heb.: I, pp. 280-81).

15. Text in S. Buber, *Midrash Shemuel* (Kraków, 1893), ch. 25, p. 123; for

introductory information on *Midrash Shemuel* see J. Elbaum, 'Midrash Samuel', *EncJud* XI, cols. 1517-18.

16. It should be noted that the background of the *Midrash* is that the rabbis interpreted the introductory phrase in Deut. 21.10 (כי תצא למלחמה) to refer to a war *outside* the Promised Land, i.e. after the occupation was completed, namely till fourteen years had passed.

17. *M. Zebaḥ.* 5.7.

PART V

REVIEW OF RESEARCH

A REVIEW OF EAST EUROPEAN
STUDIES ON THE TEMPLE SCROLL

Zdzisław J. Kapera

Kraków

Let me explain at the outset that I am not a philologist, but an archaeologist and historian of the ancient Near East by training and a librarian by profession. The Dead Sea scrolls have attracted me since my youth, when an information explosion and the antireligious fever of the Polish mass-media in the mid-fifties aroused by the discoveries at the Dead Sea first drew me into the field of Qumran research. My visit to Manchester is somewhat incidental and was caused by the kind insistence of Dr Burgmann. My topic, a short bibliographical review of research on the Temple Scroll in the East Europaean countries was chosen at the last moment. I am now preparing for print the proceedings of the first Mogilany colloquium of 1987, which was devoted to the problem of origins of the Dead Sea scrolls and to the early history of the Qumran community.[1] My current editorial work has made it impossible for me to present any original contribution about the Temple Scroll but I thought that you might be interested in the progress of Qumran research in the East European Communist countries and would appreciate a look behind the language barrier.[2] I hope to be of some help by presenting a short summary of studies on the Temple Scroll in the Eastern part of Europe.

But first of all let me exclude Dead Sea scrolls research in East Germany. The language is no obstacle in this case; besides, as far as I know, Dead Sea scrolls studies have not been very popular there since the death of Prof. Hans Bardtke in the 1970s. Also in Romania, Bulgaria and Czechoslovakia such studies are merely incidental. I have not as yet noticed any special contributions concerning the

Temple Scroll from these countries. Nor has Florentino García Martínez, editor of the *Revue de Qumrân*, who has recently published a subject bibliography on the Temple Scroll.[3] In fact among the 200 or so items listed, he mentions only a few Polish publications on the Temple Scroll. As we shall see, more has in fact been published by Polish, Russian and Hungarian scholars.

Chronologically the first information about the Temple Scroll appeared at the end of 1968 in the Hungarian journal *Világosság*; it was signed by Tibor Scher.[4] A year later the first Polish article about the manuscript appeared in the *Ruch Biblijny i Liturgiczny* (*Biblical and Liturgical Movement*); it was written by Jerzy Chmiel of the Papal Faculty of Theology in Krakow.[5] Both articles were simple presentations of preliminary announcements made in 1967 by Yigael Yadin. Russian readers were informed of the existence of the Temple Scroll by Joseph Davidovitch Amusin of the Leningrad Institute of Oriental Studies of the Soviet Academy of Sciences, in his book *Teksty Kumrana* (*The Qumran Texts*), Vol. I, published in 1971. I will turn to this contribution by Amusin a little later.

Progress in the study of the Temple Scroll is strictly connected with the publication of the monumental *editio princeps* by Yadin, first presented in Hebrew in 1977. However, it was a very expensive edition. Research in Eastern Europe became possible when these first volumes were privately brought to Poland (the copy given by Yadin to Witold Tyloch) and to Russia (where they were used by Klavdia Borisovna Starkova). Tyloch who has always been a defender of the Essene identification of the Qumran texts[6] concentrated on the study of the Temple Scroll using it for his historical research. He quickly published his first results, while working all the time on a Polish translation of the longest of the Qumran texts.

It seems that the Leningrad scholars received the publication much later and so far only Starkova has published a review of the three-volume Hebrew edition. Professor Amusin died too soon to be able to use the *editio princeps* in his last book about the Qumran community.

Now, I should like to present a more detailed account of the research of three East European scholars interested in the Temple Scroll.

Professor Tyloch from Warsaw University Oriental Department started his publications on the Temple Scroll in 1977 with an article in Polish on 'The Main Problems of the Study of the Qumran Manuscripts' in the *Studia Religioznawcze* (*Religious Studies*). The article appeared just before the publication of the *editio princeps*, so he only repeated all the information available at that time, i.e. the general description of the contents of the scroll.[1] Tyloch's second article, this time in English, 'The Dead Sea Scrolls—A Testimony of Social Ideas of Antiquity', published in 1979 in the Polish quarterly *Dialectics and Humanism* just after Yadin's publication, contained a somewhat more detailed description of the Temple Scroll and the author's first impressions.[8] Professor Tyloch accepted the connection of the text with the Qumran community and stressed some points which provided evidence that 'the author himself must have been an Essene, or at least a member of the same apocalyptic circles that adhered to the special calendar of both Qumran and the Book of Jubilees'. He went on to write that in the light of the Temple Scroll 'it is now clear that the Qumran community was an Essene community'.[9]

Tyloch's third contribution (this time in French), 'Le Rouleau du Temple et les Esséniens', in the anniversary volume of the *Rocznik Orientalistyczny* (*Orient. Annual*), 1980, dedicated to Prof. Rudolf Ranoszek (who died in 1985), was devoted to the problem of the relationship between the Temple Scroll and the Essenes.[10] Tyloch argued that two facts, namely, the solar calendar and the New Oil Festival, showed that the author of the scroll was an Essene.

Josephus (*War* 2.123) mentions that the Essenes refrained from anointing themselves with oil. Now we know that they used oil once a year (11QT 22.16) as a sign of expiation and purification. In the opinion of the writer, the passage of the Temple Scroll concerning the New Oil Festival and the rites described as connected with it are a new decisive proof to support the identification of the members of the Qumran community as Essenes. The strange information in Josephus concerning the attitude of the Essenes towards the use of oil is now explained. However, it is possible that Josephus did not know the real occasion for the feast.

Tyloch's subsequent contribution on the Temple Scroll was presented during the XIVth Congress of the International Association for the History of Religions in Ontario in 1983. In his lecture 'L'importance du Rouleau du Temple pour l'identification de la communauté de Qumrân' he took another look at the passage of the

Temple Scroll describing the Festival of the New Oil, offering his own French translation of cols. 21-22 and a more detailed interpretation which confirmed and explained Josephus' passage about the use of oil among the Essenes.[11]

In his next paper on the Temple Scroll, in the *Keller Festschrift* (1984), Tyloch reviewed the palaeographic and historical data of the text. He accepted the opinion that palaeographically the Temple Scroll could have been written in the middle of the second century BCE. Analysis of the language, which is close to that of the *Mishnah*, confirms the Hasmonean dating. Also the historical data, such as the contents of the section on Royal Authority (11QT 56.12-60.1) and the description of the method of killing sacrificial animals (col. 34) in the Jerusalem sanctuary, confirm the possibility that the Temple Scroll comes from the time of John Hyrcanus. Accepting that the Temple Scroll was the most important document of the Qumran community, Tyloch stressed that it proclaimed a Law obligatory for the whole of Israel, for the whole nation. The law was valid for and contemporary with its author's time. The Essene community treated the Temple Scroll as biblical legislation. It seems that the scroll was the mysterious book of Hagu, known from some passages in the Qumran scrolls (like 1QSa 1.7; CD 10.6, etc.).[12]

The most recent contribution by Tyloch is a series of articles published in his favourite *Euhemer* (a Polish religious quarterly). In the years 1983-1984 he produced four articles on the Temple Scroll, offering first of all a full Polish translation of the document and providing it with extensive historico-critical and philological commentaries.[13] It is worth stressing that this Polish translation was only the fourth rendering of the Temple Scroll into a modern language, after those of Florentino García Martínez (into Spanish), André Caquot (into French) and Johann Maier (into German). The English translation of Johann Maier and the Dutch of A.S. van der Woude came later, which—with ten years of research—seems to be proof that this text is not easy to translate.[14] Tyloch's translation is fluent and clear, his remarks and commentaries to the point. Tyloch can justly feel proud of his translation and commentary as it really represents a state-of-the-art pronouncement on every passage. Besides, in the introductory articles we can find full information about the acquisition of the scroll, its detailed description, an extended version of the author's previously published views on all the historical elements which suggest the Essene provenance of the scroll, and a linguistic and literary analysis which enables the author to draw certain conclusions. According to Tyloch the scroll was written down in Herodian times, but had been composed earlier in the Maccabean period, more accurately in the early Hasmonean times. This opinion can be confirmed by the section of the scroll concerning the Law of the King (cols. 56-59) and by the description of the method of killing animals in the Temple (col. 34), which suggest dating it to the time of John Hyrcanus I. It is possible to establish the milieu of the Judaic society in which the document was composed. Taking into consideration the data from the scroll concerning the Festival of the New Oil (21.12-16) and מקום יד (i.e. latrine) (46.13-16) and comparing them with the information of Josephus about the Essenes, Tyloch finds it possible to identify the group which created the document with the Essenes. Commenting on the literary character of the scroll he sees parallels between the scroll and various biblical texts. The Essene writer wanted his readers to believe that the Temple Scroll was a divine decree given by God to Moses, thus he wanted them to regard it as the real and true *Torah*. The text originated from an idea based on the concept of cultic sanctity with the Temple as its centre. It is very probable that the Qumran community regarded the scroll as its most important canonical book. Some arguments suggest that the Temple Scroll is to be identified with the ספר ההגו mentioned in other Qumran texts.

Tyloch again took up the problem of the dating and provenance of the Temple Scroll during the 1st International Symposium on the Dead Sea scrolls held in Mogilany in 1987. He repeated his previous views dating the origins of the document to the middle of the second century BCE and attributing it to the Essene community.[15]

The most recent news concerning studies on the Temple Scroll in Poland is promising. A new Ph.D. dissertation is in progress at the Biblical School of the Catholic University of Lublin. Another dissertation on the language of the Copper Scroll is in preparation at the Linguistics Department of the Poznań University. As the author, Mr Piotr Muchowski, tells me, his research reveals the existence of many very close similarities between the Copper Scroll and the Temple Scroll, which seems to suggest a lower dating for the latter.

The very well-known, now dead, Soviet qumranologist, Joseph

Davidovitsch Amusin, has unfortunately left nothing specifically
dealing with the Temple Scroll. His book of 1971, *The Qumran Texts*,
Vol. I (*Pesharim*), had in fact been finished in 1966 just before the
announcement of the acquisition of the Temple Scroll. So he could
only add a very summary report about the text in the addenda to his
book.[16]

In his description of the contents of the scroll he even used
newspaper articles from Israel. He was always a very keen observer
of the literature on the subject and was usually able to use any
important item. He agreed with Yadin that the author of the Temple
Scroll must have looked upon his text as part of Holy Scripture *sensu
stricto*. Amusin accepted Yadin's view that the Temple Scroll is
connected with Qumrano-Essenian literature. He saw this connection
not only in the palaeography, the orthography and the series of
sectarian *halakhot*, but above all in the calendar of the text. In his
opinion the author of the Temple Scroll really had been using the
Qumran calendar when describing the feast of שבעות. Furthermore
the Temple Scroll informs us about two new agricultural feasts: תירוש
and יצהר. In Amusin's opinion the hypothesis of J. Morgenstern
concerning the fifty-day calendar system gains strong support from
the book of *Jubilees* and from the Temple Scroll of Qumran.[17] In
connection with this remark Amusin reminded readers that his
colleague, M.M. Elizarova, proved the existence of the same calendar
system among Egyptian Therapeutae (cf. Philo, *Contemp. Life*
65).[18]

A little more about the Temple Scroll can be found in the last book
of Amusin, *The Qumran Community*, which came out in Moscow in
1983, but in fact had been sent to the publisher in 1977.[19] Thus, even
when he quoted Yadin's preliminary Hebrew edition, he was in fact
only able to adjust several footnotes. All his remarks were based on
the pre-publication articles by Yadin and notes by other scholars.
Amusin included the description of the Temple Scroll in a general,
but detailed analysis of the Qumran library. He noticed with interest
some rules unknown to the Bible and the *Mishnah*, for example,
concerning pregnant women being clean or unclean. He accepted
Yadin's linguistic remarks; the author of the Temple Scroll used
terms and expressions contemporary with him, and unknown to the
authors of the Bible. Amusin also stated that the plan of the temple
described in the scroll fitted the descriptions of neither the

Solomonic Temple, nor the eschatological temple of Ezekiel, nor the Second Temple. He also followed Yadin in dating 11QT to the time of the Hasmonean dynasty. Describing the calendar of the Qumran community, Amusin once again repeated his agreement with the hypothesis of Morgenstern and the calculation of the New Oil Festival by J.T. Milik involving an unpublished document.[20] According to Amusin, the Temple Scroll confirms the earlier suggestions of Elizarova concerning the calendar of the Therapeutae, who were in his opinion an Egyptian branch of the Essene movement.[21]

Discussing the family life of the Qumran community, Amusin stressed that celibacy, marriage, re-marriage and divorce remained unclear. New light was shed on the problem by a very much discussed passage of the Temple Scroll (57.17-19) concerning the king's marriage. It is evident from the passage that the Qumran sect rejected divorce, but accepted re-marriage after the death of the first wife. But in fact all we know is that this permission to re-marry concerned the king. In connection with that passage of the Temple Scroll Amusin invoked a Gospel text: Mt. 19.3-12. He noticed the existence of several parallel features in the two texts. In his opinion celibacy was alien to Judaism, but for the Qumran people an essential element of their ascetism. Its roots were not connected with Hellenistic or Iranian influences, but they were biblical, as Barbara Thiering first said in 1974.[22]

Another Soviet scholar very much interested in Qumran research, Klavdija Borisovna Starkova from Leningrad, was not yet able to use the *editio princeps* of the Temple Scroll in her book *Literary Monuments of the Qumran Community* published in 1974.[23] However, she offered several interesting remarks based only on the preliminary reports of Y. Yadin and M. Goshen-Gottstein of 1967. In her opinion we cannot now continue to say that the Qumran people were content with the interpretation of the Sinai tradition of revelation as it now stands in the Hebrew Bible. The most interesting particularity of the new scroll is that it is a pseudepigraphon which has God himself as its author. This would seem to have been inconceivable. However, in her opinion an embryo of such a work is hidden in the Bible (cf. e.g. 1 Chron. 28.19). She incidentally remarks that old Samaritan biblical manuscripts sometimes have not only a description but also some drawings of the construction of the temple.

Concerning the *halakhah* of the Temple Scroll Starkova stresses the way in which the apocryphal *Torah* changes the law of the real *Torah* without being contradictory to it in principle. This attitude is easily visible in the comment to Deut. 21.10-13 (11QT 63.11-15) where the possibility of marriage with a woman who is a war prisoner is considered. In the opinion of K.B. Starkova (and I.N. Vinnikov) the established seven-year period of mourning eliminates the possibility of marriage with a foreigner-dissenter; such marriage was absolutely unacceptable for a member of the Qumran community.[24] On another matter Starkova notes that the description of the feasts in the Temple Scroll fully confirms the theory of A. Jaubert and S. Talmon concerning the solar calendar of the Qumran community. The character of the new feasts points to the agricultural provenance of the Qumran calendar. Returning to biblical sources which could have influenced the author of the new apocryphon, Starkova points out that Josh. 24.26 proves the existence of a *Torah* of God (or *Torah* of Yahweh) which circulated widely in Israelite society (cf. Josh. 1.7-8) apart from the Mosaic *Torah*.

The new Qumran document confirms that the Qumran people considered themselves as real successors of Mosaic Israel; for the Qumran community God's revelation was continuing in addition to that in the Bible. The creation of the Temple Scroll was also influenced by the polemic with the Pharisees.[25] This halakhic document was created with a view to destroying the authority of the *Mishnah* which was beginning to be formed at this time. The document is a testimony to the real political programme of the Qumran community for a future with re-created royal power, restored theocracy and renewed Temple cult. The renewed norms of the cult were to be fulfilled in a new Temple, 'which will be the cleansed or changed temple built by Herod and his successors'.[26]

In addition to these preliminary comments, so far Starkova has expressed her views on the Temple Scroll only in a review of the *editio princeps* published in *Palestinskij Sbornik*, Vol. 27. In her opinion expressed there, this new Essene text enriches and increases our knowledge of the Qumran community and its ideology. She accepts Yadin's opinion that the language of the Temple Scroll is simple, correct and very close to the language of the late biblical books. She also repeats Yadin's dating of the Temple Scroll to the time of John Hyrcanus or Alexander Jannaeus.[27]

As far as I know, Starkova is also in charge of the preparation of the Russian translations of the Dead Sea scrolls for subsequent volumes of the series *Teksty Kumrana*. The second volume in the series with translations of all the large scrolls from Qumran is unfortunately still not published, although it was submitted to the 'Nauka' (Science) publishing house by K.B. Starkova, J.D. Amusin and F. Gazov-Ginsberg many years ago.

The situation of qumranology in the USSR at present seems tragic. It appears that Starkova is the only one who is still working in the field.[28] Amusin[29] and Elizarova died recently. As far as I know, their pupils such as F. Gazov-Ginsberg and B. Demidova have left the field for general linguistic Semitic studies. The only optimistic sign is that Ida Fröhlich of the University of Budapest, who studied and prepared her dissertation under the supervision of Amusin, continues her work, specializing in the problems of the *pesharim*.[30]

East European research on the Temple Scroll is in some respects representative of East European Qumran research as a whole. Scholars from elsewhere would probably find it repetitive and not very original. Yet the fact that only a very few scholars are interested in this branch of Semitic studies, and that they have very few pupils, must be taken into consideration. With regard to Poland, it is regrettable that neither the Biblical School of Lublin which has such an excellent scholar and qumranologist on its staff as L.R. Stachowiak, nor the Academy of Catholic Theology in Warsaw with professors like H. Muszyński and S. Mędala, nor even the Oriental Institute of Warsaw University with Professor W. Tyloch, have yet trained any young scholar in the field. This is very unfortunate at a point when for the first time the Bible has been introduced into the secondary school curriculum; and recently even Qumran has been introduced, the idea being that teachers and pupils should discuss the Qumran sect as a 'forerunner' of Christianity.[31]

Still, I hope that the current attempts of the Oriental Committee, as well as my own, will bear fruit in the future. Our first international colloquium on the origins of the Dead Sea scrolls held at Mogilany at the beginning of June 1987 was, I hope, a turning point. We got some publicity during the colloquium and some serious interest was expressed at the XXVIth all-Poland meeting of orientalists held in November. I hope to see several scholars from abroad at our second colloquium at Mogilany in mid-September 1989, at which we expect to discuss problems connected with the Teacher of Righteousness and his role in the Qumran texts. Qumran scholars world-wide can regard these words as a cordial invitation to the colloquium on behalf of the Oriental Committee of the Kraków branch of the Polish Academy of Sciences and on my own behalf as organiser.

NOTES

1. Cf. Z.J. Kapera, 'An International Colloquium on the Origins of the Dead Sea Scrolls (Mogilany, near Krakow: May 31–June 2, 1987)', *Folia Orientalia* 24 (1987), pp. 299-301; cf. Z.J. Kapera, ed., *The First International Colloquium on the Dead Sea Scrolls (Mogilany, near Cracow: May 31–June 2, 1987), Folia Orientalia* 25 (1988), pp. 5-155; Z.J. Kapera, 'I Międzynarodowe Kolokwium Qumranologiczne w Mogilanach. Krótka prezentacja wniosków', *Przegląd Orientalistyczny* (1988), pp. 169-76; F. Garcia Martinez, 'Informations Qumrâniennes', *RevQ* 12 (1985-87), pp. 603-604.

2. Some data on the progress of Qumran research in Poland can be found in the introduction to my 'Selected Polish Subject Bibliography of the Dead Sea Discoveries', *Folia Orientalia* 23 (1985-86), pp. 269-72; and in the summary article of S. Mędala, 'Recherches sur la problématique des documents de Qumran en Pologne', *Folia Orientalia* 23 (1985-86), pp. 257-68; cf. also L.W. Stefaniak, 'Les recherches polonaises sur les textes et la doctrine de Qumrân', *Les sciences bibliques en Pologne après la guerre: 1945-1970* (ed. M. Wolniewicz; Varsovie: Akademia Teologii Katolickiej, 1974), pp. 245-74; W. Tyloch, 'Główne problemy badań nad rękopisami z Qumran', *Studia Religioznawcze* 12 (Warsaw: Państwowe Wydawnictwo Naukowe, 1977), pp 128-30 (English summary, 'The Main Problems of the Study of the Qumran Manuscripts', p. 143).

3. Cf. F. García Martínez, 'El Rollo del Templo 11 Q Temple: Bibliografia sistemática', *RevQ* 12 (1985-87), pp. 425-40.

4. T. Scher, 'A kumráni Templomtekercs (The Temple Scroll from Qumran)', *Világosság* 9 (1968), pp. 636-37.

5. J. Chmiel, 'Nowe rękopisy z Qumran (New Manuscripts from Qumran)', *Ruch Biblijny i Liturgiczny* 22 (1969), pp. 302-303.

6. Cf. S. Mędala, 'Recherches sur la problématique des documents de Qumran en Pologne' (see note 2), p. 259.

7. Cf. 'Główne problemy badán nad rękopisami z Qumran' (see note 2), pp. 123-28.

8. *Dialectics and Humanism* 6 (1979), pp. 96-99.

9. 'The Dead Sea Scrolls: A Testimony of the Social Ideas of Antiquity' (see note 8), p. 99.

10. *Rocznik Orientalistyczny* 41 (1980), pp. 139-43.

11. *Traditions in Contact and Change: Selected Proceedings of the XIVth Congress of the International Association for the History of Religions* (ed. P. Slater & D. Wiebe; Waterloo, Ontario: Wilfred Laurier University Press, 1983), pp. 285-93, 707-709.

12. W. Tyloch, 'Zwój Świątynny: Najważniejszy rękopis z Qumran i czas jego powstania', *Studia Religioznawcze* 19 (Warsaw: Państwowe Wydawnictwo Naukowe, 1984), pp. 27-37 (French summary, 'Le Rouleau du Temple: le plus important manuscrit de Qumrân et l'époque de sa composition', p. 38).

13. W. Tyloch, 'Zwój Świątynny (The Temple Scroll)', *Euhemer* 27 (1983), No. 3/129, pp. 3-20; 28 (1984), No. 1/131, pp. 3-20; No. 2/132, pp. 11-28; No. 3/133, pp. 9-27; all four articles are in Polish with English summaries.

14. Cf. F. García Martínez, 'El Rollo del Templo: 11Q Temple: Bibliografía sistemática', pp. 430-31; '§3, Traducciones'.

15. W. Tyloch, 'La provenance et la date du Rouleau du Temple', *Folia Orientalia* 25 (1988), pp. 33-39.

16. *Teksty Kumrana. Vypusk 1. Perevod s drevneevrejskogo i aramejskogo, vvedenie i kommentarij* (Pamjatniki Pis'mennosti Vostoka 33.1; Moskva: Izdatel'stvo 'Nauka', 1971), § Svitok Chrama (The Temple Scroll), pp. 393-96.

17. *Teksty Kumrana*, Vol. I, p. 396, and J. Morgenstern, 'The Calendar of the Book of Jubilees, its Origin and its Character', *VT* 5 (1955), pp. 34-76.

18. M.M. Elizarova, 'Problema KalendarjaTerapevtov', *Palestinskij Sbornik* 15/78 (Moskva-Leningrad, 1966), pp. 107-16 (French summary, 'Le problème du calendrier des Therapeutes', p. 116); esp. pp. 109-12.

19. J.D. Amusin, *Kumranskaja obščina (The Qumran Community)* (Moskva: Izdatel'stvo 'Nauka', 1983) (328 pp.). Concerning the Temple Scroll see pp. 3, 33, 80, 83-85, 133, 150-51, 223.

20. *Kumranskaja obščina*, p. 133; J.T. Milik, 'Le travail d'édition des manuscrits du Désert de Juda', *Congress Volume. Strasbourg 1956* (VTSup, 4; Leiden: Brill, 1957), pp. 17-26; cf. esp. p. 25.

21. *Kumranskaja obščina*, p. 133; M.M. Elizarova, *Obščina terapevtov (The Community of the Therapeutae)* (Moskva: Izdatel'stvo 'Nauka', 1972), pp. 60-80.

22. *Kumranskaja obščina*, p. 133; B. Thiering, 'Suffering and Asceticism at Qumran as Illustrated in the Hodayot', *RevQ* 8 (1972-75), pp. 393-405.

23. K.B. Starkova, 'Literaturnye pamjatniki kumranskoj obščiny', *Palestinskij Sbornik* 24/87 (Leningrad: Izdatel'stvo 'Nauka', 1973), pp. 1-136; cf. pp. 23-26 with preliminary information about the Temple Scroll.

24. For another view of this passage see the contribution of M.R. Lehmann to this volume.

25. For some further opinion on how 11QT is polemic against the Pharisees see H. Burgmann's contribution to the present volume.

26. K.B. Starkova, 'Literaturnye pamjatniki kumranskoj obščiny', *Palestinskij Sbornik* 24/87 (1973), pp. 23-26 and 41-42 nn. 227-50.

27. 'Review' of Y. Yadin, *The Temple Scroll* (Hebrew edition), *Palestinskij Sbornik* 27/90 (Leningrad, 1981), pp. 152-53.

28. During the discussion of this paper Prof. L.H. Schiffman of New York University brought to my attention that I.S. Šifman, from Leningrad, has started research on the Dead Sea scrolls. I am glad to see that I was wrong in my statement. I have just noticed a new Qumran article by I.S. Šifman on 'Psalm 151', in the annual *Pismennye pamjatniki Vostoka: Istoriko-filologičeskie issledovanija 1978-79* (Moskva: Izdatel'stvo 'Nauka', 1987), pp. 146-55. In the meantime K.B. Starkova has informed me that she has prepared a translation of the Temple Scroll into Russian with an extensive commentary. Her manuscript will be ready for publication soon. Another Soviet scholar, I.R. Tanglevskij, has started research on the Dead Sea scrolls, including the Temple Scroll.

29. Cf. L.M. Gluskina, 'About the Life and Work of Joseph Amusin (1910-1984)' and Z.J. Kapera, 'Soviet Bibliography on the Dead Sea Scrolls. Part One: Contributions by J.D. Amusin', to be published in *RevQ*.

30. Cf. Russian summary of her dissertation: *Isotoričeskie elementy v pozdnekanoničeskoj i apokrifičeskoj literature epochi ellenizma, II v. do n.e.—I v. n.e. (Eléments historiques dans la littérature biblique tardive et dans la littérature apocryphe à l'âge de l'hellénisme, II, s. av. J.-C.—I s. ap. J.-C.)*, Leningrad: Akademija Nauk SSSR, Institut Vostokovedenija, Leningradskoe otdelenie, 1974, 23 pp.; cf. her article, 'Le genre littéraire des pesharim de Qumrân', *RevQ* 12 (1985-87), pp. 383-98.

31. Cf. W. Tyloch, 'Pochodzenie chrześcijaństwa (Origins of Christianity)', *Euhemer* 30 (1986), No. 3-4, pp. 161-83, esp. pp. 169-73.

INDEXES

INDEX OF BIBLICAL & EXTRA-BIBLICAL REFERENCES

OLD TESTAMENT

NEW TESTAMENT

APOCRYPHA

QUMRAN LITERATURE

RABBINIC LITERATURE

INDEX OF AUTHORS